The Business Response to Keynes, 1929–1964

CONTEMPORARY AMERICAN HISTORY SERIES
William E. Leuchtenburg, General Editor

The Business Response to Keynes, 1929–1964

Robert M. Collins

COLUMBIA UNIVERSITY PRESS • New York • 1981

Clothbound editions of Columbia University Press books are Smyth-sewn and printed on permanent and durable acid-free paper.

Printed in the United States of America

Columbia University Press
New York   Guildford, Surrey

Library of Congress Cataloging in Publication Data

Collins, Robert M.
    The business response to Keynes, 1929–1964.

    (Contemporary American history series)
    Bibliography: p.
    Includes index.
    1. Keynesian economics—History. 2. Industry and
state—United States—History. 3. United States—
Economic policy. I. Title. II. Series.
HB99.7.C63   338.973   81-3898
ISBN 0-231-04486-0   AACR2

For Christine and Laura

Contents

Preface and Acknowledgments

The economist Joseph Schumpeter once observed that "nothing shows so clearly the character of a society and of a civilization as does the fiscal policy that its political sector adopts." The present study dares not assess American society in so sweeping a way; but it was undertaken in the belief that an examination of business' response to the advent of the New Economics would illuminate a significant episode in the building of the modern American state. An emphasis on the political dimension of the fiscal revolution, I believe, sets this book apart from most of the existing literature on the impact of Keynes and his ideas.

Two interrelated themes emerge in the chapters that follow. The first is the flexibility of the American business system. Initially, business reacted to the proposals of others that the government's role in macroeconomic management be enlarged; as the Keynesian revolution proceeded, however, an important segment of the business community took a leading position in support of an increasingly activist fiscal and monetary policy. A second theme appears as one attempts to make sense of the most dramatic manifestations of such flexibility. The study's emphasis on change in this context also illuminates overarching elements of continuity in the history of business-government relations in the twentieth century: in their efforts to forge a new, post-Depression political economy, some businessmen embraced a neo-corporatist ideology similar in many ways to that which historians have found to have played an important role in the first thirty years of this century. The extension of this corporatist impulse into the post-Depression world constitutes an often-neglected aspect of our recent history and a central theme in this volume.

In examining these developments, I have used three important business organizations as surrogates for the American business community at large—the Chamber of Commerce of the United States, the National Association of Manufacturers, and the Committee for Economic Development. All were highly visible, and taken together the three groups represented a broad spectrum of opinion on major issues. At times I have expanded my coverage to bring in the views of other individuals and groups, but I feel confident that the three organizations provide a reasonable body of evidence from which to generalize. At the same time, it is clear to me that a full understanding of the themes elucidated in this case study of macroeconomic policy will require similar explorations of business attitudes and activities in the areas of regulation, anti-trust, defense mobilization, and environmental politics during the post–World War II period.

One of the nicest things about finishing a manuscript is that completion provides an opportunity to thank some of those who helped along the way. William Maxwell gave me that crucial first push into graduate school; and, once there, Harvey Levenstein and Lloyd Gardner taught me that the study of history can be both relevant and challenging.

To Louis Galambos, I owe a debt beyond repayment. He directed the dissertation at The Johns Hopkins University from which this book ever so slowly evolved. A demanding but unfailingly constructive critic, he has provided intellectual stimulation while helping me to express my own ideas and, as it were, take my own chances. In short, he has been an ideal mentor.

Friends and colleagues also contributed by reading various drafts of the manuscript, in part or in whole, and offering their advice. Betsy Rives tried to warn me whenever my prose became too opaque. I have benefited greatly from the criticisms and observations of Joseph Hobbs, John Higham, Anthony LaVopa, Paul Paskoff, Donald Scott, and Stanley Suval. The North Carolina Triangle Social History Workshop provided an opportunity to test my ideas on several crucial points. Ellis Hawley was especially kind in sharing with me his perceptive insights concerning the process of institution-building in modern America. Often I took the advice of my colleagues, and their suggestions have no doubt improved the final product. On some points, however, I dug in my heels and refused to budge; they are accordingly absolved from any responsibility for whatever pertinent questions remain unasked or unanswered.

Several institutions facilitated my research by their generosity. A John E. Rovensky Fellowship in Business and Economic History helped me launch the project, and research grants from the Eleanor Roosevelt Institute, the Eleutherian Mills Historical Library, the Harry S. Truman Institute, and the Faculty Research and Development Fund of North Carolina State University kept me going.

I was further aided by the kindness and experience of the professional staffs at the Eleutherian Mills Historical Library, the National Archives, the Library of Congress, and the Franklin D. Roosevelt, Harry S. Truman, Dwight D. Eisenhower, and John F. Kennedy Presidential Libraries. Archivists at Stanford and Syracuse Universities, and at the Universities of Mississippi, Rochester, and Virginia provided similar help. I owe special thanks to the representatives of several of the business groups discussed in this volume. I benefited immensely from the aid of Mrs. Rose Racine and her library staff at the Chamber of Commerce of the United States. Robert Lenhart helped me in the same spirit at the Committee for Economic Development.

Lastly, I would like to thank William Leuchtenburg, editor of the Contemporary American History Series, and Bernard Gronert and Karen Mitchell of Columbia University Press for their help in bringing this book to completion.

The Business Response to Keynes, 1929–1964

Chapter One

The Keynesian Revolution:
A Perspective

"A plague of young lawyers settled in Washington," George Peek complained, recalling the army of white collar troops that massed to fight the New Deal's war against depression.[1] Though the federal government had been expanding the scope of its activities since at least the days of Theodore Roosevelt, the Depression decade marked a sharp acceleration of this trend. The number of regular civilian employees at the federal level increased by 73 percent between 1930 and 1940, and an additional 2,892,000 Americans found employment in federal work-relief programs at the end of Franklin D. Roosevelt's second term. To support the work of this civilian army, federal expenditures soared from $3.44 billion in 1930 to $9.06 billion a decade later.[2] New agencies abounded, and more than one wag noted that the alphabet had become a primer on government.

Much of this increased government activity was directed at the solution of economic problems. Government on all levels had acted throughout the nineteenth century to encourage and subsidize some economic practices and to discourage and regulate others.[3] Yet one senses that the increased scope of federal intervention in the economy during the 1930s marks the decade as a watershed. An examination of the accretions of economic power under the New

Deal lends credence to Adolf Berle's contention that Roosevelt "intended and brought about an American economic dirigée": federal management of currency, banking, and credit was strengthened; regulation of security issues and the stock exchanges begun; systems of bank deposit insurance and social security instituted; measures for agricultural stabilization enforced; minimum wages and maximum hours legislated; regional development, as in the TVA, attempted; and mass industrial unionization fostered through Section 7(a) of the National Industrial Recovery Act and the Wagner Act. "The first duty of government," the President explained to the nation in 1938, "is to protect the economic welfare of all the people in all stations and in all groups."[4] In retrospect, such an expanded governmental role appears almost to have been preordained by the confluence of economic collapse and Roosevelt's experimentalism.

Until 1938–1939, however, it was not at all clear what the substance of this increased role would be. In answer to the demands by business that it be allowed to run its own shop in its own manner, to bring to fruition the business commonwealth long envisioned by conservatives, the New Deal advanced two alternatives: (1) a centralized, planned economy, to be brought about through structural reform; and (2) a neo-Brandeisian, atomized economy, which would restore competition and thereby reconcile economic reality with democratic ideology. Both alternatives threatened the large measure of business autonomy that had been so carefully nurtured during the 1920s. Neither policy, however, was pursued in coherent fashion, and the failure of their respective advocates to gain a clear upper hand in the councils of government, much less to bring about economic recovery, left the way open for a third solution—Keynesian spending.[5]

The path to the spending solution was a tortuous one. Although Roosevelt had come to accept deficit financing during the distressing winter of 1931–1932, his reputation as governor of New York had been that of an economy-minded executive.[6] Budget deficits posed a conflict between principle and expediency, even for a man so undoctrinaire as Roosevelt. Rexford G. Tugwell remembers that during the 1932 presidential campaign it was in the field of fiscal policy that "Franklin was most uncertain even after all our discussions."[7] Resolution of this quandary, at least for the purposes of the campaign, found traditional principle the winner. In support of a platform which called for "maintenance of the national credit by a Federal budget annually balanced," the Democratic nominee lashed out at Hoover's prodigality. "Any Government," he observed, "like any family, can for a year spend a little more than it earns. But you and I know that a continuation of that habit means the poorhouse."[8]

Once in office, the new President quickly acted to redeem such pledges of austerity. Within a week of his inauguration, he sent to Congress an economy message requesting executive power to reduce or eliminate veterans' pensions and to cut government salaries by up to 15 percent. "Too often in recent history," he warned, "liberal governments have been wrecked on rocks of loose fiscal policy. We must avoid this danger."[9] Congress embodied Roosevelt's suggestions in the Act to Maintain the Credit of the United States Government which it passed on March 20, 1933; eleven days later the President issued a series of executive orders curtailing veterans' benefits. In keeping with the spirit of fiscal rigor, Roosevelt explained to reporters that the job of his Director of the Budget, Lewis Douglas, was "to prevent the Government from spending just as hard as he can."[10] Douglas brought great ardor to the assignment, and he quickly came to exercise considerable influence. The President described him to Colonel Edward House as "in many ways the greatest 'find' of the administration." To Hiram Johnson, embittered by the new regime's treatment of veterans, he was "a young man . . . born to the purple, loves the English and their ways, and has a heart of stone."[11]

Yet there were forces at work which doomed such resolve from the outset. The first was the sheer magnitude of the economic collapse and the human distress which confronted the government. Unemployment reached its peak in early 1933, with almost 25 percent of the civilian labor force jobless. The second was the election of a Congress ready to spend in spite of principle, waiting only to be told how much.[12] As a result, the economy measures of the administration were diluted by large increases in what Roosevelt carefully labeled "emergency expenditures." This extraordinary, humanitarian spending for relief and public works made up the bulk of government expenditures, and deficits, until preparations for war began in earnest in 1940.

Some advisers, however, viewed federal spending as an economic stimulant rather than a social palliative. In 1933, Marriner Eccles, soon to be appointed chairman of the Federal Reserve System, testified before a Senate committee that government should resort to deficit spending to stimulate the economy.[13] Lauchlin Currie supported this advice and in 1934–1935 developed (with the assistance of Martin Krost) an important tool to measure the aggregate impact of government's fiscal operations on the economy, a series which came to be designated the "Net Contribution of the Federal Government to National Buying Power."[14] But through the mid-thirties these men and their viewpoint did not prevail.

Roosevelt saw deficit spending more as a condition to be overcome in the course of recovery than as a theoretical prescription to be followed. John Maynard Keynes had early written to the President urging an emphasis on "the increase of national purchasing power resulting from governmental expenditure which is financed by Loans and not by taxing present incomes," but neither such long-distance missives nor later face-to-face encounters in the summer of 1934 apparently had much effect on Roosevelt.[15] After finally meeting Keynes, the President reported to Frances Perkins that "he left a whole rigamarole of figures. He must be a mathematician rather than a political economist."[16] In May 1935 Roosevelt offered his own view of early New Deal spending:

Every authorization of expenditure . . . for recovery purposes, has been predicated not on the mere spending of money to hasten recovery, but on the sounder principle of preventing the loss of homes and farms, of saving industry from bankruptcy, of safeguarding bank deposits, and most important of all—of giving relief and jobs through public work to individuals and families faced with starvation.[17]

As the prospects of starvation and bankruptcy receded, Roosevelt's hopes for a balanced budget rose. In 1937 the President slashed spending at the same time that veterans' bonus payments were ending (the bulk of the payments had come in 1936) and the new social security taxes were taking full effect; by December the nation was again deep in the throes of depression. Roosevelt reacted conservatively to the recession which now bore his name. In mid-October 1937 he wrote to Senator John Bankhead that he proposed "to be very definite this fall in saying that if the Congress exceeds my budget estimates, which will provide a balanced budget, the Congress can stay in session or come back once a week in special session throughout the full year until they give me additional taxes to make up the loss." Nudged by Secretary of the Treasury Henry Morgenthau and others, the President agreed in early November to "turn on the old record" of fiscal conservatism and business reassurance.[18]

It was only after a bitter struggle among FDR's advisers, a battle in which Harry Hopkins finally prevailed over Morgenthau, that the President reverted in April 1938 to massive infusions of government spending to shore up the economy.

His plan to pump approximately $7 billion into the economy marked an important turning point for the New Deal—Roosevelt's first acceptance of fiscal policy as a legitimate tool for economic stabilization.[19] Of course, he probably never did abandon his belief that deficit spending could be ended; as late as 1945, he expressed hope to a Bureau of the Budget official that the national debt could quickly be repaid![20] But although he never lost his preference for balanced budgets, after the crucial 1938 reversion to spending neither he nor his successors ever again approached government spending as solely a charitable exercise.

The President's 1939 annual message made the point clearly: "By our common sense action of resuming government activities last spring, we have reversed a recession and started the new rising tide of prosperity and national income which we are now just beginning to enjoy." In the next day's budget message, Roosevelt agreed with "the most far-sighted students of our economic system" that "it would be unwise either to curtail expenditures sharply or to impose drastic new taxes at this stage of recovery." Privately, the President requested that his cabinet members "take a public position . . . in favor of the position taken in my annual message to the Congress as well as in the budget message—a policy generally known as the 'compensatory fiscal policy.' We must present our case to the country."[21]

The publication in 1936 of John Maynard Keynes's *The General Theory of Employment, Interest and Money* had eased considerably the task of the administration.[22] Following Keynes's lead, an increasing number of Americans, both within government and without, began to look at deficit spending in a new way, as a tool rather than as a condition, to be used for recovery rather than for relief. Keynes's contribution was not so much in planting the idea of deficit spending, but rather in showing how fiscal policy could be used in positive, aggressive fashion and in explaining why it offered the results that it did. Because his terminology, method, and theory lay at the center of the subsequent debate over the post-Depression American political economy, the arguments of *The General Theory* warrant a brief examination.

Keynes's analysis began with a recognition of the existence of involuntary unemployment. The argument that followed was, fundamentally, an attempt to explain the causes of such unemployment and, conversely, of employment itself. In the process, Keynes emphatically rejected the conventional belief that unemployment resulted primarily from wage rigidity—the unwillingness of workers to accept lower wages—and the concomitant suggestion that depression be combated by means of a general wage reduction. This concern with employment, or, more precisely, the problem of unemployment, in itself represented a significant shift in emphasis away from the classical theory with its focus on optimum resource allocation.

Employment, Keynes argued, is determined by the level of aggregate demand, which is equal to the aggregate income of the entire economy. This demand, or income, is in turn a function of consumption and investment. Consumption, he declared, is a relatively stable factor; the key variable in the determination of employment and national income is the more volatile one, investment.

At equilibrium, investment is equal to the excess of income over consumption. This excess, however, can be either invested or saved. If the excess is saved and not invested, aggregate income will be reduced, and with it employment. Orthodox economic theory held, however, that temporary disproportions in the savings-investment balance would be redressed by the automatic functioning of the interest-rate mechanism. In other words, an excess in savings would bring its price—the rate of interest—down, just as a glut of a commodity good reduces the price of that good, be it shoestrings or cars. With the fall in the interest rate, the incentive to invest would be increased because the money for business expansion could be had more cheaply. Thus, capitalism seemed to contain a built-in stabilizing device which would ultimately cause the economy to climb out of any slump. But the Keynesian analysis pointed out that the mechanism in fact might not work, for as depression contracted income, savings decreased. Without a surplus of savings, there would be no pressure on the interest rate and hence no expansion in investment. Without movement in this key variable, the result was equilibrium at a level which might be considerably below full employment. This conclusion, borne out all too tragically by the events of the Depression, was little short of revolutionary, for it demolished a crucial premise of classical economics, the assumption that capitalism automatically tended toward full employment of men and resources.

In addition, *The General Theory* attacked the time-honored identification of thrift with virtue. For Keynes, it was inescapable that "in contemporary conditions [the absence of full employment] the growth of wealth, so far from being dependent on the abstinence of the rich, as is commonly supposed, is more likely to be impeded by it." Thus, one of the prime justifications for inequality of wealth was removed. Such an assault was, as Joseph Schumpeter noted rather gloomily, a renunciation of "the last pillar of the bourgeois argument." It was in this sense, he claimed, that most Keynesians were radicals. As late as 1949, one American economist wrote, "What the bushy-bearded, heavy-handed German revolutionary [Marx] did with malice aforethought and by frontal attack, the English aristocrat . . . a peer of the Realm, performed neatly, skillfully, and unconsciously by flank attack."[23]

The political import of Keynesian economics has from the very outset been a matter of debate. Conservative critics

have accused Keynes of being a brazen left-wing ideol
On the other hand, one finds Soviet critics equally vehement
in their denunciation of Keynes as a shabby defender of
imperialistic capitalism.[24] Despite this confusion and despite the fact that The General Theory is replete with ambiguity, it seems clear that Keynesianism was conservative
in the broadest sense. In essence, Keynes wanted to save
free-market capitalism from both the stultifying orthodoxy
of laissez faire and the heresy of socialism.[25]

Within this broad conservatism which dictated the retention of a market economy, however, there existed a spectrum of possible varieties of capitalism. It is important to
remember that The General Theory advanced three main
recommendations for anti-depression policy (in ascending
order of importance and potential, as Keynes judged them):
(1) the maintenance of low interest rates through central
control; (2) the redistribution of wealth through taxation to
increase the propensity to consume; and (3) the augmen-
tation of insufficient private investment by government
spending.[26] These recommendations differed greatly in their
sociopolitical ramifications. Monetary policy is far more
conservative in its implications than the fiscal alternatives,
because monetary manipulation requires the smallest government bureaucracy and avoids the crucial question of the
allocation of resources and property. The result was a range
of policy recommendations broad enough to draw together
as "Keynesians" individuals from both right and left of center in America.[27]

In addition to the question of monetary versus fiscal
policy, the Keynesian analysis raised questions about the
constancy of the government's role. Again, a spectrum of
views quickly developed. At one end were the pump-
primers, those who believed that a dose of Keynes, especially of heavy deficit spending, would suffice to get the
pump of the capitalist economy back into normal operation.

To the left of these pump-primers were the compensatory spenders, those who viewed capitalism as capable of only short periods of stability under its own power, with government intervention a recurrent necessity. Furthest to the left were the interventionists or stagnationists, those who saw the existing style of capitalism as completely incapable of regeneration; they believed that only ongoing government intervention (and spending deficits) could prevent permanent depression. Thus Keynesianism, while essentially conservative, offered policy formulations which differed significantly in their ideological, political, and economic potentials.[28]

The stagnationist approach became especially persuasive in the wake of the 1937–1938 recession, a downturn which cast considerable doubt on the ability of business to step up investment when government spending was reduced. "It is all too clear," Harvard economist Alvin Hansen observed, "that 'pump priming' has not worked in the manner planned and hoped for." "Secular stagnation," he added ominously, "stalks across the stage." It was an entrance which he was prepared to chronicle in full. The stagnationist analysis had been implied in Keynes's *General Theory*, but the American Hansen and his students stressed this insight and made it a crucial element in their interpretation.[29]

Perhaps the classic formulation of this position was Hansen's presidential address to the American Economic Association in December 1938.[30] America, he told his colleagues, had reached economic maturity: population increase had slowed dramatically, and territorial expansion was now a thing of the past. Technological innovation had produced no great industrial boom since the automobile, and it was doubtful that technological change could be counted upon to stimulate the economy periodically. The result was economic stagnation, and the cure was government investment to take up the slack which was now a natural condition of the system. At first Hansen appeared to be concerned with the dangers to free enterprise posed by such a government role, but this concern soon gave way to his desire for a powerful federal program of social investment.[31] By 1941, he was calling for a "really positive expansionist" policy to replace the New Deal's tepid "salvaging program."[32]

A group of young Harvard and Tufts economists propounded another influential statement of the stagnationist analysis in 1938.[33] Their program called for heavy deficit spending in the social-welfare sector, for radical redistribution of income by means of increased taxation, for public regulation of prices and profits in oligopolistic industries, and for public ownership of such industries as a last resort if necessary. When, in February 1939, James Roosevelt discussed with his father the possibility of an educational film on the program and objectives of the New Deal, the President suggested the work of the Harvard-Tufts group as a good summation of the administration's economic philosophy.[34] Thus, in the hands of politically engaged intellectuals and those outside the scholarly community who became adherents to the cause, the stagnationist analysis from the outset comprised a complex mixture of economic ideas and political preferences. It simultaneously explained the nature of modern American capitalism and yielded a set of programs for altering that system. But also, just as importantly, it became an emphasis, a collection of attitudes, a vision of the future which assumed that economic progress and sweeping social change were not antithetical.

The New Deal did not, however, fully translate these views into action. The Spend-Lend Bill of 1939, in the words of the fiscally conservative Morgenthau, followed "a realistic approach." This last major administration spending effort before the war proposed that the Reconstruction Finance Corporation be authorized to borrow $3.8 billion to spend or lend. The entire program was designed to be self-liquidating and was touted, rather disingenuously, as being "non–deficit creating." Despite such respectability, however, the bill failed of passage. Congress proved itself able in 1939, for the first time, to defeat New Deal spending measures.[35] It was, Keynes wrote presciently in the summer of 1940, "politically impossible for a capitalistic democracy to organize expenditure on the scale necessary to prove my case—except under war conditions."[36]

I

World War II set the stage for the triumph of Keynesianism by providing striking evidence of the effectiveness of government expenditure on a huge scale. Spending for war finally ended the worst depression in American history. The victory was one to which Keynesians and their methods of analysis contributed greatly.[37]

The period 1939–1946 witnessed a great influx of Keynesian economists and administrators into positions of influence in government and the creation of numerous agencies which would serve as the institutional base for Keynesian economic policies. In November 1938, Roosevelt had established a temporary "Monetary and Fiscal Advisory Board" and described its purview as "the whole range of a great many problems that relate to fiscal and monetary policies in respect to sound and orderly recovery, and conditions essential to avoiding the peaks and valleys of boom and depressions."[38] In 1939, the Reorganization Act brought Keynesian economist Lauchlin Currie to the White House as one of six new presidential assistants and transferred the Bureau of the Budget to the Executive Office. Within the bureau, a Fiscal Division was created and Keynesian Gerhard Colm became one of its two chief economists. In the

Commerce Department, Harry Hopkins organized a new Division of Industrial Economics and named Richard Gilbert of the Harvard-Tufts group as its director.

The arrival of Hansen at Washington in 1940 as adviser to the National Resources Planning Board (NRPB) symbolized that agency's ascendence as the wartime center of left-wing Keynesianism. The Reorganization Act required the NRPB to prepare continuing six-year projections of public works, to "inform the President of the general trend of economic conditions and to recommend measures leading to their improvement of stabilization." Before its demise at the hands of Congress in 1943, the Board had proclaimed an economic bill of rights (which Roosevelt would use two years later as the basis for his 1944 State of the Union Address) and had issued a series of reports which lent more than a little substance to the attacks by conservatives who accused it of "propagandizing the program of Dr. Alvin Hansen for unlimited postwar spending of borrowed funds."[39]

With the passing of the NRPB, the views of Keynes and Hansen became centered in the numerous proposals introduced in Congress to deal with the problem of postwar employment. The debate over these proposals finally resulted in the Employment Act of 1946, legislation which institutionalized Keynesianism in the government bureaucracy. The statute declared it "the policy and responsibility of the Federal Government to use all practicable means . . . to promote maximum employment, production, and purchasing power."[40] Two instruments were established for the fulfillment of this mandate: the Council of Economic Advisers in the Executive Office of the President and the Joint Economic Committee in the Congress. It was these agencies, especially the Council, which were to coordinate economic policy in the postwar world.

Thus entrenched in the federal bureaucracy, Keynesianism also influenced the worlds of theory and scholarship.[41] Of particular importance was the publication in 1948 of Paul Samuelson's Keynesian-oriented *Economics, An Introductory Analysis,* one of the most influential texts ever written.[42] In 1951, when the prestigious American Economic Association published an "unofficial" report on the problem of economic instability, one commentator concluded, "If the report does represent a consensus of American economists, it means that our thinking has now reached a state of Keynesian conservatism."[43]

The translation of an institutional base and academic preeminence into coherent public policy was a slow process, but progress clearly was made in the years following 1946.[44] No administration, for example, denied its responsibility for aggregate economic performance, i.e., for the cultivation of economic growth and the maintenance of stability.[45] The return to power of the Republican party in 1953 was perhaps the single most important test of resolve in this area and the new administration passed it handily. As Eisenhower's economic adviser Arthur Burns put it:

Only a generation ago it was the typical view of economists and other citizens that storms of business depression must be allowed to blow themselves out, with little or no interference on the part of government. Today there is substantial agreement among Americans that the Federal government cannot remain aloof from what goes on in the private economy, that the government must strive to foster an expanding economy, and that the government has a definite responsibility to do all it can to prevent depressions.[46]

The President, any President, had indeed taken on the role of national "Manager of Prosperity."[47]

The lessons of the Keynesian revolution had been internalized, at least to the degree that no administration attempted to combat recession by belt-tightening and raising taxes to prevent a deficit. Thus, in the midst of the 1949 recession, President Truman not only accepted a deficit, but defended it as the proper policy. Perhaps even more significantly, during the recession of 1954 the Eisenhower administration—despite traditional Republican obeisance to "fiscal responsibility"—accepted a deficit and allowed previously scheduled tax cuts on the order of $7 billion to go into effect. Fiscal sophistication dictated that taxes would not be raised, as they had been in 1932, in order to combat deflation.[48]

Although American leaders accepted the passive side of the New Economics, they hesitated to implement the more active side of the Keynesian prescription. Truman and Eisenhower depended on the tendency of the federal budget to move automatically into deficit during a recession, but whenever possible they avoided dramatic, discretionary action aimed at manipulating expenditures or revenues to counteract economic instability. In this context, the Kennedy-Johnson tax cut of 1964 represented the culmination of the Keynesian revolution—the use of discretionary fiscal policy to prevent a recession and to generate a more satisfactory rate of economic growth.[49] Thus, bureaucratic institutionalization, academic predominance, and national economic policy slowly converged over time.

II

The story of the triumph of "Keynesianism" after World War II is complicated, however, by the fact that the essence of that designation changed dramatically over the years. Modern fiscal policy, we are told by contemporary observers, is merely a tool, "as ideological in its implications as a dental drill." President Kennedy viewed the choice of the mix between monetary and fiscal policy as "basically an administrative or executive problem in which political labels or cliches do not give us a solution." Despite such assertions, the Keynesian formulation of the New Deal era was *not* inherently neutral.[50] The spending solution posed a clear challenge to some of the more entrenched verities of business ideology, most especially the sanctity of the balanced budget. Nor was it clear that government involvement could or would be minimized so as to ensure continued business domination of economic decision-making. The questions of precisely how much government intervention would be undertaken and to what purposes such involvement would be put were not answered by Keynes's mathematical formulas. For example, at what point on the left-of-center continuum did Keynesian economics shade off into socialist control of the economy? Government spending cloaked in the rationale of economic stability à la Keynes and his American interpreters could lead to a super New Deal, a liberal regime endowed with planning and coordinating authority potent enough to disrupt or perhaps even overturn the power relationships of American capitalism.

Of course, such did not prove to be the case. While the seed of deficit spending was of necessity planted, the twig was early bent, its growth carefully nurtured so as to minimize change in the distribution of power and wealth. Government assumed a more active role as beneficent overseer of the economy, but the decisions that counted remained in private hands. Deficit spending was ultimately institutionalized in a military-industrial complex which devoured money in the name of national defense and Cold War rhetoric, a rationale later expanded to include for a time the needs of space-race technology. This martial imagery was borrowed for a skirmish with poverty, but by the mid-1960s it had become clear that the main thrust of the "neutral" Keynesian solution lay elsewhere.

America defined its postwar political economy by embracing the right wing of the Keynesian spectrum, a right which almost seemed like the center (as it does to historians today) as the defeated alternatives of the left receded into sectarian memories.[51] It was a formulation which opted for an active monetary policy and a passive fiscal policy, for automatic stabilizers over discretionary management, for reductions in taxation and increases in private spending over increases in public spending, for a modicum of unemployment over a modicum of inflation, and for economic stability over the redistribution of income and the reallocation of resources.

What caused this transformation to what economist Robert Lekachman has called "commercial Keynesianism"?[52] One explanation is that circumstances changed after the Great Depression and that the shift to the right wing of the Keynesian spectrum merely represented adjustment to these changed economic conditions. In some particulars this view is persuasive. Inflation, to be sure, became a more immediate problem in the post-Depression economy, a problem which the New Deal Keynesians had not foreseen as a major economic concern. During World War II Hansen and Guy Greer wrote sanguinely that "except in time of war or its aftermath, the danger of inflation is so slight as to be almost negligible."[53] The development during World War II of a broad-based system of taxation collected on a pay-as-you-go, withholding basis made tax reduction a more viable fiscal weapon than had been the case in the 1930s. Similarly, the advent of relatively large budgets in the postwar period made possible greater reliance on the cushioning effect of the economy's built-in stabilizers (corporate and personal taxes, excise and employment taxes, and unemployment compensation payments). Bigger budgets necessitated higher taxation and thus promised that the variation of revenue with a change in national income of a certain size would be larger and hopefully more stabilizing. The effect, moreover, was all the more useful because the major problem had shifted from that of generating economic recovery (the case in the 1930s) to that of minimizing an economic decline (the case in the postwar years). The resurgence of the economy after the Depression presented new problems and made possible new solutions. The transformation of American Keynesianism was in part a response to these new conditions.

Yet changed circumstances and economic performance alone cannot explain the transmogrification of Keynesianism. It was not social and economic progress which made left-wing Keynesianism obsolete. If the specter of economic stagnation was indeed vanquished, the postwar economy achieved prosperity only with the aid of massive defense budgets and federal spending which averaged 16.9 percent of the GNP per year from 1946 to 1962.[54] And many of the problems which provided the stagnationists with their social agenda remained unsolved. The maldistribution of wealth and income continued.[55] Public poverty amid private affluence remained a paradox of American life, a contradiction compounded by the periodic rediscovery of the penury afflicting tens of millions of citizens in "the other America." The Census Bureau estimated that in 1960 roughly one-fifth of the nation's housing was substandard, and American cities continued the decline which became an international scandal in the aftermath of the urban riots of the mid-1960s.[56]

A second possible explanation for the triumph of commercial Keynesianism is that political economists are basically conservative and that their analyses and policy suggestions merely reflect this fact. University of Chicago economist George Stigler has observed that the academic training of economists stresses the actions of impersonal and inexorable forces and that this in turn breeds a certain conservatism which affects both the direction and the substance of economic research.[57] This argument, however, must still confront the fact that the discipline of political economy also produces critics of conventional wisdom who sometimes have the ear of the powerful (e.g., Keynes himself, Alvin Hansen, John Kenneth Galbraith) and who often function as influential molders of elite public opinion. The conservatism Stigler describes notwithstanding, alternatives continue to be posed—early Keynesianism being a case in point.

Crucial for understanding the transformation of Keynesianism is an appreciation of the power of businessmen and business institutions in American society. Economics remains "partly a vehicle for the ruling ideology of each period as well as partly a method of scientific investigation."[58] There appears to have been a complex social and political process at work by which "radical" alternatives were filtered out, or so emasculated and transformed as to render them *relatively* harmless to those who wielded power within society. Put simply, business accommodated itself to the fiscal revolution and successfully turned aside the thrusts of those who sought to limit seriously its dominion.

However, the transmutation of Keynesian economics did not derive from business influence alone, for it was only the most important of several forces at work. The essential components included: (1) a particular body of economic theory; (2) the scientific experts who continually refined that theory and enunciated its policy implications; (3) a business power structure which was itself characterized not by unanimity but rather by a range of philosophical and political views and which naturally sought to control its political and economic environments; (4) a governmental sector which represented an even wider variety of interests and which attempted to reconcile these interests with its newly discovered responsibility for economic prosperity; and (5) a changing economic environment which was subject to conditions frequently beyond the control of either government planners or businessmen. No one of these was *solely* responsible for the process of transformation; nor can the process be explained by merely lumping the elements together. It was, rather, the interaction of these factors which led to the transformation of Keynesianism.[59]

Part I
The Depression Years

Chapter Two
Negativistic Opposition
to the New Deal

The drift from the fiscal orthodoxy of Herbert Hoover to the uncertain, incipient Keynesianism of Roosevelt's spending policies in 1938–1939 presented a major challenge to American business: the New Deal threatened to give the federal government a supreme role in the direction of the nation's economy. A significant segment of the business community responded by gradually adopting a stance of open antagonism to Roosevelt. An important voice for such disaffected businessmen was the Chamber of Commerce of the United States.

A national "organization of organizations," the Chamber at the outset of the Depression (1929) boasted a membership of 1,587 state and local chambers of commerce and trade associations, with 13,388 individuals and firms enjoying associate and individual membership; it claimed to speak for an underlying membership of nearly one million. Calvin Coolidge, expressing an opinion that was probably widespread in the twenties, said that this champion of business "very accurately reflects . . . public opinion generally." Even those who dismissed its rhetoric had to respect the strength of its financial position; the Chamber's revenue of $2,040,535 for the year 1926–1927 had fairly dwarfed the $542,284 in total receipts collected by the American Federation of Labor. The proximity of the Chamber's national headquarters to the White House, a short walk across Lafayette Park, was symbolic of the organization's influence at the end of a decade which had raised business from a vocation to a cult.[1]

It was only natural for Hoover, who had shown much solicitude for private enterprise throughout his public service, to call on the Chamber for help at the onset of the Great Depression. By the end of 1929, the Chamber had organized the National Business Survey Conference, had housed it in the group's Washington headquarters, and had made it the focal point of business-government cooperation in Hoover's voluntaristic counterattack on the economic decline. Under the leadership of Julius Barnes, Chairman of the Board of the Chamber, the Conference rejected the inevitability of the business cycle and encouraged private investment in order to increase demand. As the economic situation worsened, however, it became clear to the Chamber, and finally to Hoover himself, that the hoopla and fact-finding of such voluntarism were not equal to the task of recovery. The Business Survey Conference was quietly laid to rest in May 1931, but its passing was not mourned.[2] There was not time for that. Defeat in the battle to stave off the Depression merely meant that the struggle to balance the budget would have to be joined.

The problem appeared dreadfully simple: as the Depression cut into national income, tax receipts fell, while at the same time the worsening distress intensified demands on the public treasury. As a result, the federal government ended fiscal year 1931 (i.e., the twelve-month period ending June 30, 1931) with its first deficit since World War I and the largest peacetime deficit in its history. The response, Calvin Coolidge reported, was "a cold shiver . . . down the financial spine of the public." Though perhaps not true of the workers in the breadlines, this was certainly the reaction of Herbert Hoover. "Nothing will contribute more to the return of prosperity," the President declared in November 1931, "than to maintain the sound fiscal position of the Federal Government." He quickly embarked on a campaign to salvage the nation's fiscal respectability, and once again he found in the Chamber of Commerce a staunch and vocal ally.[3]

The Chamber's position on the deepening fiscal crisis was complex. It could agree easily enough on the desirability of a balanced budget. But exactly *how* to balance the budget was a matter of considerable delicacy. There were two extreme alternatives possible: the first was to bring the budget into balance by slashing expenditures so as to match the government's reduced receipts. To long-time advocates of small government, this solution appeared eminently attractive; but, in light of increasing demands for government succor, the political obstacles were formidable. The second approach was to raise taxes in order to bring revenues back into line with expenditures. To the Chamber, this was unconscionable.

The Chamber took refuge in that portion of the middle ground between these two extremes most favorable to the interests of business. In November 1931 its committees on federal expenditures and federal taxation called for a budget that could be balanced within the next few years. To the maximum degree practicable this was to be accomplished by reductions in expenditures. If necessary, further adjustment would come through gradually increased taxation. For the short run, however, the inescapable deficits of the current and next fiscal years were to be met by borrowing. Still, the Chamber was hardly sanguine in its acceptance of deficit spending as a temporary palliative; large deficits, it warned, were to be deplored and the continuation of even small deficits avoided.[4] In order to arrest the current drifting under deficit conditions, the Chamber in 1932 undertook a massive campaign against government spending.

Supporting Hoover's resistance to the demands of some progressives for increased public works spending, the Chamber launched a three-pronged attack on public extravagance. The opening blow was struck in April 1932 when the membership approved the fiscal formula outlined earlier by its committees.[5] Having thus gained overwhelming support for its stand, the Chamber sought to drive home its message with a barrage of publicity. The percentage of articles dealing with taxation and the cost of government that appeared in the group's house organ, *Nation's Business*, rose from 6 percent in 1926 and 4 percent in 1928 to 25 percent in 1932.[6] The assault culminated in a classic foray into pressure politics. In January 1933 Chamber president Henry I. Harriman, in a public letter to the House Appropriations Committee, called for a cut of $1 billion in the federal budget, a saving to be achieved by reducing all federal activities to 1925 levels. "By no other action," he advised, "could Congress so signally perform its constitutional duty of promoting the general welfare of the country."[7]

Although the crisis of the Depression necessitated some deviation from the strictest canons of fiscal rectitude, the Chamber attempted to stand firm for prudence in financial affairs and to hold out the balanced budget as a *sine qua non* of economic recovery. The group did temporize, for example, in its willingness to accept small deficits rather than drastic tax increases designed to bring the budget into balance. At the same time, however, the Chamber advocated "some increase in taxes to restore order to the Government finances." "The credit of the United States," it warned Congress, "must be kept upon a high plane."[8] Budget balancing was, if not quite a fetish, still a genuine concern and a high priority; in this, the Chamber was at one with the administration.

When the break between Hoover and the Chamber came, it was over an issue more dramatic than that of fiscal prudence. In 1931, Gerard Swope, president of General Electric, aroused the interest of the nation and the Chamber with a scheme for national economic planning, to be presided over by trade associations. The Chamber membership quickly and overwhelmingly approved a referendum proposing modification of the antitrust laws to allow agreements among businessmen to limit production.[9] Hoover refused, however, to follow the lead of business, calling the Swope Plan "the most gigantic proposal of monopoly ever made in history" and the Chamber variant "sheer fascism." Harriman warned the President that many businessmen would forsake the incumbent for Roosevelt unless he came out in support of the Swope scheme or some similar program. Although most businessmen almost certainly voted for the unwavering Hoover, Harriman remained personally true to his prophecy and voted for a new deal.[10]

I

It was probably without self-consciousness that the new President-elect wrote to Harriman in January 1933, "I hope to see you soon after I get back, for you and I have the same broad philosophy and I want to talk with you about a number of things."[11] Certainly the 1932 campaign had given Harriman little cause to doubt such a profession. The Democratic platform had been unexceptional, and the campaign itself had been restrained. Roosevelt did speak out in support of public power development and the regulation of both public utilities and the securities market. However, vice-presidential candidate John Nance Garner had warned, "Tell the Governor that he is the boss and we will all follow him to hell if we have to, but if he goes too far with some of these wild-eyed ideas we are going to have the shit kicked out of us." With but minor exceptions, Garner's political counsel was heeded. After a pre-election interview with Roosevelt, *Nation's Business* noted with approval the candidate's "instinctive preference . . . for a minimum of coercive action by government." "The facts to which he attached importance and the conclusions toward which he tended were strikingly similar in many respects to those heard every day from business men."[12]

For those with lingering doubts, the specter of social upheaval in the wake of increasing economic distress was enough to make the Democratic standard-bearer appear a lesser evil. On the eve of the inauguration, Merle Thorpe, editor of *Nation's Business*, wrote ominously:

Now is the winter of our discontent the chilliest. . . . Fear, bordering on panic, loss of faith in everything, our fellowman, our institutions, private and government. Worst of all, no faith in ourselves, or the future. Almost everyone ready to scuttle the ship, and not even "women and children first."[13]

If the new administration seemed to some to threaten change, the prospect was not entirely unwelcome to America's businessmen.

The Chamber's policy of cooperation with government and its hope for business self-regulation quickly came to fruition in the National Industrial Recovery Act (NIRA). In the fluidity of the First Hundred Days, the advantage lay with those who were organized and who had a plan; the Chamber met both criteria, and its representatives played an important role in the formulation of the NIRA.[14] Harriman had corresponded and talked with Roosevelt, Raymond Moley, and Rexford Tugwell often during 1932 and early

1933 concerning the problem of industrial recovery.[15] In mid-April, he sent the President a memo regarding "the vital necessity of establishing minimum wages, maximum hours of labor, and possibly minimum prices in order to stop the downward spiral of wages and prices and to check the ruthless competition from which we are suffering."[16]

Such was precisely the kind of program which Roosevelt had in mind when he addressed the Chamber's annual convention on May 4. Though other interest groups had also contributed to the President's thinking, the reception of the business community would be crucial to the success of the administration's plan for industrial recovery. Pointing to the disorder of the industrial system, he declared:

You and I acknowledge the existence of unfair methods of competition, of cut-throat prices and of general chaos. You and I agree that this condition must be rectified and that order must be restored. The attainment of that objective depends upon your willingness to cooperate with one another to this end and also your willingness to cooperate with your Government.[17]

The Chamber quickly made its desire for cooperation apparent; the *New York Times* reported that "the President's speech was received with an enthusiasm which can hardly be overemphasized."[18] The significance of Roosevelt's appearance, his intimation of pending action, and the reaction of his audience were soon translated into furious activity. On May 17, 1933, the President sent his bill to Congress; "I believe," he wrote to Harriman, "the industrial recovery bill will meet with your approval."[19]

Harriman's immediate reaction was euphoric. The NIRA, he declared just a few days after the administration's proposal had gone to the Hill, was a "Magna Charta of industry and labor." At last business and government were to join hands in an effort to rationalize America's industrial system. Laissez faire, Harriman told the Philadelphia Chamber of Commerce, "must be replaced by a philosophy of planned national economy."[20]

The Chamber acted quickly to ensure that the interests of business would be well represented under the new arrangement. Even before passage of the measure by Congress, the Chamber's legal department drafted model codes; and as soon as the act was signed into law, the Chamber rushed a letter to its local affiliates suggesting eight ways in which they could contribute to the code-making process. On June 22, the Board of Directors adopted a policy of encouraging trade associations to support the Recovery Act.[21]

Such cooperation typified Chamber–New Deal relations during the early halcyon days of the NRA. It resulted from a modicum of trust in Roosevelt, a definite fear of further economic collapse, and a genuine hope for the rationalization of the national economy under the auspices of organized business. Though there were risks involved in cooperation, they were outweighed by the perils of further drift. "Some ancient cornerstones of business undoubtedly are being moved," Nation's Business admitted, "but there is strong sentiment that they are landing on solider ground."[22]

The early spirit of cooperation manifested itself in other areas as well. The administration's early economy moves, in particular, gave rise to Chamber expectations that the budget would quickly and finally be balanced. The Chamber mobilized its affiliate organizations in support of the Economy Act passed by Congress in March 1933 and warmly commended efforts to reduce expenditures. Such actions, Nation's Business observed, offered "the promise of a budget balanced or nearly balanced with no considerable increase in the burden on the taxpayer." President Roosevelt, it added effusively, "has done a fine job."[23]

The Chamber recognized that the situation confronting the administration was unusual in many respects, and this perception also colored its roseate view of New Deal fiscal policy. One key Chamber committee reported that matters were in a constant state of flux and feared that events were outrunning even the most determined efforts to embody the Chamber's interests in relevant policy. Under such conditions, the committee warned, it was impossible to make policy recommendations with any finality.[24]

Such temporizing was accentuated by a willingness to accept increased public works spending, called for under Title II of the NIRA, as a legitimate part of the recovery effort. Though it had some misgivings over the apparent "eagerness to spend," *Nation's Business* was hopeful: "Inevitably under such a system there will be some hasty and ill considered action, some errors, and perhaps some regrets. But . . . there is evident a conscious attempt to reduce mistakes to a minimum and to make expended funds produce maximum results." Translating this tacit approval into action, the Chamber sent to its affiliated local chambers a memo describing the most effective manner in which local communities could apply for some of the $3.8 billion available under Title II.[25]

As during the Hoover years, the Chamber appreciated the direness of the economic situation and accordingly tempered its adherence to the traditional creed of fiscal responsibility. Uncertainty regarding the political and economic environment militated against a vehement defense of the balanced budget, and hopes for the New Deal and most particularly for the NRA caused the Chamber to stifle criticism that might have been advanced under less unusual circumstances. An important contributor to early New Deal economic policymaking, including the NRA and AAA, the Chamber spoke in muted tones so long as the outcome of its handiwork appeared favorable.

II

Although business dominated both the code-making process and the NRA authorities which were established to administer the new economic canons, by the fall of 1933 observers began to note increasing antagonism toward the Blue Eagle among businessmen. In its enthusiasm, *Nation's Business* might report nearly unanimous support for the NRA, but by September, Roosevelt was receiving warnings of "growing skepticism and pessimism in the mind of the average business man." By the end of 1933 it was obvious that many were beginning to view the NRA as a bureaucratic tool of oppression, wielded unmercifully by monopolists in collusion with the federal government. Small businessmen complained bitterly that the competitive edge often enjoyed by smaller firms would be destroyed by NRA compulsion to accept unionization and pay higher wages while being barred from meaningful price competition. The proscription of price-fixing in the summer of 1934, however, only served to alienate those other interests within the business community for whom domination of the codes had been the *raison d'être* of the whole endeavor. When government intervened to redress the most obvious imbalances, these interests felt betrayed.[26]

Opposition to the NRA could not, moreover, be categorized solely along big business–small business lines. Disapproval also spread along functional boundaries. The durable goods industries, for example, drifted into resolute opposition to the NRA. Having no problem of sweatshop competition, the durable goods producers found that the codes merely resulted in higher prices for materials without any corresponding advantages. The natural resource industries like coal and oil, on the other hand, were plagued by overcapacity and so welcomed NRA production controls; after the Recovery Act's demise, these interests continued to work for government-sponsored cartelization. Thus, the reaction of business to the NRA divided according to size and sector. The determining factor was whose ox was being gored.[27]

On one point, however, the entire business community seemed to unite; the NRA's labor provisions antagonized businessmen of every stripe. Section 7(a), which guaranteed the right of collective bargaining to workers under NRA codes, reinvigorated the torpid labor movement. The resulting burst of labor activism caused more work stoppages in 1933 than the nation had experienced in any year since 1921. In 1934 nearly one-seventh of the national work force was involved in industrial conflict. The gains of organized labor under the NRA were counterbalanced by the growth of company unions under 7(a). But this development resulted from a dramatic counteroffensive by management, one costly in time, money, energy, and principle. Business' success in temporarily stemming the tide—at least until the Wagner Act of 1935—in no way diminished its vexation at having to fight the battle in the first place. The Chamber believed that most of the strikes during the NRA period were "the result, not of unsatisfactory conditions but of a clause in the Recovery Act."[28]

Within the NRA the forces of consumerism, small business, labor, and the federal bureaucracy all appeared to be impinging seriously on the freedom of action of the once-dominant trade associations. As the initial advantage of the organized and the ready diminished, the euphoria of the Chamber membership dissipated. In September 1933 Harriman warned that 7(a) was "giving rise to confusion and misunderstanding which should receive the attention of all business men and their organization."[29] An index of the organization's more general dissatisfaction was its response to the proposal of a second Swope Plan. In November 1933 Swope presented to the Department of Commerce's Business Advisory and Planning Council another program "for achieving self-government of industry." He suggested replacing the NRA with a National Chamber of Commerce and Industry "which may well be an enlargement and development of the present Chamber of Commerce of the United States"; the government was to step aside and permit business to organize the economy without interference.[30] Harriman supported the proposition; and when the Chamber's Board of Directors met later that month, it appointed a special committee to study the NRA and to examine the merits and feasibility of the latest Swope scheme.[31]

Misgivings about the administration of the Recovery Act were not limited to the leaders of the Chamber. A survey of reactions to NRA operations in over one hundred cities made evident the disenchantment of the membership at large. Released on the eve of the Chamber's 1934 convention, the canvass reported many complaints, with favorable evaluations of the NRA running only slightly ahead of critical responses.[32] The amalgam of deep despair and exaggerated hope which had characterized the Chamber at the dawn of the New Deal was giving way to a new realism.

The Chamber's 1934 meeting reflected this change in mood. Though speakers were hesitant to attack the New Deal in toto, they subjected some of the specifics of FDR's program to caustic analysis. Roosevelt declined to address the gathering in person. Instead he sent a cautious message, one which could not be called unfriendly but which had an unmistakable edge to it: "It is time," he wrote, "to stop crying 'wolf' and to cooperate in working for recovery and for the continued elimination of evil conditions of the past. I confidently count on the loyalty and continued support of the Chamber."[33] Of this last, the Chamber was less certain than ever.

Still, Chamber leaders minimized the rift, warning that "too often we deal entirely in criticism and do not recognize the great amount of good that may be done." In the end Harriman attempted to put the best face possible on the proceedings. It was difficult, he wrote the President several days after the convention, to find unanimity among so many businessmen. He took some satisfaction, however, in the fact that

Neither the right nor the left wing, whatever that may mean, was in ascendency. Parts of your program were not agreed to, but, on the whole, I feel that American business recognizes the magnificent effort you have made to assist recovery, appreciates your absolute sincerity, and agrees with many of the basic principles, if not the details, of your program. Above all . . . it earnestly desires to cooperate with the government to the end that permanent and lasting prosperity may be restored.

The sentiments were undoubtedly sincere. It was becoming increasingly uncertain, however, whether such feelings were representative of either the Chamber or business in general.[34]

The Chamber was not the only disgruntled element in the business community in the summer of 1934. A generalized fear that the New Deal threatened business autonomy developed among businessmen of all sorts. In June, Roosevelt signed into law the controversial Securities Exchange Act, which established a new agency to regulate the securities market and eliminate some of the worst abuses of the speculative 1920s; he also announced plans to send a sweeping social welfare program to Congress in 1935. Two months later, FDR's staunchly conservative Director of the Budget, Lewis Douglas, resigned, and that same August the American Liberty League was incorporated. *Time* magazine reported that "private fulminations and public carpings against the New Deal" had become "almost a routine of the business day."[35]

Finally, on September 21, 1934, the Chamber's NRA Committee presented to the Board a preliminary report recommending that the Recovery Act not be extended upon its expiration the following June, but rather that it be replaced by new legislation applying only to interstate firms on a wholly voluntary basis. The new law would ban the closed union shop and stretch the guarantee of collective bargaining to ensure the right of minorities and even individuals to make their own contracts with employers.[36] Government involvement was to be limited to the approval or disapproval of codes written by business. In effect, the plan demanded pure and simple business self-government, without the concessions to labor and to a vaguely defined but bothersome "public interest" that had begun to complicate the NRA.

Characteristically, Harriman sought once more to cushion the blow. Troubled by "so many garbled and misleading statements" appearing in the press, he wrote a personal letter to the President assuring him that neither the Chamber's special committee nor its Board opposed "the basic principles of the NRA." Harriman, however, was falling out of step with the Chamber's rank and file. In December 1934 the membership voted in a referendum 1,708 to 254 to allow the NIRA as originally formulated to die upon its legal expiration in June 1935. The Chamber counterproposal, for industrial self-government played solitaire, was overwhelmingly approved.[37] Since the beginning of the New Deal, the Blue Eagle experiment had held the Chamber, however tenuously, in Roosevelt's national coalition, but as business soured on the NRA it became progressively more difficult to maintain peace on other fronts.

III

Broad Chamber opposition to the New Deal broke surface with the publication on September 24, 1934, of a letter from the Board to Roosevelt. Duly noting that for the past eighteen months the Chamber had "whole heartedly supported" the administration, the message expressed concern over the "general state of apprehension among the business men of the country" and propounded questions regarding the direction of New Deal policy in six major areas. The queries went publicly unanswered, but a private response was apparently provided.[38] In an unsigned letter to "My dear Mr. Harriman," Roosevelt vented his spleen. Attached to the draft was a "Memo for Mac" asking, "What do you think of this letter?" The President's assistant secretary, Marvin McIntyre, did not commit his opinion to paper but noted, "Bring to President on Wednesday morning when Mr. Harriman comes in to see him"; thus, we can assume that the gist of FDR's draft was indeed communicated to the Chamber, or at least to its president. "I am annoyed," he wrote, "by the request . . . that the President make categorical answer to . . . questions propounded by a wholly private organization." Leaping to the offensive, he argued that the Chamber leaders would be more helpful if they offered their own views, "not along the lines of glittering generalities, but on practical methods for accomplishing what they believe to be the correct procedure."[39]

Roosevelt apparently expressed these sentiments with considerable vigor, for several days later Harriman replied in a politely indignant letter that the Board had been "very careful to adopt language which would express its earnest feeling that a public expression regarding the six subjects would be of great public value." The President's press secretary Stephen Early responded curtly that both the President and the press had viewed the statement as a questionnaire. The Chamber, he said, had done nothing to correct this impression.[40] By this point, the Chamber and the administration were drifting dangerously apart.

The stunning Democratic victory in the November 1934 elections temporarily closed the widening breach. Fearful of the radical potential of the new Congress, the Chamber moved quickly to make peace with the administration. Harriman explained:

Business has come to regard the realities of the situation. It recognizes that the country has given a mandate to the President. It is our hope that his policies will be wise and helpful to business and, further, it is our belief that they will be. . . . All we want, all we can ask for and all the country needs is a thorough spirit of cooperation. And when I say "cooperation" I mean a condition in which government does not attack business and business does not attack the government.[41]

The truce, however, proved short-lived.

In the early months of 1935, Chamber-administration relations steadily worsened. With a large public employment program already proposed, Roosevelt on January 17 asked Congress for a comprehensive social security program; on the next day, the Board of Directors authorized the appointment of a committee to study past and pending legislation "to determine whether such legislation may be demonstrated as leading definitely to the complete socialization of the United States."[42] When Chamber members gathered in the nation's capital for their annual meeting at the end of April 1935, dissatisfaction was the order of the day.

As retiring president of the Chamber, Harriman opened the convention on April 30 with a critical but conciliatory address in which he described the NRA and AAA as "extraordinarily daring experiments" and urged their reconsideration with "critical sympathy." But such dulcification quickly gave way to acrimonious criticism of the New Deal, which increased as it became clear that the President did not intend to send the traditional message to the convention. For almost an hour on May 1, Harriman, his associates, and certain key Chamber staff members met to try to avert a total break. On that day too the permanent staff and several of the leaders of the more important committees attempted to forestall some of the critical resolutions that had been drawn up—unsuccessfully.[43]

On the very next day, rebellion erupted on the floor during a general session on resolutions, and the membership struck out in unprecedented fashion against both the New Deal and the Chamber leadership. The delegates approved resolutions attacking the NRA extension suggested by the administration, government interference with "the proper functions of trade associations," the proposed Utility Bill of 1935, Title II of the pending banking legislation (affecting the Federal Reserve), and the AAA. Even this was not enough for the mood of the membership; soon a struggle ensued over a seemingly innocuous resolution calling for the establishment of uniform highway standards. After a melodramatic debate, the convention defeated the original measure and substituted a states'-rights resolution in its stead.[44] Events quickly moved beyond the control of Harriman, who was presiding, and the other Chamber moderates.

The representatives of the Illinois Manufacturers' Association struck the most serious blow of the assault in attacking a Chamber resolution which called for the postponement, pending further study by Congress, of the administration's proposed social security program. Even this far-from-friendly resolution was swept away and replaced with a substitute which eliminated the original veiled approval of federal-state cooperation on old age pensions. An exasperated Harriman tried to save the original resolution by reminding those assembled that a vote for the amendment meant opposition to federal aid for the aged indigent, but the audience shouted him down. Amendment sponsor George Houston of the Baldwin Locomotive Works demanded sharply that the vote be taken without interpretation from the chair, and the amendment was passed. The break with the New Deal was now public and complete.[45]

The transition from the politics of cooperation to that of opposition can be seen in the evolution of Chamber policy on federal finance during 1934–1935. As relations with the administration cooled, concern over fiscal policy increased. At the September 1934 Board meeting which issued the Chamber's notorious "questionnaire," the chairman of the Committee on Federal Finance (COFF) warned that government spending and borrowing practices were retarding recovery.[46] In this, as in other areas, the results of the 1934 elections prompted a reassessment. In January 1935 the Committee, mindful of the renewed post-election spirit of cooperation, found that after prolonged discussion it was unable to agree on a publishable statement concerning federal fiscal policy. Among the reasons the Committee offered for its hesitance to make a public statement were the advisability of supporting FDR's budget policy for fear that a worse one could be forthcoming from the new Congress and the realization that demands for a smaller deficit might be seized upon by New Dealers anxious to impose new taxes on businessmen.[47] In July 1935, ten weeks after the uproarious convention, the Chamber announced a nationwide campaign against Roosevelt's "soak-the-rich" tax proposal, accusing the administration of pursuing social reform under the guise of raising revenue. By the end of the Second Hundred Days, with their Wagner Act, social security legislation, and passage of the Wealth Tax Act of 1935, the Committee's rationale for moderation rang hollow. Hence, when the Committee submitted its formal report in November, its earlier indecision had changed to certainty: New Deal taxes, it argued unambiguously, retarded recovery and threatened the very existence of the American economic system. Government would either have to restrain itself or be restrained.[48]

In its approach to fiscal affairs, as in other matters, the Chamber's days of expedience had passed. In early 1936, the membership followed the lead of the Committee's November attack on New Deal finance with its overwhelming approval of a referendum statement which called for a balanced budget, without increased taxes, "in the near future" and, once that balance was achieved, a further reduction in taxes "at the earliest practicable date."[49]

There were many reasons for this change in the Chamber's views on fiscal policy. In part, the group reacted to developments in national economic policies. The Chamber found it increasingly difficult to dismiss the administration's deficit spending as a passing aberration; each successive deficit was harder to accept. In addition, the organization believed that the Wealth Tax of 1935 aimed the weapon of taxation directly at business, thus bearing out the Chamber's earlier contention that budget deficits ultimately necessitated additional taxation. New Deal economics seemed to be a crazy amalgam of spending, deficits, and taxation—a combination which simultaneously defied conventional economic wisdom, courted inflation, fostered rule by bureaucracy, and soaked the successful.[50]

The new stance represented a response to more general pressures as well. The initial sense of crisis which had dulled business reaction to the early New Deal deficits had clearly passed. A revival of optimism regarding business recovery made criticism easier than it had been earlier.[51] As the new Chamber president, Harper Sibley, related, "The life preserver which is so necessary when the ship is sinking becomes a heavy burden when man is back on dry land."[52] The "life preserver" seemed all the heavier as Chamber hopes for the NRA crumbled. The disintegration of that business-government condominium was particularly a blow to Harriman's leadership.[53] His retirement from the Chamber's presidency in May 1935 further meant that an important mediating influence had been lost. Although incoming president Harper Sibley was no hard-shell reactionary, his leadership was clearly less friendly to the administration and to the tenets of the New Deal. Harriman had stressed flexibility and change; Sibley emphasized the defense of fundamental principles. The distinction involved both style and substance.[54]

The growing antagonism of the New Deal toward business also contributed to the Chamber's shift in policy. Whether the transition from the First to the Second New Deal in 1934–1935 was a turn to the right or the left is still a point of contention among historians, but the increase in antibusiness sentiment among the purveyors of the Second New Deal was palpable. "Fighting with a businessman," New Dealer Tommy Corcoran told Raymond Moley in the spring of 1935, "is like fighting with a Polack. You can give no quarter."[55] In this context, it is easy to understand why the Chamber moved beyond expediency to a position of negativistic opposition to Roosevelt and his works.

IV

An ever-increasing defensiveness characterized the Chamber's new stance in the period after its formal break with the New Deal in 1935. As the administration stepped up its rhetorical assault on "the royalists of the economic order," the Chamber slowly but perceptibly slouched into a posture of uncomprehending innocence. Finding business "a stranger in its own house," *Nation's Business* was bewildered by the "mental fog about business" which threatened the free enterprise system.[56] To combat this generalized antagonism, the Chamber embarked in 1937–1938 on a $500,000 public relations campaign built around a series of advertisements in *Nation's Business* (preaching largely, as it were, to those already converted) and the *Saturday Evening Post*. More than 12,000 billboards nationwide aimed at a broader audience with the message, "What Helps Business Helps You."[57]

As the Chamber grew more defensive, it adopted an increasingly rigid position on matters of public policy. Unquestioned opposition to government and adherence to the verities of the classical laissez-faire business creed became the hallmarks of Chamber policy pronouncements. Of the 1936 convention, one participant reported:

Practically all speakers were critical of government activities. . . . However, in these discussions constructive criticism was noticeably lacking, most of the speakers limiting themselves to criticisms of existing laws, regulations, etc. without making any suggestions as to what changes should be made or how such changes could be made. In other words, business . . . did not seem to have any definite ideas as to just what course to sail.[58]

The topic of fiscal policy quickly came to the fore in the campaign to roll back the New Deal. One reason for this was the widespread concern among businessmen over the propriety of the government's spending and taxing efforts. A second reason was the general popularity—in the abstract, at least—of calls for "governmental economy."[59] In addition, the fiscal issue proved particularly useful because it seemed to lie at the center of a whole constellation of concerns and fears. Deficit spending not only threatened economic disaster but also exemplified moral decay. Taxation not only appeared exorbitant and unfair but also served as the foundation for the growth of big government, promising rule by bureaucracy and, ultimately, a drift into socialism.[60] Spending was, in short, a mainspring of the New Deal; in the Chamber's view it thus constituted a moral and political as well as an economic problem.

Despite the Chamber's emphasis on fiscal questions, however, its policy of negativistic opposition left it unable to influence the New Deal's most important fiscal decision—the determination to resume spending in the wake of the 1937–1938 recession. Roosevelt initially reacted to this slump, the most precipitous downturn in American history, by continuing the conservative fiscal policies which had helped to bring it on. Important support for this tack came from Secretary of the Treasury Morgenthau, who argued vigorously for a balanced budget and a courting of business favor. But as conditions steadily worsened, the spending bloc among the President's advisers grew in numbers and influence.[61] The tide of battle finally swung in favor of the spenders when the President went to Warm Springs in late March 1938. Away from the influence of Morgenthau, Roosevelt fell prey to the entreaties of Harry Hopkins, who came armed with arguments prepared by Leon Henderson, Aubrey Williams, and the businessman Beardsley Ruml. On April 14, the President announced a program calling for $3.05 billion in additional relief ($1.5 billion of this to be in the form of RFC loans); a credit expansion of $2.15 billion by means of a reduction in reserve requirements and the desterilization of Treasury gold; and the spending or lending of $1.912 billion for public works ("definite additions to the purchasing power of the nation").[62] The decision was one made almost wholly within the executive branch. Administrators and advisers fought the battle, expert advice was mustered in support, and Roosevelt was finally swayed.

The Chamber realized that the President's program was a departure from earlier spending for relief. It meant that spending as a "defensive against distress" had been supplanted by spending "as an offensive to create and sustain prosperity."[63] The change was a crucial one. Yet the business organization which had helped to shape other New Deal landmarks—the NIRA and AAA—stood silent, without influence.

The reason for this impotence lay in part in the gen-

erally poor relations between the Chamber and the administration. With the passing of Harriman's leadership, a curtain had fallen across Lafayette Park, effectively interrupting
discourse between the Chamber and the White House. Those
who had experienced the intimacy of earlier days particularly noticed the change. Julius Barnes, Chamber president
from 1921 to 1924, complained that Chamber presidents
were no longer invited to the White House for consultation,
a "very unhealthy situation" as he saw it.[64] In 1925, *Nation's
Business* had crowed that the American businessman was
"the most influential person in the nation . . . perhaps the
most influential figure in the world"; in 1939, however,
Secretary of Commerce Hopkins dismissed the resolutions
of the Chamber as "defeatist" and "dull reading."[65]

The Chamber's policy of negativism had left the organization unable to offer any suggestions for economic recovery short of a total repeal of the New Deal. The Chamber
remained resolute in its denunciation of continued deficits.
Despite its realization that large expenditures stimulated the
economy, the group attacked deficit spending as the greatest
single obstacle to faith in the free-enterprise system and to
recovery from the Depression.[66] Instead it offered a program
which reached to "the roots of existing difficulties." The
prescription ran the anti-New Deal litany: tax relief, amendment of the Wagner Act, budget balancing through cuts in
expenditures, an easing of securities regulation, cessation
of government competition with private utilities, and return
of relief programs to local authority.[67] In short, the Chamber
responded to crisis by calling for the restoration of the status
quo ante bellum. It is hardly surprising that such a platform
elicited only emnity from the administration.

The executive was not the whole of government, however, and the Chamber was already turning to the Congress
to stem the New Deal tide. Conservatives had long considered the Supreme Court the last bastion of laissez-faire cap-

italism. This view had been seemingly justified by the
Court's willingness, at least through 1936, to declare invalid
significant components of the administration's legislative
program. Such actions provoked Roosevelt's ire and in 1937
he attempted to ensure the New Deal's control of the Court
by expanding its membership. In a technical sense, the President lost the battle to "pack" the Court but won the war;
for a combination of reasons, the Justices soon began to
uphold New Deal initiatives. Accordingly, conservatives
turned increasingly to Congress for help. This was particularly true as fiscal issues came to the fore; in this area the
New Deal's constitutional mandate was beyond challenge.
"In 1935," George Houston told the 1938 Chamber convention, "many of us said, 'Thank God for the Supreme Court.'
In 1938, and again I hope in 1939, we are saying 'Thank
God for an independent Congress.'"[68] Despite such hopes,
congressional conservatives could not prevent the implementation of FDR's April 1938 decision to resume massive
federal spending. Fearful of opposing renewed spending in
the midst of a serious downturn—an election-year slump
at that—Congress actually gave the administration more
money than it had requested.[69]

But when conditions improved in 1939, Congress for
the first time defeated a New Deal spending measure. The
Works Financing Bill of 1939 proposed the creation of a
$3.06 billion revolving fund for self-liquidating projects, to
begin with an outlay of $870 million in fiscal year 1940; the
money would be either lent or spent by the RFC directly,
or made available to other agencies (the Department of Agriculture, the Public Works Administration, the Public
Roads Administration, and the Rural Electrification Administration) to spend or lend. Moreover, the borrowing authority of the U.S. Housing Authority was to be increased
by another $800 million.[70] Many spenders thought the pro-
posal too weak. Morgenthau found it "respectable" and saw

its self-liquidating feature as a way to spend or lend without incurring a budgetary liability.[71] The program would not add to the deficit, it was claimed, unless in the future the loans (with both interest and principal guaranteed by the federal government) were defaulted. Such bookkeeping distinctions were lost on conservative critics, however. They saw the bill as a rather clever attempt to camouflage deficit spending and continued infiltration of the economy by the federal government.[72] A watered-down version finally passed the Senate on July 31, 1939, but the House killed the proposal the next day when, by a 193–166 vote, it refused to consider the bill. On August 3, the $800 million housing measure, being considered separately, met the same fate by a vote of 191–170.

Just how much the Chamber contributed to the congressional attack on New Deal fiscal policy is impossible to measure, but the Chamber's constant drum beat of government frugality appears to have finally had some effect. The court fight had weakened Roosevelt politically, and he had suffered a further defeat when he intervened unsuccessfully in several 1938 congressional primaries in an attempt to secure the election of Democratic liberals. Capitalizing on these failures and on the fact that recovery from the recession was making spending a somewhat less attractive policy, conservative bodies like the Chamber combined with ideological allies to frustrate the New Deal's fiscal plans.

One such kindred group was the National Association of Manufacturers. The NAM had a smaller membership than the Chamber, one drawn wholly from the manufacturing sector of the economy. It generally took a more conservative position on public issues and had long enjoyed a reputation as "the shock troop brigade" of the American business community.[73] Founded in 1895, the organization in its early years concentrated on the development of foreign trade, but after 1903 the Association turned its attention to combating the rise of organized labor. During the 1920s the NAM became a national leader in business' drive for the open shop. The Depression hit the Association hard, however, and its membership—primarily small and medium-sized manufacturers—fell off precipitously. By 1932 resignations were averaging sixty-five a month, and the Association was "perilously close to its last dollar and its last member."[74]

Ironically, the New Deal was the salvation of the NAM. The group never fully participated in the "honeymoon" phase of the early New Deal; and although it had lobbied for some sort of industrial coordination, it was more critical of the National Industrial Recovery Act and especially Section 7(a) than was the Chamber. Led by president Robert Lund of Lambert Pharmaceutical and a cadre of particularly conservative executives known as the "Brass Hats," in 1934 the Association consciously set out to make itself the rallying point for business opposition to the Roosevelt regime.[75] Membership, which had dropped to 1,469 in 1933, shot up to 3,008 in 1937 and to 9,418 by 1943; support by large firms increased significantly.[76] Throughout the 1930s, the NAM retained its leadership in the struggle against organized labor, but its opposition to the New Deal was broad in scope and never confined to one issue. Alfred Cleveland has found that of thirty-eight major legislative proposals enacted into law between 1933 and 1941, the NAM opposed all but seven. Association criticism was sharpened by the belief that "in opposing unsound economic and social measures it is unnecessary to propose alternatives."[77]

The opposition of the NAM to New Deal fiscal policy reflected this general stance; its congenital fiscal conservatism hardened as deficit spending became an emotional political issue as well as an economic problem. In 1933, concern over the "crisis" in federal finance prompted the NAM to recommend the imposition of a federal sales tax and a broadening of the income tax base. Opposition to deficit spending was a recurrent theme throughout the Depression years.[78] When Roosevelt increased spending in 1938, the NAM remained critical: "Pouring public funds into pump-priming projects, no matter how freely," the NAM directors announced, "cannot provide permanent jobs and economic stability if private enterprise is not encouraged simultaneously to proceed and expand. On the other hand, if all possible encouragement is given to private enterprise, then little, if any, pump-priming will be necessary."[79] Such rhetoric caused Senator Claude Pepper (D-Fla.), shortly after the defeat of the administration's spend-lend proposal in 1939, to denounce a "designing alliance" for attempting to destroy the New Deal, accusing the conspirators of "having prostituted their power to serve the U.S. Chamber of Commerce, the Manufacturer's Association, and the beneficiaries of special privilege."[80]

The situation, then, was one of apparent stalemate. With the April 1938 spending decision, the administration embraced an expansionary fiscal program, largely for Keynesian reasons. Though the commitment was not total, and the theoretical purity of the motives not completely beyond cavil, the change in direction was nevertheless clear. By 1939, however, there had arisen in Congress a conservative bloc able to frustrate the administration's proposals for all but military spending. To some unknown degree, the Chamber and the NAM contributed to this foiling of New Deal fiscal policy. At last the cost of negativistic opposition—a stunning loss of influence in the executive branch—appeared to be balanced by the rewards flowing from congressional resistance. The New Deal contagion had been, if not eradicated, at least contained.

Closer analysis indicates that this stalemate was fraught with danger. Negativism left the Chamber and the NAM unable to provide positive alternatives aimed at achieving recovery. The position allowed no middle ground; it made impossible any recognition that government did have an important leadership role to play in economic and especially in fiscal affairs. The organization of the Chamber exemplified this rigidity. Without the need to develop new answers to the problems posed by the Depression, the Chamber felt no need to modernize its research and policymaking apparatus. Policy continued to be made for businessmen by businessmen. The organization hired no economists, employed no specially trained experts.[81]

The resignation of Edward A. Filene from the Chamber in 1936 set the problem in stark relief. Head of a well-established Boston department store, Filene was the founder and president of the Twentieth Century Fund, a research foundation created to generate critical analyses of major political, social, and economic issues. He had been one of the Chamber's organizers in 1912 and was generally considered the father of the group's referendum system. In a public letter to the Board of Directors, he complained:

The United States Chamber of Commerce, as at present organized, is not an organization of *business* but rather an organization of *business men*—meeting not to study business in a business way, nor even to find out what the needs of business in general may be, but either to promote the special views of certain prominent people in the business world, or at best to discover and express the fixed opinion of the membership concerning matters which, in the most successful modern business organizations, would be referred as a matter of course to fact-finding research. . . .

. . . By this, I do not mean merely that it is alienating progressive minds: I mean, rather, that such a policy cannot be constructive—cannot produce the results by which the members, whether liberal or conservative, may realize that they are getting their money's worth. The Chamber as at present organized may function as a successful club of business men when times are good, or as a potent center of reaction when changing times make some great new forward step necessary; but in neither role can it furnish any real help to business, either to business in general or to the particular business of the average member.[82]

The Chamber's ideological and institutional rigidity contrasted markedly with the willingness of the federal government to respond positively to a rapidly changing environment by making increasing use of expertise. The much publicized Brains Trust had been merely the professorial vanguard.[83] In a shrewd analysis of the Second New Deal's advocates of the spending solution, contemporary observers noted that "they are like nothing so much as the clever liberated younger professors in a big urban university." Tommy Corcoran, Ben Cohen, and Jerome Frank were all lawyers with strong academic connections. Isador Lubin, Leon Henderson, Mordecai Ezekiel, and Lauchlin Currie were trained economists.[84] Roosevelt had said early on that "while there is a certain amount of comment about the use of brains in the national government, it seems to me a pretty good practice—a practice which will continue—this practice of calling on trained people for tasks that require trained people."[85] By contrast, the Chamber and its allies were bogged down in nay-saying and uninterested in finding the "trained people" they would clearly need in the days ahead.

In the confines of academe, meanwhile, liberal intellectuals, led by Alvin Hansen of Harvard, were formulating a version of Keynesianism which made the spending decision of April 1938 appear timid by comparison. The stagnationist prescription called for increased, heavily progressive taxation, continued deficit spending for massive public welfare projects, and a generally expanded role for the federal government in the economy. In short, the program promised a super New Deal, and found a receptive audience among liberals.[86] Hansen's appearance before the Temporary National Economic Committee was a tour de force, carefully orchestrated by friendly New Dealers. Currie recalls "arranging for him to be our star witness . . . rehearsing together our testimony and going over a long list of 'good' and 'bad' words prepared for the use of the government witnesses by Stuart Chase."[87]

Businessmen responded to Hansen's ideas in a variety of ways. For some, his views merely confirmed the belief the Keynesian economics was New Deal liberalism in a fancy package. Others were more receptive: in 1939 the participants in the *Fortune* Round-Table found "indefinite stagnation and chronic unemployment" to be the greatest danger facing the nation.[88] Still other businessmen expressed cautious support for countercyclical spending, grasping at the politically less potent versions of Keynesianism in hope of warding off the solution of the stagnationists.[89] But the policy of negativistic opposition left the Chamber and the NAM unable to maneuver in this flexible way. It discouraged the development of an institutional apparatus which could translate flexibility into cogent policy options. Despite the apparent ability of congressional conservatives to frustrate New Deal fiscal policy, the Chamber and the NAM were left without the ability to influence the formation of policy within the executive branch or to formulate viable alternatives. Business' leading spokesmen in Washington could react to events, but appeared unable to plan effectively for the future. The stagnationists were, by comparison, activists who at least offered an assertive program.

Other elements in the business community, however, reacted more positively to the developments of the Depression years. These businessmen sought to define a new, more active macroeconomic role for government which would generate recovery and promise economic stability while avoiding statist regimentation. In their attempts to forge a new partnership between government, academe, and business, they manifested a significant continuity with the activities of those who had labored since the turn of the century to establish what James Weinstein has called "the corporate ideal in the liberal state."[90]

Chapter Three
Patterns of Positive Business Response

With negativism firmly entrenched in the most visible business organizations, it is not surprising that both contemporary observers and subsequent historians have emphasized conflict as the dominant theme in business-government relations during the New Deal.[1] As we have seen, this view is built on a foundation of truth. It has, however, caused students to neglect one of the most significant dimensions of business-government interaction in the twentieth century—that is, the pattern of accommodation or compromise that persists beneath the surface of conflict-centered events. Even during the bitterest moments of the 1930s, some businessmen within the Chamber of Commerce believed that outright opposition to so popular a figure as Roosevelt was politically inexpedient and doomed to failure. Although efforts to move the Chamber back to a more moderate position were not immediately successful, they did keep alive a hope for greater flexibility which would flourish in the more favorable atmosphere of World War II.

Rumblings of discontent with the Chamber's negativism sounded soon after the more or less formal adoption of that position at the controversial 1935 convention.[2] Though negativism was a rallying point for those elements within the Chamber which were completely estranged from the New

Deal, it repelled those who hoped for some sort of rapprochement. In April 1936, the Automobile Manufacturers Association, one of the original members of the Chamber, withdrew. *Business Week* explained, "While the automobile makers may object to the Roosevelt philosophy, they are enjoying a perfectly grand business with prospects of a record season. Also political advisors suggest that, like it or not, the chances are for four more years of Roosevelt."[3]

Meanwhile, both the national organization and its local chambers suffered from a lack of support by big business, a problem that was exacerbated by the Chamber's defensive stance. The National Firms Committee of the National Association of Commercial Organization Secretaries (NACOS) reported in 1938, "The present programs of many local Chambers and the National Chamber are not understood or sympathized with by many of our most active businessmen. . . . On the other hand, the management of large corporations is getting closer to government either by choice or necessity."[4]

The inability of the Chamber to "get close" to government prompted some members to speak out against the rigidity of its opposition to the New Deal. Marion Folsom, treasurer of Eastman-Kodak and president of the relatively progressive Rochester chamber, reminded the professionals of NACOS in 1937 that "most of the social reforms which require governmental action have not . . . been helped very much by business organizations and have not been foreseen." He continued:

Now, the result has been that influence of business organizations has been somewhat discredited and we have not had nearly as much to do with the writing of this legislation as we should have had. Much of the legislation has been written without the practical assistance of business men. As a result, we have legislation that is too radical in many respects and not altogether practical. . . .

As our civilization becomes more complex, it is only natural the government will have a little more to do with it than it had in the past. . . . We must not lose all the good we have obtained in the past and yet we must adjust ourselves to changed conditions. It seems to me the Chamber of Commerce should provide this need; study the present situation; see what these trends are, and try to prepare business men for changes which are inevitable; when it is necessary to have legislation, assist in drafting that legislation so that it will be along sound and practical lines.[5]

Such sentiments, moreover, were not limited to those associated with "big business." In May 1939, for example, the chamber in Walla Walla, Washington, sent a letter to both Secretary of Commerce Hopkins and Chamber President W. Gibson Carey calling for "greater coordination and a better understanding" between business and government.[6] At the same time, local chamber and trade association executives were becoming restive over what they considered to be a decline in the quality of service rendered to members by the national organization.[7] Chamber operations seemed to be lagging both in Washington and in the field.

The Chamber's leaders were slow to recognize this mounting dissatisfaction with their negativistic stance. At times they seemed almost to wallow in the adversity which they had done so much to create. Resolute opposition to the New Deal and all its works became a symbol of spiritual purity: "It is this continuing adherence to principle," proclaimed Executive Committee Chairman John O'Leary, "unaffected by expediency or by temporary pressure to be so-called 'cooperative' or 'not always opposed' that has kept the Chamber through the period of this policy in a position of regard and respect."[8] Similarly, the relaxation of tension between the Chamber and the administration was not a goal to be sought but rather prima facie evidence of failure: "When we fail of being attacked or criticized by these forces, we must need watch our step for fear that we are not doing our full part in protecting the business system."[9] The moderates and pragmatists within the Chamber failed to make much headway against such views during the 1930s, but their continued complaints would later serve as the basis for a dramatic movement to force the Chamber into a positive accommodation with the changes wrought by the Depression experience.

I

Other businessmen outside the traditional peak business associations also reacted positively to the challenge of the New Deal. Their responses reflected not merely a concern with political expediency but also a philosophical view of the state quite different from that held by the negativists of the Chamber and the NAM. Such businessmen shared an organic view of society and believed the business-government conflict of the period not only politically impractical but in a larger sense dysfunctional for the operation of a modern capitalist economy. Eschewing the emotionalism and sloganeering which seemed to pervade the spirited opposition of the negativists, these corporatists accented the need for expert analysis in order to define the government's proper role in the economy. One expression of this viewpoint was the establishment within the federal bureaucracy of a Business Advisory Council (BAC), whose members combined political pragmatism with an awareness of the failings of laissez-faire capitalism. A second group of businessmen, some connected with the BAC but others not, came directly to a recognition of the need for deficit spending to generate economic recovery. A third group opened another front toward the end of the Depression decade; this campaign began at the University of Chicago and brought together a small circle of academics and business executives who shared the belief that businessmen should now appropriate the economic wisdom of the scholarly community. Such efforts gave business leaders important experience in working regularly with government, helped to develop a new appreciation of Keynesian economics among businessmen, and influenced the course of public policy. These same three groups would later come together in the establishment of a new business organization, the Committee for Economic Development, which would become one of the nation's most glamorous spokesmen for "enlightened business sentiment" and a crucial factor in the shaping of America's postwar political economy.

Created in 1933, the Business Advisory and Planning Council—a name shortened to Business Advisory Council two years later—was the brainchild of Secretary of Commerce Daniel Roper, who hoped that regular consultation would bring about "a more harmonious relationship between government and business."[10] After discussing the idea with his friends and advisers, Roper suggested to the Chamber of Commerce convention in early May 1933 that a "President's council of business" be established to supply the administration with "the most experienced . . . advice as to proper ways of stimulating and reviving" the nation's sagging economy.[11] A preliminary meeting in early June elicited the support of many leaders in America's corporate community—among those in attendance were Henry I. Harriman of the Chamber, Gerard Swope of General Electric, Alexander Legge of International Harvester, Walter Teagle of Standard Oil, and Alfred Sloan of General Motors—and invitations to serve on the council were sent out to forty-one eminent businessmen. On June 26, the BAC was officially established.[12]

The original members were chosen with an eye toward industrial and geographic representation, but "more farsighted businessmen with a broad public conception of the obligations of business" were especially sought after. The resulting membership consisted of several liberal executives from medium-sized firms and a disproportionate number of businessmen from truly giant corporations. The latter included Myron Taylor of U.S. Steel, Alfred Sloan of General Motors, Robert Wood of Sears Roebuck, Walter Gifford of A.T.&T., and Pierre duPont.[13] Gerard Swope, intellectual progenitor of the New Deal's NRA, served as chairman of the group.

Membership quickly expanded to over fifty and the Council began its work almost at once. In its first year and a half of operation the BAC established twenty-one separate committees and completed studies on topics ranging from the decentralization of industry to uniform statistical reporting and accounting methods for industry.[14] Businessmen drawn from the BAC's membership on a rotating basis staffed the NRA's Industrial Advisory Board. Following the resignation of NRA overlord Hugh Johnson in September 1934, S. Clay Williams of R. J. Reynolds Tobacco left the BAC to become titular head of the recovery effort as chairman of the National Industrial Recovery Board.

As the New Deal program took shape, however, the position of the Council became increasingly uncertain. On the one hand, the NRA, for which such high hopes had been entertained, was rent by dissension. On the other hand, the rising tide of reform legislation made the Council increasingly uneasy. In March 1934, the BAC labeled the proposed Fletcher-Rayburn Stock Exchange Bill "a national disaster."[15] A direct confrontation finally came in May 1935, when Roosevelt attempted to exploit the Council in his battle with the national Chamber of Commerce. With his programs under blistering attack by the Chamber, the President welcomed a delegation from the BAC and accepted from them several reports which were then publicized as favorable to the very policies—social security and the NRA—most vehemently criticized by the Chamber convention.[16] In fact, the BAC report on the extension of the NRA was much more qualified than Roosevelt admitted, and an additional, generally hostile report on the public utilities issue was simply not made public.[17] Many members felt that the President, in collusion with a group of Council liberals, had used the imprimatur of the BAC in an effort to persuade the public that the Chamber was an isolated foe of the New Deal's programs. In addition, they feared that a kind of censorship had been imposed, with only favorable reports destined to see the light of day, unfavorable commentaries being relegated to dark recesses of the White House. Despite a plea by Ernest Draper of the Commerce Department that Council members not "disregard the future . . . in a burst of petulant disgust," resignations poured in.[18]

The Council was quickly reconstituted with some changes in both leadership and membership, but the hopes of the First Hundred Days had been permanently damped. Members continued to find much to criticize in Roosevelt's program, especially in his fiscal policies.[19] As economic conditions slowly improved in 1936 and early 1937, the Council became more insistent in its demand for a fiscal reckoning. The time had come, at last, for the New Deal to stop viewing the balanced budget as "a desirable objective" and to fix it, finally and firmly, as "a definite and positive goal."[20] The Council resolutely advocated a balanced budget even as the economy fell into deeper depression in late 1937. While the administration debated what course to follow, the BAC plumped for fiscal retrenchment. Further pump-priming, it warned, would "seriously interfere with, if not completely prevent, the resumption of fundamentally sound recovery."[21]

The Council greeted with dismay FDR's announcement on April 14, 1938, that the government was reverting to massive—in the context of the times—federal spending to generate recovery. Roper had argued that retrenchment would not necessarily breed prosperity, and in December he had reminded the BAC that recession conditions sometimes made it "not only desirable but necessary to expand government credit by unbalancing the budget." In February 1938 the Council requested that the federal government accelerate its spending during slack periods, but by implication this was to be done within the limits of a balanced budget. Further than this the BAC would not go. As the New Deal moved hesitatingly to embrace the spending solution, it left behind its most important formal link with the business community.[22]

Moreover, a sense of general dissatisfaction on the part of both the BAC and the administration lurked behind such particular disagreements. Council members felt isolated and doubted their ability to influence policy; the arrangement lacked the intimacy they had hoped for originally. The realization that business was not the only group enjoying access to the administration compounded their frustration. Harry Hopkins, Roper's successor as Secretary of Commerce, made it clear that the BAC faced stiff competition from other organized constituencies, observing that he did not "think for a moment that this group [the BAC] . . . have any more wisdom about what ought to be done than a group of labor people, or a group of farmers, or of necessity a group of unemployed."[23]

Roosevelt, for his part, disliked the council format and complained to one member that meetings with the BAC as a body were "useless from the point of view of facts and policies and . . . only good for the dissemination of morale and a few ethical fundamentals." Even more exasperating, from the President's view, was the unwillingness of his business critics to advance positive alternatives to administration policies. When Council member Fred Kent complained in general terms about the New Deal's unbalanced budgets,

Roosevelt sent him a copy of the budget and asked pointedly that Kent note exactly where he would make his cuts to bring the budget into balance.[24]

Yet, even amid the squabbling and criticism there existed some significant areas of agreement between the BAC and the New Deal. The Council was the staunchest advocate within the business community of a social security system.[25] Four members served on the advisory committee which helped draft the legislation, and Gerard Swope called the Social Security Act "one of the great milestones of [the] . . . administration."[26] In this instance, as in the case of the Wagner Act, one very important difference between the BAC and the New Deal's more vocal critics in the business community was the Council's willingness to admit the need for reform legislation and then to debate the particulars. In part this reflected a shrewd recognition of the value of positive public relations. It also represented greater agreement with the ultimate goals of the New Deal than other business organizations were able to muster.

In addition, the BAC served as a locus for the planning impulse among America's businessmen. Although the word "planning" was dropped from its title in early 1935, the BAC never lost its desire to order the business environment. From the beginning its members had a strong interest in "the engineering approach" and in national economic planning. Morris Leeds found particular hope in the "possibility of taking over that procedure through which industry has so fruitfully used the findings of the physical sciences, into the realm in which we hope society may learn to make equally fruitful use of the social sciences." "Coordination and long range examination," Henry Dennison told the Council, "must be made realities."[27]

Throughout the 1930s, the BAC remained a bastion of those who dreamed of a business commonwealth—a system involving national planning and regulation of industry, with government cooperation but without government control. After the demise of the NRA, the Council struggled to keep alive the possibility "for businessmen in cooperation with Government to anticipate and correct maladjustments, existing or threatened, and to engage in useful industrial planning."[28] The old deity of laissez faire, worshiped devotedly by some critics of the New Deal, was held in low esteem by the businessmen of the Council. For them, the question was not whether the economy should be managed, but by whom and to what ends.

Because of their hope that the issue might ultimately be settled in favor of business, the members of the BAC worked to maintain their link to the New Deal. Despite Roper's disappointment at his inability either to get the Council to endorse the New Deal wholeheartedly or to have the administration meet with the group more frequently, the Secretary of Commerce could gain some satisfaction from the fact that the BAC remained in effective contact with the Roosevelt regime.

Continuous interaction proved to be an educational experience for the businessmen involved, and the tie to the administration would become particularly important in the early forties when war supplanted depression as the government's major concern. The BAC's members were, Ralph Flanders recalled, "trained in the knowledge of government operations. They were trained in their insight as to working with and in government. They were trained in patience. They were trained in mutual cooperation and understanding with each other." Roper observed, "No other group or affiliation of business men . . . has had the composite experience of working so closely with the Federal Government." Later, during World War II, the administration would fill many of the top positions in the mobilization agencies with BAC personnel; Roosevelt too would seek to capitalize on the BAC's decade of experience in the government.[29]

II

Although the pragmatic business liberalism which characterized the BAC in the 1930s did not include acceptance of deficit spending, some businessmen did recognize the possibilities of Keynesian fiscal policy. For them, the Council's accommodation to the New Deal's popularity was not enough. In 1935, Ralph Flanders, Morris Leeds, Lincoln Filene, and Henry Dennison, all charter members of the BAC, embarked on an inquiry into the root causes of capitalism's debacle, an investigation which led them to an essentially Keynesian analysis of the American economy and to a clear formulation of compensatory fiscal policy. They reached this conclusion at a time when the administration was still fumbling its way toward the spending decision of April 1938.

At first glance, the four made an incongruous team. Flanders, a flinty New Englander, had risen from a machinist apprenticeship to the presidency of the medium-sized Jones and Lamson Machine Company of Springfield, Vermont. Filene, the son of a Prussian immigrant, served as chairman of William Filene's Sons Company, one of Boston's largest department stores. He had been elected to Phi Beta Kappa in 1922 despite his lack of formal education beyond high school. Dennison, by contrast, came from an upper-class Boston home and had been educated at the Roxbury Latin School and Harvard before taking over the management of his family's long-established paper products manufacturing firm. Leeds headed the Leeds and Northrup Company of Philadelphia, which specialized in electrical instruments. This pattern of diversity was reflected also in the political proclivities of the group. Leeds, Dennison, and Filene were, in general, supporters of the New Deal, but Flanders believed the Roosevelt regime "a national calamity and maybe an irreparable one." Often the butt of his friends' gibes for his political heresy, he explained patiently, "I am sure I am not a Bourbon; I am not effective enough to be a Tory; and am coming to conclude that I may be a Diplodocus, or some other extinct and completely unnecessary animal."[30]

The disparate group did, however, share some important experiences and attitudes. One such experience was their BAC membership, service which Flanders considered the most significant of his life. All were drawn from the Business Advisory Council to staff the NRA's Industrial Advisory Board. In 1935, the four sat on the BAC's Capital Goods Expenditures Committee, and in the process presumably discovered mutual interests which led them into a common search for the path to recovery. They shared also a disenchantment with laissez-faire political economy. Dennison derided as "Lazy Fairies" those who believed in a Never Never Land of invisible hands, perfectly functioning markets, and limitless economic frontiers. All thought that man could, and should, control the economic environment. The planning impulse was perhaps strongest in Leeds and Dennison—the latter a hard-working adviser to Roosevelt's National Resources Committee (the forerunner of the National Resources Planning Board)—but even Flanders wanted to "bring the teaching of correct underlying theory to the solution of practical problems."[31]

Recognizing as early as 1933 the "unrealized possibility in a budgetary system . . . applied to the period of the business cycle instead of to the fiscal year," the four undertook in 1935 to develop a recovery program which would bring to public policy the latest advances in economic thought. They consulted both among themselves and with a wide circle of academic and business economists, asking the scholars to read over and criticize their ideas. To ensure that their final conclusions were properly informed by economic doctrine, they employed a young but impressive

Harvard economist, John Kenneth Galbraith, to "ghost" their manuscript.[32]

The resultant program, which was published in 1938 under the title *Toward Full Employment*, reflected a Keynesian view of the economy. The authors brandished modern analytical devices, such as the multiplier concept, and argued, as had Keynes, that there existed under capitalism no self-correcting mechanism to deal with the problem of excessive savings. The interest rate, that old standby of the classical formulation, was simply not up to the job; capitalism did not enjoy a built-in tendency toward equilibrium at a high level of employment. Their basic policy prescription was similarly Keynesian: the Depression-ridden economy required government spending in excess of receipts to shift money from the savings stream to the consumption stream. In short, the need was for a compensatory fiscal policy which would "operate at times with an unbalanced budget and at other times with an overbalanced budget."[33]

To implement such a policy, they advanced the idea of a "flexible budget." Normal expenditures were to be authorized in the usual way. Additional contingent funds would also be appropriated, but these would be spent only if unemployment increased over a certain acceptable level. Should unemployment rise above this level, the government would initiate contingent spending according to a prearranged schedule, i.e., so much additional spending (e.g., $200,000) for each additional increment of unemployment (e.g., 1,000 more jobless) over the maximum acceptable level.[34]

The authors sought to continue and extend on a more rational basis what the administration had been doing haphazardly for years. They recognized that such a policy would inevitably lead to deficit spending; indeed, this was the *raison d'être* of the exercise. At the same time, they rejected a policy of permanently unbalanced budgets and were keenly aware of the dangers of deficit finance. Their fears of inflation and of overwhelming debt were tempered, however, by their recognition that, contrary to conservative doctrine, government finance was not directly analogous to family finance. They also appreciated the benefits business would reap from judicious public spending.[35] Flanders, the most conservative of the foursome, believed the spending solution inevitable, no matter who might occupy the White House; the wisest approach, therefore, was "to organize the thing, develop, emphasize, and apply the constructive elements in the process and by so doing reduce the magnitude of the crises to which the remedies will have to be applied."[36] This, of course, left wide latitude for criticism of New Deal fiscal policy, which even the kindest of the authors felt was plagued by partisan politics and a paradoxical blend of intolerable delay and inappropriate haste.[37] On balance, the program advanced in *Toward Full Employment* differed from the New Deal chiefly in its coherence. It is not surprising, therefore, that the program was, on the whole, warmly received by New Dealers. Jerome Frank and Marriner Eccles were both enthusiastic; Henry A. Wallace sent his advance copy of the manuscript to FDR, noting the "most enlightened attitude" of the authors.[38]

The authors' goal, however, was not merely to win the administration's kudos. As Flanders told his collaborators several days after the resumption of federal spending in April 1938, converting administration liberals was like bringing coals to Newcastle. The real need was to convince their fellow businessmen of the efficacy of a wisely administered fiscal policy. But the work of conversion was difficult. Sales of their book were slow, and a considerable number of the copies sold were purchased by the authors themselves. In December 1938, Leeds confided to his friends that it was "improbable" that business would rally to the kind of program proposed in *Toward Full Employment*.

"The average businessman," he lamented, "is apparently convinced that industry will take care of the unemployment problem if government will give it a chance, and is not sufficiently interested even to consider any other suggestions at the present time."[39]

Leeds's assessment was perhaps too harsh. Some executives responded favorably to the group's educational campaign. Walter Teagle, for one, subscribed "entirely" to the objective of smoothing out the business cycle by the timely expansion and contraction of government debt. Other individual businessmen were by the late 1930s developing an appreciation of the potential utility of fiscal policy as an economic balance wheel. *Fortune* magazine's first "Round Table" in early 1939 came far closer to the views of Leeds and his compatriots than to those of the New Deal's more negativistic critics in assessing the effects of government spending. Even if only a small minority of the nation's businessmen matched the pace set by Messrs. Filene, Dennison, Leeds, and Flanders, it is significant that they had formulated a businessman's version of a compensatory fiscal policy grounded in a Keynesian analysis of the economy.[40]

They had done so just as the New Deal was drifting toward a spending solution, and, in fact, Roosevelt's April 1938 decision to embark on what he later termed "compensatory fiscal policy" was influenced to a degree by another businessman who, on his own, had reached conclusions similar to those of the authors of *Toward Full Employment*. Beardsley Ruml had a very rare combination of academic accomplishments and business acumen.[41] Political scientist Louis Brownlow has described him as possessing "one of the most complex and comprehensive minds of modern times."[42] He received his Ph.D. from the University of Chicago in 1917, specializing in psychometry, the study of intelligence measurement. During the 1920s Ruml served as director of the $80 million Laura Spelman Rockefeller Memorial Fund and was at one point considered for the presidency of his midwestern alma mater, only to be rejected as too young and too fat to fit the trustees' conception of a university head.[43] In 1931, he nevertheless left the Memorial Fund to serve under the equally young but considerably slimmer Robert Hutchins as dean of the social science division and professor of education at the university on the Midway. Three years later, he departed academe for good to become treasurer of R. H. Macy's, the New York department store. As Maude Phelps Hutchins observed, he "left ideas for notions."

Ruml nonetheless took with him into the world of business a set of interests, ideas, and values which reflected his early experiences. Under his direction, the Laura Spelman Rockefeller Memorial had been one of the first national foundations to systematically encourage the social sciences. Ruml hoped that the disciplinary boundaries separating sociology, ethnology, anthropology, psychology, history, political science, biology, and economics could be broken down and that a body of knowledge and techniques—"a social science"—could be created which would lend itself to immediate application in the solution of pressing societal problems.[44] Among such problems would be those of public policy, and as director of the Memorial Fund he had an important part in the establishment of the Public Administration Clearing House in Chicago, an attempt to encourage a scientific approach to government administration.[45]

Despite his departure from the social science community, Ruml continued to play a role which he once described as that of a "coordinator." Such a person, he was to write in the twilight of his career,

should know what is going on, should have time enough to think about it and should be friend and counselor to every operating agency. He should have time to travel at home and abroad, should have time to write and time to make speeches. He should have no ambitions for political or administrative power and should not want to get rich.[46]

Accordingly, Ruml involved himself in public affairs while at Macy's, and in January 1937 he became a director of the Federal Reserve Bank of New York. Throughout the 1930s, he maintained contact with many New Dealers, including Charles Merriam and Frederic Delano of the National Resources Committee, and came to know many of those in the administration who advocated a Keynesian solution.[47]

This background and his interest in retail trade naturally led Ruml to take a keen interest in the problems of the economy and especially in the question of how to maintain purchasing power in a depression. In October 1937, he perceived that the nation was heading once again toward economic collapse. "Washington *could* turn the situation," he remarked, "but it is improbable that Washington will act in time." Instead, he predicted, the government would at first respond by speechmaking and confidence-building, efforts which would "produce little purchasing power and . . . fail as Hoover's did."[48] The problem was that the administration had mistakenly embraced a "socio-financial" policy, an approach which tied policy decisions to the financial necessity of striking a bookkeeping balance between expenditure and income. The alternative, he suggested, was a "socio-economic" policy, which would establish as the criterion for success not a balanced budget but rather "the production of goods and services and the elimination of physical and human waste."[49]

Partly through happenstance and partly because of his success in playing the role of "coordinator," Ruml was soon called upon to marshall these arguments in an effort to win over the President to the spending solution. The "spenders" within the administration lobbied for their approach throughout the winter of 1937–1938, but Roosevelt hesitated. In November 1937 Morgenthau, in a speech cleared with the President, proclaimed the administration's determination "to do everything possible to promote a continuation of recovery and to balance the budget through cutting expenditures." The struggle took an important turn in late March 1938, however, when FDR left Washington for a brief vacation in Warm Springs. There he was met by Harry Hopkins, who attempted once again to persuade Roosevelt to increase federal spending. Hopkins asked Aubrey Williams of the National Youth Administration and the government economist Leon Henderson to go to Pine Mountain Valley, near the presidential retreat, to aid him in his struggle to convert the President. En route, Williams and Henderson met Ruml, who was traveling by train to Atlanta on business; knowing his views and appreciating his talent, they asked him to join them in their task.[50]

The three proceeded to Pine Mountain Valley where they formulated arguments for Hopkins to use to convert the President, a process in which Ruml appears to have played an important part. On April 1, he drafted a memorandum which was given to Hopkins and Roosevelt that same day. Ruml's unique contribution was his historical justification for the seemingly abrupt break with tradition involved in large-scale deficit spending. The federal government had always created purchasing power—through the somewhat indirect process of alienation of the national domain. Land grants to railroads were but one example. The unlimited coinage of gold discovered in California was another: "From the national domain to purchasing power in one jump." Franchises and the tariff were merely less obvious manifestations of the same process. "It follows," he concluded, "that the competitive capitalist system has been sustained from the beginning by federal intervention to create purchasing power."[51] This claim for historical continuity appealed to Roosevelt. On April 2, the President left Warm Springs and returned to Washington "rarin' to go."[52]

The spenders had finally won. After frantic consultation, they devised a specific program, and on April 14, the President went before the nation, explaining the spending approach and justifying it as just another measure of federal intervention in that long line described by Ruml. "It is following tradition as well as necessity," he explained, "if Government strives to put idle money and idle men to work."[53] One suspects that this line of reasoning had greater effect on Roosevelt himself than on his national radio audience; the cloak of historical precedent was no doubt comforting to a leader who, although a fiscal conservative at heart, was deserting his natural inclination and stepping out into the chilly realm of Keynesian economics.

III

While Flanders, Dennison, Leeds, and Filene sought to persuade their fellow businessmen and Ruml attempted to nudge the New Deal toward a Keynesian fiscal policy, another strand of the positive business response to the Depression and the New Deal developed in the exciting environment of the University of Chicago. In 1936, William Benton, who had retired at the age of thirty-six from the advertising agency of Benton and Bowles, came to Chicago to make a brief study of the public image of the University; the youthful salesman so impressed President Hutchins that he appointed Benton vice-president of the University, a post he held for ten years. Benton came to his new career disheartened by the fact that American business seemed to lack a constructive program for dealing with the major problems of the day, especially unemployment. At Chicago, contact with such distinguished faculty members as Henry Simons,

Frank Knight, and Paul Douglas taught him "how much I had to learn, and how much the academic world had to convey to our business leaders—if they would only listen."[54]

Benton suggested to a friend, Lewis Brown, president of Johns-Manville, that they organize a seminar to be attended by the chief executives of the country's one hundred largest corporations and by top-flight scholars; Brown would provide the businessmen, Benton the economists. The idea did not blossom immediately. When, in 1939, Benton approached the Department of Commerce suggesting that the government sponsor such a meeting, the agency refused, fearing that administration involvement would make any such effort suspect. But the concept was resurrected the following year when Paul Hoffman, president of Studebaker Motors, complained to Benton and Hutchins after a University of Chicago trustees meeting that the school was not playing an influential enough role in public affairs.[55]

Benton and Hoffman, sharing an interest in public policy and an appreciation of academic expertise, set about to establish an organization that would fill the void. Political scientist Harold Lasswell contributed a name—the American Policy Commission—and in the summer of 1941 produced a memorandum outlining an agenda for the proposed group. Benton used Lasswell's memo as a prospectus to win recruits to the cause.[56] The organization was to be composed of influential men "united by their desire to clarify their own minds and the minds of their fellow citizens about the major alternatives of national policy." To "close the gap between knowledge and policy," the Commission would remain in close consultation with the faculty of the University of Chicago. Together, these businessmen and scholars would address themselves to what Lasswell called "the main object" of the group: the clarification of the basic principles of a free society. If the "free society" was indeed a "balanced society," how was that balance to be struck? What were the proper spheres of government and private enterprise? A fruitful conjunction of experience and academic knowledge, it was hoped, would provide the answers to such questions.

With this agenda, Hoffman and Benton approached several of the nation's most noteworthy businessmen, including the Charles E. Wilsons of General Electric and General Motors, General Robert Wood of Sears Roebuck, Henning W. Prentis of Armstrong Cork, *Time-Life* publisher Henry Luce, Clarence Francis of General Foods, and Beardsley Ruml.[57] The attack on Pearl Harbor and American entry into World War II interrupted their efforts for a time, but later they were encouraged to press forward when the BAC and the Department of Commerce began to consider proposals aimed at stimulating business planning for the reconversion and postwar periods. It was around these wartime plans that the three groups advocating a positive business response to the Depression—the pragmatic business liberals of the BAC, the inquiring proto-Keynesians, and the advocates of a partnership of business and academe—finally coalesced. When they did, it was not the result of circumstances that suddenly emerged during World War II, but was instead a culmination of important developments rooted in the 1930s and earlier years. Their wartime efforts would extend, rather than begin, the long-run trend of business-government collaboration in organizing the modern American welfare state.

Part II

The Experience of War

Chapter Four

Precious Room for Maneuver

Where were you on December 7? The currency of the question over the years and the fact that so many Americans could, decades later, answer it in striking detail illustrate the impact of the war on the nation's historical consciousness. The group most directly touched by the war probably were the sixteen million men and women who joined the armed forces, many to fight and almost 300,000 to die in combat, others only to "hurry up and wait" in typical GI fashion at bases and outposts scattered around the nation and the world. But the war impinged on those who stayed behind as well. For civilians, life at home included a sense of both loss—separation from loved ones and distance from the events that seemed to matter most dramatically—and participation, the feeling that war work or even the cultivation of a victory garden bound one with others enlisted in the cause of victory. "There are no two fronts for America in this war," Roosevelt observed in 1944. "There is only one front. . . . When we speak of our total effort, we speak of the factory and the field, and the mine as well as of the battleground—we speak of the soldier and the civilian."[1]

At home, as elsewhere in the world, the war both generated forces of change and strengthened elements of the status quo; it was a time of flux and inertia, of gains by both liberals and conservatives. But impact of the war cannot be fully understood by simply weighing and comparing the victories of the left and the right; the war's influence was too dynamic and complex for such either/or judgments. Rather, the war experience embodied change *and* stasis, and presented new challenges and opportunities to groups all along America's political spectrum.

In the economic realm, one development overshadowed all others. The war brought to a close the worst depression in American history. In so doing, it ended the stalemate in Washington over fiscal policy. The explosion of government spending for the weapons of war finally generated recovery, and the decline in unemployment from 17.2 percent of the work force in 1939 to 1.2 percent in 1944 provided striking evidence of the power of the Keynesian prescription—when it was adopted on a sufficient scale.

The flood of war orders also fostered the rapid rise of businessmen such as Andrew J. Higgins and Henry J. Kaiser. Both men combined the traditional hustle of the self-made entrepreneur with a shrewd ability to take full advantage of the government's wartime largess. Constantly on the phone—Kaiser's long-distance telephone bill during the war hovered at around $250,000 a year—cultivating contacts such as former New Dealer Thomas G. Corcoran, Kaiser parlayed government aid into an industrial empire. Such was the triumph of "free enterprise" during the war.[2]

The success of Kaiser and Higgins symbolized the industrial maturation of the West and the South, and the economic development of these areas was significantly accelerated by the war. By 1944, California had received 9.7 percent of the dollar value of war contracts let by the federal government, and a flood of workers followed in the wake of defense spending. Much of the internal migration of the war years flowed from the countryside to the city, and between 1940 and 1945 the nation's farm population dropped

17 percent; but movement to the West and South was an equally striking dimension of wartime relocation. California attracted 1.4 million migrants, and a Census Bureau list of the ten areas most congested by the influx of defense workers included eight locations on the Pacific coast and in the South. As one man headed for Olympia, Washington, observed, "It wouldn't take any imagination at all to think that you were going west on a covered wagon and were a pioneer again. It made me think of 'The Grapes of Wrath,' minus the poverty and hopelessness."[3]

Many such workers experienced collective bargaining for the first time during the war. In 1941, such bastions of antiunion sentiment as Ford and "Little Steel" fell before the onslaught of organized labor. A year later, the War Labor Board promulgated the "maintenance of membership" rule which provided that workers would have a fifteen-day period during which they could resign from a union; if they did not, they had to remain union members for the life of the contract then in force. Although the rule was a compromise measure, union membership increased from 10.5 million in December 1941 to 14.75 million in June 1945.[4]

The war also witnessed significant political changes that strengthened New Deal liberalism in several ways. The presidency emerged from the conflict greatly enhanced if not quite yet imperial. The belief that government had both the responsibility and the capacity to guide the economy into prosperity underlay much of the planning, both private and public, for the conversion to peace. The activities of the Office of Price Administration gave more people than ever before actual experience in administering the economy from Washington. Although conservatives took advantage of the war to dismantle such New Deal agencies as the National Youth Administration, the National Resources Planning Board, and the Farm Security Administration, important vestiges of reform liberalism lived on in the efforts to provide for the returning veterans. The displacement of Dr. New Deal by Dr. Win-the-War did not completely vitiate American liberalism.[5]

The political gains of liberals were in many ways counterbalanced by the wartime revitalization of American conservatives, however. The 1942 congressional elections brought impressive conservative gains, and Roosevelt's victory in 1944 did not seriously impede the consolidation of a conservative coalition in Congress which was both more active and more tenacious during the war years than it had been during the late 1930s. In early 1944, the President complained to Budget Director Harold Smith that for all practical purposes he was forced to deal with a Republican Congress—a tribute to the strength of the alliance between Southern Democrats and Republicans.[6]

Moreover, the economic changes of the war period took place within the context of a "confirmation of size" which perpetuated the broad outlines of prewar· institutional arrangements. The wartime expansion of the federal government was matched by the further growth of big business, big agriculture, and big labor. Despite the shift of economic activity along regional lines, the war strengthened big business far more than small, and the bulk of prime contracts went to large firms. In 1942, Roosevelt ordered a halt to antitrust actions which might interfere with the war effort, and soon after trust-buster Thurman Arnold left the Department of Justice for a federal judgeship in a move of both practical and symbolic significance. The war sounded a death knell for whatever quixotic hopes remained among the neo-Brandeisians left over from the 1930s that the American economy could somehow be made safe for the "little man."[7]

At the same time, World War II gave the business community a welcome respite from the tensions of the Depression and the New Deal. As the prosecution of the war engaged liberal energies and diverted liberal attention away from domestic issues, the attacks on business—both actual and rhetorical—of the late 1930s petered out. Businessmen flocked into government service in unprecedented numbers; as *Nation's Business* noted gleefully, "They're Whistling Business Out of the Doghouse."[8] The capitalism that had been damned as bankrupt just a few years before was now celebrated for its prodigious feats of production. The war presented businessmen with the incentive both to reinvigorate their own private organizations and to form new groups in the shadowy area where the private and public spheres intersected. In short, the war provided American business with room for maneuver that had been lacking under the New Deal.

I

It was in this favorable atmosphere that the positive patterns of the 1930s came together in the formation of a new organization, the Committee for Economic Development, which ultimately would play a major role in shaping the fiscal revolution. The direct impetus behind the CED was business' concern for the shape of the "post-armament" economy. Early in 1941, the Business Advisory Council appointed a Committee on Economic Policy to consider the problem of postwar planning under the leadership of Marion Folsom, treasurer of Eastman Kodak. The BAC feared that if businessmen remained mute, the problems of reconversion and employment might be solved in ways inimical to the private enterprise system; it also recognized the need for a new and more positive approach. As BAC chairman R. R. Deupree put it: "The Challenge which business will face when this war is over cannot be met by a laissez-faire philosophy or by uncontrolled forces of supply and demand. Intelligent planning, faith in the future and courage will be needed to carry us through the reconstruction period."[9]

Secretary of Commerce Jesse H. Jones, a Texas businessman turned administrator whose commitment to the New Deal and attachment to Roosevelt as an individual were minimal, shared these concerns.[10] Under Jones's aegis, the Department began to seek mechanisms by which business influence could be brought to bear more effectively on public policy. In late January 1942, Carroll Wilson, director of the Bureau of Foreign and Domestic Commerce, proposed to the BAC that a new, permanent, businessman's committee be established under the sponsorship of the Commerce Department to encourage postwar planning by individual firms and to "bring together the results of the planning activities of many firms and agencies so as to make clear their implications for the economy as a whole, i.e., to weld many separate plans into a unified program."[11]

The BAC reacted favorably to Wilson's proposal and referred it to the Council's Committee on Economic Policy. There it was further discussed, along with other proposals drawn up by individual businessmen but conceived in a similar spirit and dedicated to the same ends.[12] Finally, after much discussion with Commerce Department officials, the BAC in April 1942 suggested the establishment of an "Institute of Business Enterprise." The new organization would be formed along the lines suggested by Wilson; its tasks would be to induce firms to plan for the postwar period, to gather data on probable postwar demand and employment patterns, and to "attempt to formulate a suggested overall program for business and industry."[13] Thus, under the cosponsorship of the redoubtable Jones and the BAC, America's businessmen made ready to order their postwar environment.

Before these plans were implemented, however, businessmen added another element to the planning equation. At the urging of Paul Hoffman, William Benton, who was still hoping to establish his University of Chicago–based organization, approached Folsom "to discuss plans here at the University and how they may correlate with your current activities on behalf of the Department of Commerce and American business."[14] To his disappointment, Benton found that Folsom's enthusiasm for business planning failed to encompass the less directly applicable "research" which the Chicago group wanted to emphasize. Undaunted, Hoffman and Benton approached Secretary of Commerce Jones and indicated that their involvement in the project was contingent upon provision for just such broad-gauged activity. To their surprise, Jones found their proposal eminently practical. He agreed on the spot that the proposed group be allowed to spend up to 50 percent of its budget for scholarly research on questions of broad public policy.[15]

Over the course of the summer of 1942, a series of meetings was held and agreement reached on the details of organizing the new body. The group was given a new name— the Committee for Economic Development—and a basic, functional bifurcation was agreed upon: the Field Development Division was to encourage and monitor plant-by-plant business planning through the establishment of a network of regional and local committees; the Research Division would "bring to light information . . . to aid in bringing into being an economic climate more favorable to continued high employment."[16] The Research Division would also generate the organization's policy recommendations through the Research and Policy Committee. The latter group was to be composed entirely of businessmen, who would be advised by a Research Advisory Board of distinguished scholars and by an in-house research staff of hired experts. By the end of the summer, Jones had handpicked an eighteen-member board of trustees. On September

3, 1942, the CED was legally incorporated. "When I started this job," Hoffman remarked, "I thought we were going to hatch a hen egg. It has turned out to be an eagle."[17]

The positive business responses of the 1930s were fully represented in the new group. The BAC acted as a sounding board for the original proposal and as cosponsor of the organization during its gestation. Most of the leaders of the CED came from the ranks of the Advisory Council; of the 20 trustees who served on the CED board in 1942, 14 had served or were then serving on the BAC, and 3 of the remaining 6 were appointed to the Council the next year (1943).[18] Similarly, the University of Chicago group was responsible for the CED's Research Division and also provided the Committee's chairman and vice-chairman, Paul Hoffman and William Benton. The Chicago economist Theodore Yntema became staff research director, and Neil Jacoby, professor of finance and secretary of the University, served on the Research Advisory Board (as did Theodore Schultz, a professor of agricultural economics who within the year would leave Iowa State to take a position at Chicago). From among the proto-Keynesians of the 1930s, Ralph Flanders chaired the all-important Research and Policy Committee, and the irrepressible Ruml became that committee's most fecund idea-man and intellectual catalyst.

The CED manifested a continuity with the past that went beyond the matter of personnel. The ideology of the new group was strikingly similar to the techno-corporatist formulations of the National Civic Federation during the Progressive era, of the collectivists who organized America's mobilization during World War I, and of Herbert Hoover and the advocates of an associative state during the 1920s.[19] American corporatism had been less visible after the demise of the NRA experiment in the early 1930s, but the corporate ideal was kept alive during the Second New Deal and after by the very men who came together during World War II to form the Committee. American corporatists sought a middle path between statist formulas for the organization of society and the traditional laissez-faire creed of conservatives. They stressed the importance of expertise and tried wherever possible to transform political decisions into technical ones. Corporatism placed private, functionally defined groups in the crucial role of partners with a cooperative, rather than oppressive, state apparatus; together they were to pursue an objectively recognizable general interest.[20]

Thus, the CED's first chairman, Paul Hoffman, held that it was "very important that we as a group think of ourselves not as 'right', 'left', 'conservative' or 'radical' but as 'responsible'." The Committee's faith in its own objectivity was so deeply rooted that in 1962 Herbert Stein, the group's research director, could indignantly rebuke those who viewed society "as sharply divided into a certain number of classes,—business, labor and possibly others." In contrast, he observed that the CED "believes that there is a general interest, and a truth independent of class interest."[21]

The pursuit of responsible objectivity led the Committee to embrace expertise with a fervor still new to the majority of their peers in the business world. Businessmen, the CED announced, stood "in need of the economist and social scientist, just as much as . . . the engineer and the chemist."[22] The system of research which the group developed was sophisticated and well organized. The members of the Research and Policy Committee—the only body authorized to issue policy statements for the organization—drew from three different wells of expert opinion: (1) the resident research staff headed by University of Chicago economist Theodore Yntema; (2) the Research Advisory Board made up of six prominent economists and one political scientist; and (3) the reports of outside consultants who were hired for specific projects.

In emphasizing the importance of research and incorporating experts into the organization, both on the permanent staff and as consultants, the CED recognized that on issues of broad economic policy, the day of the practical but theoretically untutored amateur had passed. Because businessmen had been suspicious of new economic ideas, research director Yntema advised, the basic thinking on those policies which determined the economic climate had been the work "chiefly . . . of men in the employment of government or in academic positions, men who have been usually somewhat remote from the realities of business."[23] Like the proto-Keynesian businessmen of the 1930s, the CED would now utilize the knowledge of experts to seek ends which were acceptable to the friends of modern capitalism.

Thus armed with expertise, the Committee sought to define a new, expanded role for the federal government in the pursuit of economic stability. The state had a crucial part to play if capitalism was to survive. As Hoffman told his compatriots, "Private business has little to do with maintaining high levels of employment, and . . . there is little that local government can do. It follows, therefore, that the government must take certain steps if we are to achieve high levels of employment."[24] National fiscal and monetary policy would have to act as a balance wheel in order to mitigate economic fluctuations.

Acceptance of a Keynesian role for the federal government and of the wisdom of occasional deficit spending did not, however, signify adoption of the liberal, stagnationist position. The Committee explicitly repudiated the concept of economic maturity, proclaiming instead that the envisioned new relationship between business and government would guarantee the profitable exploitation of America's remaining internal frontier.[25] Rejecting both the older laissez-faire mentality of conservatives and the solution of the stagnationists, the CED sought to harness the New Economics for the purpose of ensuring the retention of a private-enterprise political economy. Although the details of the Committee's policy prescriptions would not be fully articulated until later in the decade, the group from the outset took a thoroughly modern view of the role of the state.

II

The impact of the war on the champions of negativistic opposition in the 1930s—the NAM and the Chamber of Commerce—was more uneven. During the war years the NAM changed its style slightly but not its substance. True, by the end of the 1930s several chinks had appeared in the NAM's fiscal orthodoxy. Privately, one of the NAM's departments admitted that Keynesian economics contained elements of both fact and logic. Within the association's Economic Policy Committee, it was conceded that, with proper safeguards, deficit finance might sometimes be desirable.[26] But approval of the New Economics foundered on the inability of the NAM to envision deficit finance in any form other than that prescribed by the New Deal and the stagnationists. Government spending was perceived as the key to the Keynesian system and entailed, it was feared, "the mass surrender of personal liberties and substitution of an unknown measure of the government operation of the economy for private enterprise."[27] Keynesianism was equated with the stagnationist formulation, and was therefore unacceptable. "The Hansen debt philosophy," NAM Secretary Noel Sargent announced, "is a job-destroying concept; perhaps its real significance is to be found in the Hansen admission that the public debt is one means of regulating the distribution of income. Those who advocate socialistic proposals should do so openly." "The Hansen theory," observed George Ray, Jr., a member of the NAM's Committee on Postwar Problems, "should be hit and hit hard. Either industry will expose the Hansen theory, or extravagant government spending will be with us forever."[28]

Neither a major reorganization of the NAM in 1945 nor a concerted attempt to rid itself of its negativistic image altered the group's fiscal proposals.[29] The structural upheaval pushed to the fore no charismatic leader and did not result in any dramatic infusion of expertise into the organization. Plans for a business journal which would "offer an unbiased and scholarly analysis of fundamental economic proposals emanating from outside industry" were considered but never implemented.[30] Although the NAM overhauled its structure and revamped its public relations program, its fiscal policies changed not at all.

The Chamber, on the other hand, responded more positively and more effectively to the challenges presented by the war. Given the group's history of negativism during the 1930s, the Chamber's wartime experience provides a striking example of the way in which the war worked to foster flexibility on the part of organized business. The Chamber's annual meeting at Chicago in May 1942 unleashed within the organization forces of modernity which had been constrained since 1935. Under the cover of Eric A. Johnston's leadership, these forces wrought a virtual revolution in the organization of the Chamber: economic expertise was institutionalized; a functionally specialized apparatus for the mobilization of political opinion was created; and a new, positive outlook and image were cultivated. Thus, when the debate on fiscal policy broke out anew in 1945 over the issue of full employment, the Chamber was able to act with a vigor which it had lacked in the late 1930s. Accepting Keynesianism in its most attenuated, conservative form, the Chamber played a critical role in the framing of America's postwar economic constitution, the Employment Act of 1946.

The first step away from the negativism of the late 1930s was unwittingly taken by the Chamber's old guard itself. In nominating Eric A. Johnston of Spokane, Washington, for the organization's presidency in 1942, the Chamber establishment sought to capitalize on the abilities and appeal of a young, handsome, and successful businessman. Johnston had received a law degree from the University of Washington and served four years as an officer in the Marine Corps, only to be invalided out of the service in 1922 after suffering a severe head injury while stationed in Peking. He began his business career by selling vacuum cleaners door to door, and later formed the Brown-Johnston Company, one of the Northwest's largest appliance distributors. The Chamber's leaders hoped that Johnston's Western ties would restore the regional balance of the group's politics, since the previous president had been Albert Hawkes of New Jersey.[31] Johnston was not nominated to lead a revolution or to blaze new trails, but rather to guide the Chamber more effectively down a path already chosen.

As if to prove this point, the old guard attempted at the 1942 convention to solidify its position. In 1937, after a series of disastrous administrative experiments, John O'Leary, an archconservative, successful Chicago businessman, and past-president of the Chamber, had been hired at $40,000 per year to run the Chamber as permanent chairman of the Executive Committee. His position had never been formally recognized, however, and an attempt to do so at the Chicago convention by means of a by-law amendment finally ignited smoldering resentment against the O'Leary regime and its policies. A bloc of over 100 delegates mobilized to oppose "the O'Leary Amendment." Fearing defeat in a savage floor fight, O'Leary and outgoing-president Hawkes agreed to withdraw the amendment and to refer the matter to the Chamber's Board for resolution.[32]

At their first post-convention meeting, the directors found themselves confronted by two ad hoc committees—one representing affiliated local chambers and the other state organizations—demanding a complete revamping of the Chamber. The problem, both groups agreed, was not that the organization was too conservative, but rather that it was not getting results; they quarreled not with the Chamber's goals but with the means used to achieve them. The Chamber's management, they concluded, was inept and its structure unwieldy and old-fashioned.

These basic flaws had in turn left the Chamber unable effectively to influence national legislation or to formulate compelling alternatives to New Deal policies. Rejecting the argument that but for Chamber opposition even more serious defeats would have been suffered at the hands of the New Deal, the complainants noted caustically that the record could not have been much worse. The process of effectuating Chamber policy needed to be rationalized; the ad hoc "country club" style of lobbying which had been the Chamber's forte needed to be complemented by a more highly organized method of influencing opinion.[33]

The petitioners received a sympathetic hearing, and it quickly became apparent that the newly elected Johnston was more in tune with the insurgents than with the regime which had nominated him.[34] The Chamber's directors empowered Johnston to appoint a committee to study the complaints and recommend any necessary changes in the organization's structure and administration. Within a month the president's committee returned to the Board with John O'Leary's scalp on its belt, announcing that the venerable ex-president had resigned his position as permanent, paid chairman of the Executive Committee and recommending acceptance of the resignation.[35]

Almost immediately there began a perceptible shift in the orientation of the Chamber. The emphasis moved from opposition to "areas of accord."[36] "Instead of talking about the great calamities that are going to happen to us," Johnston explained, "I have been advocating a positive program directed toward improving our system and making it better."[37] The Chamber's new tack was highlighted by an affirmative attitude toward change, which was recognized as the rule of life; capitalism was touted as "a human institution, vibrant and evolutionary, capable constantly of adjusting itself to new conditions." Failure to recognize the natural law of change, it was claimed, had been business' greatest sin in the preceding decades.[38] Under the politics of negativism, change had been a process fraught with danger, but for the new regime opportunity counterbalanced the threat:

If we are to survive, we must become the leaders rather than the victims of changing conditions and the readjustments that we will have to make will be less radical, more tolerable, and less likely to wreck us if we have ameliorated their more drastic aspects by intelligently preparing to meet them.[39]

Foremost among the changed conditions confronting the Chamber were the increased stature and power of labor and government; recognition that these rivals had valid roles to play in the political economy constituted another element in the Chamber's new *Weltanschauung*. Believing firmly that the old free-booting laissez faire of the nineteenth century was dead, Johnston advocated a "new capitalism," which, while resolute in its opposition to "super-statism," recognized nonetheless that "the role of government must keep pace with change—the game has become so complicated that government in its legitimate character of umpire has vastly more to do."[40] Similarly, he viewed most labor-management antagonism as a holdover from "a more primitive stage in the history of American labor"; liberation from "illogical prejudices and blind opposition" required acceptance of collective bargaining as "an established and useful reality."[41] An amendment of the by-laws in early 1943 extended formal recognition to these countervailing powers; the Chamber proclaimed its concern with questions of "economic, civic and public welfare" and announced its readiness "to cooperate with government, with other organized commercial groups, with labor, with agriculture and with all men of good will."[42]

With Johnston now clearly at their head, the insurgents stove diligently to give the Chamber a new image. In his first months in office, Johnston opened the Chamber to the outside worlds of agriculture, labor, and government. In mid-July 1942, he met with the heads of the Farm Bureau Federation and the Illinois Agricultural Association, and one week later arranged a White House meeting with the President and representatives of the NAM, AFL, and CIO. These gatherings were followed by a personal conference with Roosevelt in September for a review of business proposals to strengthen the war effort and ease the eventual conversion to peacetime production. "My God, Eric," the President is reported to have exclaimed at their first meeting, "how did they ever elect you president of the chamber!" In October 1942, Roosevelt appointed Johnston to be one of the two business representatives on the new Economic Stabilization Board.[43]

Although the practical results of such efforts are difficult to gauge, Johnston had indeed taken off the curse and become the symbol of the Chamber's regeneration. When *Reader's Digest*, America's most widely circulated magazine, characterized him as "about the most dynamic spokesman the American businessman has found in many a year," the Chamber basked in his reflected glory and attracted both new members and new money. In 1946, a poll taken by the Psychological Corporation found the Chamber to be thought "well of" by 65 percent of those interviewed, far ahead of

its most immediate competitors in the associational sweep-
stakes (the AFL—50 percent; the NAM—37 percent; and the
CIO—26 percent).[44] As Chamber General Manager Ralph
Bradford explained,

Under the leadership of Eric Johnston, the Chamber has become
a part of what goes on in Washington. . . . We can no more remain
aloof from government than from any other element of society. . . .
We have not changed our base, only our approach. Our job is not
merely to announce our principles, but to make them work.[45]

The search for a way to make principles "work" went
deeper than Johnston's activism. The Chamber also made
structural changes in its organization designed to comple-
ment its energetic new leadership and to implement its re-
oriented policy. One major achievement was a centralization
of authority within the association. Ralph Bradford, a vet-
eran Chamber administrator, assumed the newly created
post of General Manager (effective October 1, 1942) and
began to oversee all Chamber activities. The Board of Directors was also strengthened. Amendment of the by-laws
in 1943 gave the Board definite policymaking power, provided that 20 percent of the Chamber's total voting membership, representing at least twenty different states, did not
register disapproval before the expiration of a Board-im-
posed time limit. In addition, the Board was authorized to
take informal polls to supplement its referenda, the results
of such soundings being advisory rather than binding.[46]
    Most important, the reorganization created two new
divisions: the Departments of Economic Research and of
Governmental Affairs. The task of the former was to bring
economic expertise to bear on the formulation of Chamber
policy, and the duty of the latter was to see that such policies
influenced government actions. The Department of Economic Research evolved slowly out of a recognition of the

complexity of wartime problems and a desire to view such issues in the context of the economy as a whole. The first step in the evolutionary process came in September 1941, when the Board created a Committee on Economic Policy to study the problems of mobilization and post-defense reconversion. In 1942, the Chamber hired Dr. Arthur Upgren, a professor of economics at the University of Minnesota, to serve as adviser to the new committee. When Upgren resigned after only a few months to take a position with the Federal Reserve, he suggested his Minnesota officemate, Professor Emerson P. Schmidt, as his replacement. Starting work without any supporting staff in January 1943, Schmidt was given as his primary task the preparation of business views on postwar reconversion. Finally, in mid-1944 he became the director of a new Economic Research Department, whose main function was to study the economic aspects of legislation.[47]

Academic economists were not entirely new to the Chamber. Several had served on Chamber committees before, and Fred Fairchild, professor of political economy at Yale, had sat on the Committee on Federal Finance throughout the thirties. It was not clear, however, what value the old regime had placed on such advisory expertise. As late as 1942, the chairman of the COFF could remark that "we use Fred to tell us what all the theories propounded by the professors in Washington mean to an ordinary layman. His answer invariably is: 'Nothing!'"[48] The new leadership, on the other hand, viewed expertise more favorably. Addressing a meeting of business economists called by the Chamber in March 1944, Eric Johnston observed that the Depression had caused government to turn to the economist for diagnoses and prescriptions, although it was not certain whether the advice proffered was either correct or "consistent with the true inwardness of a free-functioning, private-enterprise economy." He added, "Had the business economists been more vocal and more articulate in pointing out other ways and remedies when these things were done to our society, I daresay the results would have been better for all concerned—except for the few who thrive on pathological conditions and unrest." Planning was being done; to forswear the use of economic expertise, Schmidt warned, "simply means that we are not helping to determine the shape of things to come."[49]

Determination of the future called for more than the mere formulation of policy. To ensure that the pronouncements of the Chamber would be heeded, General Manager Bradford in 1942 created a Department of Governmental Affairs to communicate Chamber policy to federal officials and to gather information for members regarding government actions.[50] The new agency focused its attention on Congress; as the Chamber explained to its members, "In that body are found most often the beginning and the end of the governmental affairs with which Business is most concerned."[51] To mobilize public opinion and exert pressure on legislators, the department became the liaison between the Chamber and the approximately 800 national affairs committees set up locally by organization members. To facilitate communication on congressional activities, it began publication of the *Governmental Affairs Legislative Daily* in three editions: a daily version published during congressional sessions, providing a résumé of congressional action, pending legislation, and calendars of committee hearings; a weekly edition subtitled *Bill Digest*; and a series of special numbers which discussed particularly important legislation. In addition, the Chamber strengthened its divisional offices to enable them to encourage more effectively local chamber participation in national affairs, and to oversee the entire effort Johnston appointed an Advisory Committee on National Affairs.[52]

Thus transformed, the Chamber faced the postwar

world with a newly found flexibility, a refurbished image, and a revitalized organizational machine. During the war the Chamber's active minority accommodated itself to the principle of an increased government role in the economy. It remained to be seen, however, precisely how that role would ultimately be defined. The Chamber sought to limit the government's area of responsibility to the minimum necessary for economic stability. But there were other forces in Washington which wanted to use the lever of economic stabilization to increase the federal government's power.

III

Particularly troubling to conservatives were liberal plans, rooted in the stagnationist analysis of the political economy, to "impose" a super New Deal on America. In 1945, the business economist George Terborgh warned that the debate over the mature economy thesis was no idle academic exercise. The stagnation theory was "now in effect an official creed," with disciples occupying "most of the high policy-making and advisory positions in the executive agencies"; what had begun as an intellectual formulation was "becoming increasingly an unstated assumption of government policy and planning."[53] The danger lay in the nature of the political economy that might result from such an analysis. Stuart Chase, an influential popularizer of the Hansen school, admitted privately that the compensatory fiscal policies of the stagnationists would ultimately require "a super duper planning agency." Hansen himself suggested the creation of two new agencies in the executive branch— a Central Fiscal Authority and a Central Planning Agency— which would operate as "an economic government composed of specialists."[54] A state dedicated to continuously high federal spending for education, social welfare, public works, regional development, public health, and urban renewal could hardly be expected to elicit cheers from men who had viewed the TVA as the opening wedge of American socialism.[55]

The Chamber forthrightly denounced such heresy. "We can take no stock," Johnston told the Colmer Committee on Postwar Economic Policy and Planning, "in the theory that our economy has attained such a degree of maturity as to offer insufficient opportunity for private investment and thus to require a constant stream of government investment in public projects." But the insidious argument would not die. The Chamber's two new economists proclaimed themselves "shocked to find how deeply this set of ideas, skillfully propagated, about the mature economy had apparently paralyzed the men with the know-how, the capital, and the experience," and wrote a book to refute the maturity thesis. They argued that the probable outcome of the stagnationist program would be "continued high taxes and the destruction of individual initiative; and/or, eventually, destructive price inflation and the consequent redistribution of income and wealth among a minority." With such dire consequences in the offing, it is no wonder that the Chamber experts saw in the "Keynes-Hansen school" an ideology "not greatly distant from neo-Marxian thinking."[56]

Even those who believed that the stagnationists were pessimistically mistaken found their influence disturbing, for they had come to Washington in great numbers, and Hansen especially attracted a wide following among American liberals.[57] His thinking was clearly reflected in the National Resources Planning Board's 1943 program for postwar America, a proposal calling for the creation of a welfare state far surpassing in vigor and scope both the hopes and accomplishments of the New Deal of the 1930s.[58] There were, in addition, several particularly articulate and powerful converts to the cause. Henry Wallace, who had become the drum major of American liberalism after Roosevelt turned his attention to the prosecution of the war, hoped for the emergence of a "People's Century," the economic basis of which was to be a peacetime Keynesian welfare state drawn along the lines advocated by the NRPB. Hansen extolled Wallace's call for *Sixty Million Jobs* as "an education in applied economics" which should be "read and reread by every voter" and "studied in every high school and college in America."[59] It was, in fact, Wallace's commitment to an expansionary, developmental economy based on the stagnationist analysis that in large part inspired the vehement opposition to his appointment as Secretary of Commerce in early 1945. The thought of this liberal ideologue in control of the Reconstruction Finance Corporation's $14 billion revolving loan fund terrified conservatives.[60]

Roosevelt's relationship to this brand of left-wing Keynesianism was, as usual, unclear. FDR's feelings about the kind of master planning which underlay the whole approach had always been ambivalent. In 1939, for example, he had complained to Morgenthau of being "sick and tired of having a lot of long-haired people around here who want a billion dollars for schools, a billion dollars for public health." And in 1943, his reaction to the threatened abolition of the NRPB was mild indeed: "I don't care how planning is done. They can abolish the . . . Board, if they set up some other organization to do the work." Yet, as the end of the war approached, even the President seemed to adopt at least the trappings of a program rooted in Hansen's analysis. He included in his 1944 State of the Union Address the economic bill of rights first propounded by the NRPB in 1942, and in October he called for a postwar economy that would provide sixty million jobs, a goal which at the time surprised even Wallace as "perhaps high." In January 1945, he included in his budget message a Keynesian accounting device—a national budget—breaking down the nation's gross national product into the component contributions of consumers, business, and all levels of government. He concluded his report by recommending the adoption of an expansionary national economic policy, which would include "provision for extending social security, including medical care; for better education, public health, and nutrition; for the improvement of our homes, cities, and farms; and for the development of transportation facilities and river valleys." The voice was weak and tired, the lyrics were ambiguous, but the tune was unmistakably that of Alvin Hansen.[61]

IV

The stagnationist influence took tangible form in the proposals advanced by liberals for full employment legislation. Fear of renewed depression was widespread, and even those businessmen who correctly foresaw a postwar burst of prosperity were not entirely certain that such a boomlet would not merely postpone the inevitable crash.[62] The problem of how to maintain full employment in the postwar period was hotly debated throughout the war. What would happen when the arsenal of democracy had to readjust to a world at peace, when spending for war—which reached $250 million per day—simply stopped? Would America's twelve-million-man fighting force disband only to sell apples on street corners? Opinion polls conducted during the war found that economic readjustment was considered the single most important problem for the postwar period. Between 1943 and 1945 hundreds of books and articles on the employment question appeared.[63] Interest in the issue ran so high that the Pabst Brewing Company of Milwaukee decided to celebrate its one-hundredth anniversary in 1944 by sponsoring an essay contest calling for two-thousand-word so-

lutions to the problem of postwar employment. Awards to-
taling $50,000 were announced on December 1, 1943, and
by February 7, 1944, 35,767 entries had been received.[64]
Out of this ferment of concern there emerged in 1945 a
liberal program which suggested a stagnationist cure for the
anticipated ills of the postwar economy.

On January 22, 1945, Senator James Murray (D-Mont.)
introduced the Full Employment Bill of 1945, S.380. The
bill consisted of three main elements. First, it proclaimed
the right of all Americans "able to work and seeking work"
to useful, regular, and fulltime employment and affirmed
the responsibility of the government to guarantee that right.
Second, it provided a planning mechanism, the National
Production and Employment Budget, by which such a guarantee would be executed. The National Budget would es-
timate in advance the gross national product necessary to
provide full employment, and also the volume of investment
and expenditure anticipated from both the private and public sectors. Third, the bill directed that if a gap existed between the full employment requirement and the original
estimated expenditures and investment, the deficiency
should be made up first by the encouragement of nonfederal
and private spending, and, if that was insufficient, finally
by government spending. The preparation of the National
Budget was to be the responsibility of the Executive Office
under "the general direction and supervision of the President," and the chief executive was to be given discretion
over the rate of federal investment when such was required.[65]

The Chamber quite correctly traced the Murray proposal back to the theories of Hansen and the stagnationists.[66]
The assumption underlying the bill was that private business would not be able to invest enough money year in and
year out to keep the economy operating at full employment.
The accounting concept of the National Budget—calculat-
ing the aggregate needs of a full-employment economy and

estimating the contributions of major economic groupings (business, government, consumers) to the fulfillment of these requirements—was Keynesian in conception. Although the measure did give passing mention to the reduction of aggregate investment and expenditure in periods of inflation, it emphasized expansionary spending. Indeed, in its call for a report on the distribution of incomes and in its proviso that action be taken "to assure that monopolistic practices with respect to prices, production, or distribution . . . not interfere with the achievement of the purposes of this Act," the original bill was reminiscent of the program set forth by the Harvard-Tufts economists in 1938.[67] Liberals viewed the Full Employment Bill of 1945 as a lever of reform rather than a mere technocratic tooі for application to intermittent crises.

Although state and local chambers of commerce reacted to S.380 with vehement hostility,[68] the attitude of the national Chamber was more complex. The Washington leadership recognized that a return to the mass unemployment of the 1930s would spell disaster. Although Johnston predicted a boom in the immediate postwar period, he acknowledged that the task facing the nation was to ensure that prosperity would continue even after the war's pent-up demand for goods had been met. The stakes were high, for mass unemployment was "the one thing, more than any other, which might doom capitalism and rivet a bureaucratic slave state on us forever."[69]

The Chamber had addressed the possibility of renewed mass unemployment in its Albert Lea Survey of 1943. At the suggestion of Chamber director John Cameron Thomson (vice-chairman of the new Committee on Economic Policy), the small town of Albert Lea, Minnesota, was chosen for an experiment in community postwar planning. The local chamber, the Committee for Economic Development, the University of Minnesota, and the Minneapolis Federal Reserve Bank worked together to produce an extraordinarily detailed projection for postwar Albert Lea. Researchers gathered data on anticipated peacetime income patterns and on projected consumer demand. A survey of employers found 5,978 probable jobs for a labor force estimated at 6,571. The residual 593, for whom no work promised to appear, represented the crux of the postwar problem. It was not at all certain whether private, voluntary efforts and careful analysis could do more than illuminate the issue. To be sure, Albert Lea had, as a result, a better idea of what the future held in store—down to the detail of anticipating demand for 646 refrigerators in the first two years of peace. But how this mass of self-knowledge could be translated into 593 new jobs was never made clear. Perhaps it was an awareness of this problem which prompted Johnston to admit that no one segment of the economy could singlehandedly prevent a postwar slump.[70]

Fear of the consequences of renewed mass unemployment and realization of the obvious limitations of local efforts to deal with the problem left the Chamber ready to accept a stabilizing role for the federal government. But the desired government commitment was not one founded in a stagnationist analysis and promising continued heavy deficit spending for social welfare projects. "We can't afford to go into another tail spin," Johnston explained to the Chamber staff in midsummer 1945. "We can't afford to go into another depression which would mean the loss of our system." But he added: "I don't think the Murray full employment bill is the answer. We might get full employment under that bill, all right, but in the process we'd lose our democracy and have a regimented state."[71]

Emerson Schmidt, the Chamber's Director of Economic Research, analyzed S.380 and compared it to the British White Paper on Employment Policy of 1944 and to the full employment plan advanced by Britain's William Beveridge.

All were basically Keynesian, but Schmidt recognized the politico-ideological gradations within the Keynesian spectrum: "The Beveridge Plan goes all the way. In comparison, the British White Paper and the Murray Bill are effete, temperate, halting and ineffectual."[72] Still, there was enough in S.380 to evoke a strong attack by Schmidt, who was especially critical of the role of forecasting (the National Budget concept) and of the very wide discretion such a proposal would of necessity grant the executive branch. The characterization of Schmidt's pamphlet, however, as "one of the earliest full-fledged attacks on S.380" misses a very important point: he attacked the substance of the bill, not the principle that government did indeed have a new and enlarged role to play.[73] The problem, for Schmidt and for the Chamber, was the "proper" specification of the federal government's sphere:

The Murray bill (S.380), if it forces us to examine honestly and realistically every proposed bill, rule and regulation and every public and private policy in order to determine whether each contributes or hinders in the process of absorbing our whole labor force into productive economic activity, could serve a useful purpose.[74]

The Chamber's ambivalence was reflected in the slowness of its public response to the Full Employment Bill. In April 1945, *Nation's Business* presented an analysis of the Murray proposal which emphasized its endorsement by Henry Wallace—the kiss of death as far as conservatives were concerned. Johnston, however, did not testify at the Senate hearings on the measure. He was troubled, he intimated to the Chamber's division managers in September, by indications that the Chamber was drifting back into its old negativism, and he refused to testify on S.380 until the Chamber developed a positive position on the employment question. He reiterated that he did not think the Murray bill workable in its original form. But he was hesitant to face Congress armed only with a negative attitude. With the Chamber (and most of the conservative community) largely on the sidelines, a slightly modified S.380 was passed by a Senate vote of 71–10 on September 28. Although the bill's original exclusive commitment to the goal of "full employment" was diluted by amendment, the final Senate version retained intact the measure's economic planning mechanism.[75]

By late September, when the scene shifted to the House, the Chamber was prepared to act decisively through its newly renovated organizational machinery to provide a more acceptable definition of the government's economic role. The House Committee on Expenditures in the Executive Departments actually considered three versions of the bill: the measure as originally introduced in the House by Democrat Wright Patman of Texas (H.R. 2202, virtually identical to the original Senate bill, S.380); the Senate version as finally passed; and a strengthened liberal substitute measure, H.R. 4181, introduced by Republican Representative Charles La Follette of Indiana. Chairman Carter Manasco of Alabama chose the committee's witnesses from a list provided by James Ingebretsen, who had been the first manager of the Chamber's Department of Governmental Affairs and who was now working for General Motors' vice-chairman Donaldson Brown in a concerted lobbying effort against the Full Employment Bill. Not surprisingly, their testimony was considerably more hostile than that which had been offered during the Senate hearings.[76]

Ultimately, none of three measures proved acceptable to the conservative committee, and a subcommittee was appointed to draft a substitute. From a subcommittee of five, with two staunch conservatives and two equally committed liberals, Will Whittington, a moderately conservative Democrat from Mississippi's Delta region, emerged as the swing man and assumed major responsibility for drafting the House substitute.[77] Whittington vigorously opposed the initial Senate and House Full Employment bills, particularly the idea of a government "guarantee" of the "right" to employment and the deficit spending bias of the original proposal. He nevertheless recognized the need for some legislation "to keep people who desire to work in employment." Congress had hesitated too long before acting during the 1930s, he wrote to a constituent, and "we ought not to repeat the error following the depression of 1929."[78]

The ambivalence of the Delta Democrat mirrored rather remarkably that of the Chamber leadership, making them natural allies in this political struggle. Indeed Whittington had served his local Greenwood, Mississippi chamber of commerce in the past as National Councillor (representative to the national Chamber convention) and had been a contributor to *Nation's Business.*[79] It was understandable that he turned to the Chamber for help in drafting the House substitute. At Whittington's request, the Chamber's Department of Governmental Affairs submitted to him on October 22 three drafts; according to Department Director Howard Volgenau, these were meant to aid the congressman in proposing amendments designed to render the bill harmless.[80] With the drafts as his guide, Whittington drew up a substitute measure which did just that: it diluted the bill by extending its scope beyond employment to the problems of production and the maintenance of purchasing power; it emasculated the spending provisions by limiting them to loans and public works consistent with "sound fiscal policy"; and it eliminated the National Production and Employment Budget, replacing it with a less powerful President's Economic Report, to be prepared with the assistance of a Council of Economic Advisers.[81] Of the five fundamental principles embodied in the original bill—points which the sponsors believed beyond compromise—only one, the provision for a Joint Congressional Committee on economic affairs, remained in the Whittington version. This proposal, endorsed by the Chamber draft, had actually long been a Chamber goal.[82]

Whittington's handiwork, in substantial measure a product of the Chamber, was reported out of committee on December 5 and passed by the House on December 14, 1945. Both versions of the bill, the Senate-passed and modified S.380 and the Whittington substitute, then proceeded to a joint conference committee, which had the task of working out a final compromise. The Chamber, having provided the conference committee with a conservative benchmark in the House substitute, had already embarked upon an energetic campaign to ensure that the final bill would most closely resemble the Whittington version.

On December 7, even before the House vote on the Whittington substitute, the Department of Governmental Affairs published a special number of the *Legislative Daily*. Presenting an analysis of both the House and the Senate bills, the bulletin left little room for doubt as to which was the more desirable. After linking S.380 with such bugbears as Alvin Hansen, Keynes, Henry Wallace, and a nameless totalitarianism, the Department likened it to the Beveridge Plan, noting that the House substitute was "void of any such connotations." The issue was not the desirability of high employment, but rather the role of government: "Will the operation of such proposals . . . require widely expanded Governmental controls of a nature foreign to and in conflict with American peacetime ways?" Interestingly, the bulletin stopped short of an outright endorsement of the House substitute, and did not intimate the role of the Chamber in drafting it. The reason for this lay no doubt in the vigorous opposition already displayed by many local members to any governmental commitment whatsoever. The message, nonetheless, was clear: the Chamber explicitly recommended the creation of a permanent economic commission and a joint congressional committee, and these could only be obtained through support of the Whittington bill.[83]

To ensure the proper grass-roots response, the Department directed the Chamber division managers in New York, Atlanta, Dallas, Chicago, Minneapolis, and San Francisco to urge important member organizations to take action on the full employment question. The department called attention to the Chamber's analysis of the proposals before Congress, and distributed 150,000 copies of the *Legislative Daily* special edition on employment legislation.[84] One week before the conference committee began its formal deliberations, Volgenau wrote to Whittington and his fellow conferee Clare Hoffman (R-Mich.) that while "both bills evidently seek the same goals . . . the means provided are at variance." Noting that the Senate bill was "clearly at odds with policies long advocated by the National Chamber," he recommended its rejection. "The same," he continued, "cannot be said of the House bill, the obvious intent of which is to place main reliance upon private initiative in the attainment of high level employment."[85] He knew whereof he spoke.

When the conference committee concluded its work on February 2, the Employment Act of 1946 was a mere shell of the original Senate bill; in detail as well as in essence, it resembled the draft the Chamber had given Whittington in October. Despite President Truman's support for the Senate version, the House substitute served as the point of reference in the deliberations of the conference committee, and the final bill was reconciled to it rather than to the Senate measure.[86] As Whittington told his fellow representatives, "The conference agreement contains the essential provisions of the House bill and it rejects the philosophy of the Senate bill." Gone were the planning mechanism of the National Budget and the unambiguous commitment to full employment. Alvin Hansen later claimed that everything in the original bill except the spending provisions had been window dressing; when Truman signed the act on February 20, 1946, the window dressing was all that was left.[87] For the Chamber, accommodation had indeed been a rewarding experience.

The final vote on the Employment Act of 1946 (320–84 in the House, approved without opposition in the Senate) indicates that many liberals felt compelled to accept what Charles La Follette called "a half loaf."[88] Leon Keyserling, who played an important role in the legislative struggle and who later became chairman of the Council of Economic Advisers under Truman, has since argued that the outcome was not a liberal defeat at all. "The final legislation," he maintained, "met the need for a plenary planning statute." Yet Keyserling himself became a vociferous critic of the administration of the act. His major criticisms, which warrant examination for the light they shed on the 1946 law, were: (1) that subsequent economic policy failed to set in motion "a real planning process," and that the lack of a "unified program and policy" resulted in "a congeries of scattered and *ad hoc* short-range efforts"; (2) that the "distributional aspects of Keynes' teaching were neglected," i.e., that "it mattered not much who got the tax reduction or where the increased spending went, and even not much whether tax reductions or increased spending was resorted to, so long as on paper the quantitative addition to the total potential spending stream was adequate to restore full employment"; (3) that subsequent policy "worked directly counter to the needed shifts from the private to the public sector"; and (4) that later administration of the act evidenced an "obsessionary preoccupation with inflation."[89]

The crucial first steps down the path Keyserling found so objectionable, however, were taken before the Employment Act went to the White House for Truman's signature.

Keyserling's critique of the implementation of the act is persuasive, at least for the period 1946–1964, but the process he describes began when the House substitute diluted the commitment to full employment and substituted the Council of Economic Advisers for the National Production and Employment Budget. The original full employment proposals offered, through the National Budget apparatus, a more unified, almost single-minded approach to long-range economic policy. It was an approach, moreover, that had an obvious spending bias which promised increased allocation of resources to the public sector. The original Murray measure called for "a report on the distribution of the national income" and "an evaluation of the effect upon the distribution of the national income of the programs set forth in . . . the [National] Budget."[90] For Keyserling, "the real purposes" of the Employment Act of 1946 were circumvented and subverted by the ensuing administration of the law. In truth, however, the trend of subsequent policy merely fulfilled the conservative intent and expectations of those responsible for the final outcome of the legislative struggle over full employment.

V

The dilution of the original Full Employment Bill was a significant victory for moderate conservatives in general and for the Chamber in particular. Under the daring leadership of an active minority which advanced progressively farther ahead of its "troops," the Chamber seized the opportunities presented to it by the fluid wartime situation and successfully accommodated both its outlook and its organization to the inevitable intervention by government in the economy. By so doing, it helped shape the governmental role which it had in principle finally come to accept.

In one sense, the Chamber defined that role in negative terms. In its defeat of the left-wing Keynesianism, the Chamber in effect stipulated what the government's role would *not* be. It did this by politically defeating a program based on a stagnationist analysis of the American political economy and bent on creating a super New Deal grounded in a left-wing brand of Keynesian principles and liberal social concerns.

Yet, from a different perspective, the Chamber appears to have acted constructively as well. Confronted with widespread fear of renewed depression and massive unemployment, the Chamber faced the issue squarely and recognized the need for some government role in the stabilization of the economy. It compromised on issues which, during the period of negativistic opposition, had been considered beyond negotiation. In a public pronouncement issued at the height of the full employment controversy, the Chamber's Committee on Economic Policy called for a program of countercyclical public works and tax reduction in hard times, accepted the necessity of deficit spending in periods of depression, and subscribed to the concept of balancing the budget over the business cycle rather than annually.[91] By its private maneuvering, the Chamber also made a crucial contribution to the establishment of the Council of Economic Advisers, which helped institutionalize the use of economic expertise to oversee the national economy.

The contrast between these actions and the Chamber's generally lackluster, negative performance in the late thirties is striking. Three major factors made for the difference: (1) the propitious setting provided by World War II; (2) the charismatic leadership of Eric A. Johnston, who strengthened the Chamber immensely in its moment of need; and (3) the organizational changes wrought by the new leadership, changes which allowed the Chamber to exploit effectively the opportunities presented by the war. The war gave busi-

ness a renewed sense of collective self-confidence and security while at the same time confronting business with a
challenging problem—determining the shape of the postwar
world. The combination of security and challenge is one,
social scientists tell us, particularly conducive to innovation, either on a personal or organizational level.[92] In the
case at hand, the innovations were both individual and collective, and together they left the Chamber in a position to
play a leading role in the definition of America's postwar
political economy.

The Chamber's success during World War II was
marred, however, by one critical flaw—the gulf which was
developing between the active minority leadership and the
bulk of the membership. As the Chamber gradually accepted
a government commitment to economic stabilization, the
membership seems to have fallen behind. The resulting gap
was often camouflaged by the device of making policy statements without labeling them as such, thus obviating the
necessity of submitting each question to the membership by
means of a referendum or a resolution at the annual meeting.
Emerson Schmidt's series of Post-War Readjustment Bul-
letins provides a perfect example: all were capable of being
construed as representing the views of the Chamber, but
were carefully prefaced with disclaimers that they did not
"necessarily" represent the opinions of the organization.
Rather, they were published "for the purpose of raising
questions, providing information and presenting views that
may be helpful in the consideration of policies."[93] Despite
such subterfuge, the differing initial responses of the national Chamber and its local affiliates to the Murray-Patman
Full Employment bills made the rift apparent; only considerable Chamber circumspection kept the employment issue
from becoming divisive.

The Chamber had reacted effectively to liberal agitation
for employment legislation and had played a key role in the

formulation of the Employment Act of 1946. In so doing, it had stymied the thrust of an incipient reform movement rooted in left-wing Keynesianism. However, the question remained whether, once the need to respond to the proposals of others had passed, the business community would be able to formulate its own positive version of the New Economics.

Part III

The Postwar Period

Chapter Five
The Struggle to Develop an Alternative

For a brief moment at the end of World War II, it appeared to many Americans that the nation—indeed, the world—had entered what publisher Henry Luce four years earlier had called "the American Century." The new era, it was hoped, would produce a new, peaceful world order, presided over by a beneficent and omnipotent United States. Victorious on two fronts against enemies of whose villainy there was virtually no popular doubt and possessing a new secret weapon which harnessed the most basic force of the universe, America seemed destined to shoulder the burden of world leadership more self-consciously than ever before. The basis for American power would be the most productive economy in history, reinvigorated by war but untouched by physical destruction. The vision reflected presciently the way in which postwar America would be influenced by the interaction of its involvement in the world and its affluence at home.[1]

Missing from this view of the future, however, was a full appreciation of the problems and anxieties that would also beset the United States in the years after the war. Relations with the Soviet Union, uneasy at best throughout the war, soured as the Allies disagreed over the fate of Eastern Europe. By early 1946, when Winston Churchill observed that an iron curtain had descended across Europe, it was becoming apparent that the postwar world would not conform exactly or automatically to American specifications.

The early years of the Cold War proved especially vexing because America seemed strangely unable to translate its vast power into unchallenged dominion. The Truman period witnessed the solidification of Soviet control throughout Eastern Europe, the "loss" of China, the end of America's atomic monopoly, and a costly, undeclared war in Korea. The frustration that resulted from such developments both hardened the resolve of policymakers to contain further Communist expansion and fueled an increasingly shrill search at home for those traitors and fellow-travelers some thought must be responsible for such a disparity between power and performance.

Just as America's world leadership colored the postwar experience, so did the affluence that underlay the nation's global role. A wave of consumer spending eased considerably the reconversion to peace as purchasers sought to satisfy a pent-up yearning for the civilian "good life." By the end of the forties, network television had made its commercial debut and Milton Berle was becoming the medium's initial "star" performer; the first Levittown—a prepackaged, planned suburban community—had sprung up on Long Island offering the American Dream for under $10,000; and the materialistic lineaments of the consumer culture had been established.

The transition to peacetime prosperity was not without controversy. The resolve of liberals to continue wartime controls into the reconversion period sparked strong opposition from those who wanted to dismantle the intrusive Office of Price Administration bureaucracy; and the ultimate lifting of controls aggravated a postwar inflation which simultaneously drove the cost of living up and Truman's popularity down. Caught in the squeeze of rising prices, and determined to demand wages that would compensate for the loss of war-related overtime pay, workers struck industry after industry. In April 1946, John L. Lewis called his 400,000 soft coal miners out of the pits, and a month later the nation suffered a brief but paralyzing national railroad stoppage. The President's threat to draft striking rail workers was never acted upon, but served to antagonize both the union supporters of the left and the constitutionalists of the right.

Beneath the optimism, frustration, and uproar, one disquieting fear ran through the immediate postwar years. A roving reporter in St. Louis touched the hidden nerve when asking a young mother about her expectations for the future. "Oh, things are going along just wonderfully." Her husband had a good job and the couple a new baby. But, she asked, "Do you think it's really all going to last?"[2] The postwar boom proved to be very real, but many wondered what lay ahead once the consumer splurge had spent itself.

Businessmen and their organizations shared the concern. Could prosperity be guaranteed? Seeking an answer, some businessmen continued to struggle to devise new means by which government could ensure economic stability. Others retreated to the comfort of traditional laissez-faire verities. In the midst of a Cold War abroad and affluence at home, the echoes of the Great Depression continued to influence national life.

I

The Chamber's time of ferment did not long outlast the war. As the postwar world took shape, it became increasingly apparent that the modernizers had lost touch with the membership. When Johnston left the Chamber in 1946 to become America's movie czar (as head of the powerful Motion Picture Association), the Chamber of Commerce sought to return to peacetime normalcy.

The impact of this retreat on the Chamber's response to the New Economics was significant. Under the Johnston regime important elements within the Chamber had cautiously accepted the tools of Keynesian economic analysis, the conception of government as the overall director of the national economy, and the prescription of deficit financing as a device for increasing aggregate demand in times of serious recession. The elite holding this forward position became isolated, however, as the tide of change ebbed; widespread support for such views did not materialize. The Chamber was unable to accept and transform into policy the recognition of its own experts that government action was the key to economic stability. Instead, the organization drifted, sometimes borrowing Keynesian rhetoric to support policies chosen on other grounds, but never really internalizing the lessons of the New Economics.

Behind the scenes, the Chamber's fiscal modernists waged a long and initially losing struggle to integrate the most basic tenets of Keynesian doctrine into Chamber policy. The origins of the intraorganizational debate on fiscal policy lay in the acceptance of the New Economics in 1945–1946 by those elements within the Chamber most expert in economic affairs: the newly developed Economic Research Department, lair of the staff economists; and the Department's affiliated Committee on Economic Policy, a membership group in which business economists were heavily represented. At the same time that the Chamber was acting to shape the content of the Employment Act, these groups were making their peace with some of the fundamentals of Keynesian economics. Chamber economists Emerson Schmidt and Ernst Swanson admitted that the Keynesian analytical techniques provided "a new insight into the operations of the monetary-fiscal system and its influence upon the flow of investment." Economists, they agreed, were indebted to Keynes for "having gotten them out of an impasse in the thinking about the causes of economic fluctuations."[3]

The modernists accepted the concept, which lay at the heart of Keynesian doctrine, that government must of necessity play a major role in stabilizing the economy. George Terborgh, who joined the Chamber's Committee on Economic Policy in 1946, noted that "the day has passed when government can deal with depressions simply by whistling or wringing its hands."[4] The government could not only ease the plight of the unemployed but could also "through monetary-fiscal policy bring about adjustments in money flows that again will spur on reemployment."[5] In any case, henceforth the government was fated to "play a dominant role in the determination of the general level of economic activity" by virtue of its "sheer size." Because of this fact of life, the proper coordination of government programs for taxing, spending, lending, and credit control became supremely important. To provide such coordination, the Committee on Economic Policy proposed the formation of an economic council, which would report to the President and to a special joint congressional committee "with a view toward recommendations as to the inner consistency of government policies."[6]

Regarding the government policies which might be implemented to sustain employment, the Committee offered proposals which revealed a surprisingly flexible attitude toward that centerpiece of orthodox economics, the balanced budget. Arguing that raising taxes and tapping new tax sources during the Depression had worked "a great hardship on the taxpayer" and had exerted "a depressing effect on enterprise and jobs," the Committee suggested that in the future taxes be reduced in times of distress. It also advised that public works be postponed when possible during prosperity and expanded in periods of depression, a program which would make "a substantial contribution . . . towards mitigating the business cycle." The convergence of reduced taxes and increased expenditures could only result in deficit spending. This was to be tolerated, however, in the knowledge that the government would henceforth seek to balance its budget "over the course of the business cycle," rather than annually.[7]

The Committee artistically couched its proposals in language which accepted the new approach without ever really recommending it and qualified them with warnings that such policies were particularly open to abuse. There was always the problem that such useful weapons against depression would be treated as panaceas, their dangers forgotten or ignored. Deficit spending could be used for political or ideological purposes, and compensatory fiscal policy in undisciplined hands might result in large deficits during slack periods and only slightly smaller ones in prosperous times.[8] It would take statesmanship of a high order to avoid drowning the nation in a sea of red ink. And of course stagnationist formulations remained beyond the pale of respectability; the "Keynes-Hansen school" would "freeze the economy" and initiate "a general decline in the standard of living for all."[9] But despite such caveats, the Committee on Economic Policy advocated "a contracyclical fiscal policy to be used at times with discretion and moderation."[10] "Deficit spending," the Chamber's staff economists agreed, "has a limited but definite place in a monetary fiscal program."[11]

Just as these elements within the Chamber were accepting a diluted brand of Keynes, however, the rest of the organization began to retreat from the hyperactivism and relative liberalism of the war years. Johnston grew fearful in 1945 that his hold on the organization was weakening and that the Chamber was drifting to the right.[12] Perhaps he sensed the growing suspicion among the members that their dashing president was intent not on serving the Chamber but rather on using it as a vehicle for his personal political ambitions.[13] Aware in any case that the wave of his popularity had crested, Johnston informed the Board in September 1945 that he would leave his Chamber post at the end of his term (April 1946) to become president of the Motion Picture Association; *Business Week* reported that "more than one of the Chamber's conservative wheelhorses was heard to murmur that Hollywood was a more fitting arena for his talents."[14]

The retreat from Johnston's brand of corporate liberalism became apparent at the Chamber's 1946 convention. Only after a vigorous behind-the-scenes struggle were Chamber liberals able to kill a policy resolution calling for repeal of the Wagner Act; at the last moment the convention opted instead for a resolution recommending revision of the act so as to give employers equal rights and protection under the law. The retiring president suffered an added rebuff when the delegates called for the termination of all price controls (except rent) by October 31—after Johnston had told reporters that the hasty abolition of price controls would be suicidal.[15] Incoming president William Jackson— a self-styled "social-minded conservative" and vice-president of the United Fruit Company—was elected largely in the hope that he would provide less flamboyant leadership.[16] Though Jackson's acceptance speech made reference to the "unusual obligation of leadership" involved in trying to follow "the brilliant record that has been made by our retiring President," conservatives undoubtedly found the heart of his message in the observation that the Chamber "is not a man, but an institution; not a personality, but a principle."[17]

Eric Johnston took the occasion of his valedictory address to call one last time for a "new capitalism," one

stripped of the ancient prejudices against organized labor,
government activity, and community planning. "We in business," he warned, "must liberalize or face the threat of
economic liquidation. The law of life applies: adapt or
die."[18] The performance struck at least one in the audience
as "Wagnerian, in a sense—'The Twilight of the Gods.'" As
John Beukema, the manager of a Michigan chamber, confided to General Manager Ralph Bradford:

I sat through it with mixed emotions. I am sure you sensed the
drama—the cold audience, immune to his quondam eloquence
and personal magnetism; Eric fighting to the last for his principles.
He was a Roman gladiator entering the arena for the last time.[19]

To Beukema, the significance of the spectacle was clear;
the Chamber had "changed . . . clothes once more" and
"gone Conservative."[20] Bradford agreed that Johnston's fare-
well marked the end of an era, noting that during the past
year there had been a loss of support for some of Johnston's
more liberal positions. But he cautioned against overesti-
mating the shift, and observed that Jackson, although more
traditionally conservative than Johnston, was not a reactionary.[21] Bradford was correct. Johnston's departure did
indeed signify a shift to the right, but not a reversion to the
sullen negativism of the late thirties. This was scant solace
for the Chamber's fiscal modernists, who now found themselves isolated, far ahead of both the membership and the
leadership in their willingness to accept a positive formulation of Keynesian economics.

II

Because of the return of the Chamber to a more traditional,
conservative stance, Chamber policy on fiscal questions in
the postwar forties failed to follow the lead of the organi-

zation's own experts. At the same time that the Committee on Economic Policy was cautiously suggesting the adoption of a moderate compensatory program for the downward side of the business cycle, the Chamber was putting itself on record in support of the annually balanced budget to which prewar businessmen had been so attached.[22] Fiscal policy remained during the postwar years an issue of primary concern, but the Chamber's approach to fiscal questions seldom evidenced the flexibility which had been apparent during the Johnston regime.

With peace, tax reduction became the nation's overriding fiscal issue. In 1945, taxes were cut with the approval of the administration.[23] The Revenue Act of 1945 repealed the wartime excess profits tax, lowered the corporate tax, and reduced personal income tax rates across the board. Despite its hopes for a return to a balanced budget, the Chamber supported the cut, calling in fact for even more drastic action, including a flat reduction of 20 to 25 percent in the personal income tax rates. It maintained that such changes would ease the conversion from war to peace by increasing business' incentive to invest. The Chamber countered criticism that tax cuts would be inflationary with the argument that increased incentives (i.e., lower taxes) would bring forth increased production and so raise supply to the level of demand.[24]

The Revenue Act of 1945 merely served to whet the conservative appetite, and the election of a Republican majority to the 80th Congress in November 1946 elevated further tax reduction and the revision of the Wagner Act to the top of the legislature's list of priorities. As soon as the new Congress convened, Harold Knutson (R-Minn.), new chairman of the House Ways and Means Committee, introduced H.R. 1, a bill calling for a 20 percent cut in rates on personal income under $302,000 and an additional $500 exemption for those over sixty-five.[25] Once again the Chamber called for even more dramatic changes: a 25 percent across-the-board reduction in the individual income tax; a step-by-step cut in the corporation tax from 38 percent in 1947 to less than 25 percent in 1949; a reduction of the effective capital gains tax rate by half; and a general lowering of gift and estate taxes.[26] Despite the relative moderation of the Republican congressional version (which was made even milder by concessions in committee), the Chamber found H.R. 1 "constructive and statesmanlike" and close enough to the Chamber's own proposal to warrant prompt enactment.[27] When Truman vetoed the bill, describing it as "the wrong kind of tax reduction, at the wrong time," Chamber president Earl Shreve called for enactment of the bill over the President's veto.[28] Congress' attempt to override failed, however.

In July 1947 the same bill was reintroduced (with only the effective date changed), passed by Congress, but again vetoed as "unsound"—inflationary in a period of inflation—and "unfair"—inequitable to the low income taxpayer. Once more, the Chamber clamored for passage over the veto, but to no avail.[29] Finally, in January 1948, Knutson introduced H.R. 4790, a bill which removed some of the inequities of the earlier versions. Again the Chamber supported the Knutson measure, and again Truman vetoed it.[30] This time, however, Congress overrode the veto and tax reduction triumphed. The cut of $5 billion—as large relative to the size of the budget and the national income as the more widely heralded reduction of 1964—finally became law. The tax struggle had been a study in ironies. Liberal Democrat Harry Truman stood as the guardian of fiscal integrity, defending the nation against inflation. Conservatives, on the other hand, insisted that high taxes were too steep a price to pay for sizable reduction of the national debt.[31]

Particularly confusing was the fact that the Chamber used Keynesian rhetoric throughout the struggle to support policies which were in fact pursued for other reasons. Often such arguments were combined with more traditional ones. For example, in testifying in support of H.R. 1 in April 1947, the chairman of the Chamber's Committee on Federal Finance emphasized the need for tax reduction as an incentive for increased production: "[A] tax cut now is anti-inflationary in its encouragement to production, savings and investment and in reducing the pressure to expand bank and other sources of credit." At the same time, however, he conjured up the specter of an impending recession or worse to justify tax reduction:

Shortages are decreasing, inventories are at record high levels, orders are leveling off, prices are wobbling, costs are increasing, earning forecasts are less bright, and the entire economy is vulnerable to a variety of unfavorable influences. We cannot await further development of these influences unfavorable to the continuation of a high level of national income and of a dynamic and progressive economy. We should buy insurance now, through encouragement to incentive and by tax reduction.[32]

In June 1947, Chamber president Earl Shreve warned of the possibility of a recession and noted that the proposed tax reduction would encourage greater capital investment and increase purchasing power.[33] The Chamber expressed this view even more forcefully during the final hearings in March 1948:

The greater purchasing power for those in the low-income classes would be helpful to the economy as a whole. Scarce goods are becoming more plentiful . . . and the time is not far distant when manufacturers and distributors will need new markets if they are to maintain present production schedules and a high level of employment.[34]

Thus, the crowning irony of the postwar tax reduction struggle was the Chamber's apparent advocacy of a tax cut in order to avoid a recession.

Had the Chamber indeed accepted the New Economics in calling for tax reduction in 1947–1948? At first glance, it would appear that the only thing that could have made the prescription more clearly Keynesian would have been a lowering of taxes to the point of purposely creating a deficit. But on closer analysis, the answer must be a qualified no. The Chamber had been calling for large, across-the-board tax cuts since 1945; in October of that year, it had proposed a reduction even more drastic than that advocated by congressional Republicans, at a time when the existence of a postwar boomlet was widely acknowledged.[35] Arguments emphasizing the need for increased incentives were then considered justification enough for such a proposal. In reality, the Chamber adopted the fear-of-recession argument to gain support for a policy which had been pursued for other reasons—mainly, a longstanding devotion to low taxes and the small government that it was hoped such taxes would guarantee.

Nor is it entirely clear that the Chamber believed recession to be an immediate threat. It is true that fear of a slump was widespread in the first half of 1947. For example, a *Fortune* survey of over 25,000 executives in May 1947 found fully 74 percent expecting a downturn by the end of the year. But by November, *Fortune* pollers found "a boom psychology for 1948 . . . pervasive."[36] And the Chamber's own staff economist told a congressional committee in July 1947 that he foresaw a period of continued inflation ahead, a condition which tax reduction "certainly would not help."[37] It would probably be unwise—and unjust—to dismiss entirely the Chamber's fear of recession as a motivation for its support for tax reduction. But it would be unrealistic to see this concern as the primary motive; it was more than anything a handy argument, a weapon grasped after the brawl had begun. That the argument was used at all, however, did represent a forward step of sorts in the Chamber's acceptance of Keynesian economics.

The sincerity of the Chamber's call for an expansionary fiscal program to combat a downturn received its severest test in 1949, when recession became a reality. Then, the Chamber failed badly. The slump began in November 1948, at a time when both the Chamber and the administration seemed to be primarily concerned with inflation. In January 1949, Truman asked for a $4 billion tax increase to provide a budget surplus, which, he argued, would be "our most effective weapon against inflation now."[38] The recession went largely unnoticed at first, despite the fact that the potential "postwar readjustment" had been talked about and feared for several years. Only after much hesitation did the administration formally abandon its battle against inflation. The President's *Mid-Year Economic Report* in July noted that "a moderate downward trend" now characterized the economy, and most importantly, the administration accepted the deficit brought about by declining revenues.[39] Either to raise taxes or reduce expenditures in such a downturn, the Council of Economic Advisers warned, would aggravate the deflation already under way.[40]

The Chamber, however, shared only that half of this prescription congenial with its traditional low taxes–small government orientation. It agreed wholeheartedly that taxes should not be raised to balance the budget in the middle of the slump. But this position reflected the organization's longstanding aversion to taxation more than advocacy of compensatory fiscal policy. The Chamber's demand that the budget be balanced by immediate reductions in expenditures despite the recession evidenced little regard for the expansionary effects of deficit spending.[41]

As the deficit became a reality, the Chamber called for

stricter economy in government. On June 13, 1949, the Senate Committee on Expenditures in the Executive Departments approved a joint resolution (S.J. Resolution 108, or the McClellan Resolution as it came to be called) which directed the President to slash the budget (which had been submitted in January) by between 5 and 10 percent.[42] On June 24, at the height of the controversy ignited by this recommendation, the Chamber's Board of Directors announced its support of the McClellan Resolution.[43] The proposal ultimately died because of procedural obstacles, but it and the backing that it received stand as monuments to pre-Keynesian orthodoxy.

In December 1949, the economic philosophy which underlay the Chamber's actions during the recession was neatly summarized in the statement which the Chamber's Finance Department Committee and Committee on Federal Finance presented to the Douglas subcommittee of the Joint Committee on the Economic Report. The Chamber's stand was forthright; it "viewed with skepticism specific proposals for compensatory spending stabilization" and reiterated its belief that "rigorous economy" was the key to economic stability. It recommended once again an annually balanced budget and the rejection of "temporizing proposals for budget balancing only in years of an expanding and prosperous economy."[44]

Thus, despite an auspicious receptivity to a conservative formulation of compensatory economics on the part of the Chamber's own economic experts in 1945–1946, neither the Chamber's declared policy nor its performance during the 1947–1948 tax cut struggle and the 1949 recession indicated a departure from prewar fiscal orthodoxy. Although the rhetoric of Keynesian economics was sometimes invoked, the new ideas were used to defend goals deeply rooted in traditional Chamber concerns.

The Chamber's retreat from its earlier accommodation

to the New Economics resulted partly from the enduring strength of its more conservative faction and partly from the very nature of the organization. Despite wartime changes in the Chamber's style and structure, the group remained what social scientists call a "peak association," a confederation of organizations with a very broad base. The diversity of so large a membership—differences in background, interests, and outlook—made a forthrightly positive stand on so controversial an issue as Keynesian economics impossible. The inability of the Chamber to seize the initiative in this area had been obscured during the war by Johnston's dazzling leadership and by the fact that the organization was still reacting to the proposals of others. To formulate its views in a more positive fashion proved to be a difficult matter.

The Chamber's hesitation adversely affected its leadership within the business community. Its brief period of flexibility during the war had enabled it to play a significant role in the defeat of the stagnationist program; but its retreat from that position left it unable to help fill the policy vacuum which it had done so much to create. As a result, the task of developing a business alternative to left-wing Keynesianism in the postwar years fell to a much smaller, more cohesive organization, with a membership more unified in both background and outlook—the Committee for Economic Development (CED).

III

Organizationally better suited for the task of leadership in so controversial an area, the CED became in the immediate postwar period the major influence in the development of business Keynesianism. The formal process of defining the CED's Keynesian stance began with the publication in August 1944 of a policy statement proposing *A Postwar Federal*

Tax Plan for High Employment. Eighteen months in preparation, the product of "at least a dozen" meetings and
twelve to fifteen major drafts, the report was, in Beardsley
Ruml's words, "by all odds the most difficult to produce"
of all the Committee's statements on fiscal policy.[45]

The Committee proposed a major reformation of the
nation's tax structure. The goal was a revenue system which
would be both fair and adequate while imposing "the least
possible restriction upon an expansion of production and
employment."[46] The personal income tax was to be the heart
of the revised system; rates would be reduced and exemp-
tions raised. Excise and sales taxes would be lowered and
the corporate earnings tax reduced to a flat rate no greater
than that applied to the first bracket of personal income.
Supposed inequities, such as the double taxation of divi-
dend income and the failure to tax state and local security
issues, would be eliminated in an attempt to encourage risk-
taking. Business commentators generally applauded the
package, an approval that was informed by an acute sense
of self-interest. On similar grounds, a liberal critic castigated
the proposal as "an Intelligent Rich Man's Guide to Profits
and Prosperity."[47] Many of the recommendations were so
obviously progressive, however, that even *The Nation* could
characterize the CED plan as the "most deserving of close
study" of all such suggestions put forth by business.[48]

Debate over the substantive recommendations obscured
the highly significant fiscal context in which the proposals
were placed. The statement itself left little doubt of the
Committee's concern over the preceding fifteen years of
uninterrupted federal deficits. Still, the CED refused to be
forced into the position of demanding a balanced budget
regardless of economic conditions. "The Committee," it
noted, "does not consider justified the apprehensions sometimes voiced about the size of the federal debt, so long as
there is a manifest national resolution to stop its further

increase except under clear conditions of slump in industry and trade." The CED recognized that the crux of the tax problem lay in the reconciliation of the desire for a balanced budget and reduction of the national debt, on the one hand, with the necessity of maintaining maximum employment and production on the other. The issue was finally resolved with the proposal that:

the tax structure and budget should be so drawn as to make possible substantial reduction of the federal debt at a high level of employment. As much debt should then be retired as is consistent with maintaining high levels of employment and production.[49]

This simple, two-sentence formula had taken hours to write and was to serve as the foundation for the future work of the CED.

The particular tax structure proposed by the Committee was designed to yield a budget surplus at a national income of $140 billion, a figure consistent with "a satisfactory high level of employment."[50] If the economy generated a higher national income, the size of the surplus would naturally increase; should the economy slump and national income fall below $140 billion, the surplus would gradually disappear and at some point turn into a deficit. The language of the proposal was vague, its implications largely left undrawn, and compensatory finance was nowhere mentioned; but the import was nevertheless clear. As the analysts of *Fortune* commented, "Double talk aside, the C.E.D. advocates deficit financing when there is unemployment."[51]

Whereas the CED's 1944 tax proposal struck a glancing blow to the edifice of fiscal orthodoxy, the publication in November 1947 of the Committee's full-blown program for "prosperity in a free economy" launched a frontal assault against the balanced budget. The 1947 policy statement was the handiwork of a committee of businessmen headed by

Cameron Thomson (head of the Northwest Bancorporation) in consultation with CED staff economist Herbert Stein, and was a culmination of the CED's research activity. "Their report," Hoffman wrote to Ralph Flanders shortly before publication, "will have an even greater impact than did the 1944 . . . tax study."[52]

The CED's deliberations made it clear that the sense of urgency which drove the group had not been cooled by the relatively easy transition to a peacetime economy. Fear of recession remained strong in the minds of prominent CED members, despite the postwar boom. The "collapse," Stein warned the Research and Policy Committee in July 1946, was "still in the future" and "only extraordinarily skillful and energetic policy can avert the slump."[53] If anything, the intensification of the Cold War with Russia had upped the ante. A severe depression, Hoffman warned, would "put our free economy to the greatest hazard" and "play directly into the hands of the Russians."[54]

Goaded by such apprehensions, the Committee expanded the argument broached in its 1944 tax proposal. The circumlocution which had characterized the earlier statement disappeared; now the CED made a candid assessment of the range of possible fiscal policies. The traditional approach of balancing the budget on an annual basis, regardless of economic conditions, was examined, attacked, and dismissed. Implementation of such a policy, the CED warned, necessarily meant the adjustment of tax rates and spending programs "at times and in directions most harmful to high employment and stable prices." Tax rates would be raised and expenditures cut when income was falling and unemployment spreading; conversely, taxes would be cut and expenditures increased during booms, at precisely the time when fiscal restraint was required. The historical record of tax reductions in the prosperous 1920s and tax increases during the Depression was adduced as testimony to the folly of traditional approaches. Nor would such a policy foster government economy in the long run. Potential surpluses were likely to be dissipated through increased spending in good times, and attempts at retrenchment in hard times were "certain to be ineffective." The attack was a spirited one, and the balanced-budget principle, which had been held so dear by so many for so long, was given short shrift by the corporate liberals of the CED.[55]

The Committee based its alternative to the annually balanced budget on the high employment budget first suggested in 1944: "Set tax rates to balance the budget and provide a surplus for debt retirement at an agreed high level of employment and national income." This time, however, the formulation was more carefully drawn and the variables calculated. The surplus to be sought was $3 billion at a national income figure which would yield employment of 96 percent of the labor force. A figure of 4 percent unemployment was judged acceptable because at that point "most involuntary idleness is of the between-jobs variety."[56] A second amplification of the high employment budget provided that tax rates, having been set to yield a surplus at high employment, would then be left alone barring "some major change in national policy or condition of national life."[57] Thus, an economic tool—the basic high employment budget formula—was made the basis for a full-fledged policy prescription, which the CED called the "stabilizing budget policy."

Under the stabilizing budget, tax rates would be set according to the formula described above. In prosperous times, national income would rise and so also would the amount of taxes collected, even though the tax *rates* would remain the same; the size of the budget surplus would increase, and this in turn would tend to dampen any inflationary tendencies generated by the economic surge. Conversely, in periods of recession national income and federal revenues would shrink, and government expenditures such as unemployment compensation would rise; the budget surplus would decrease, and at some point an expansionary deficit would be incurred. Thus, stable tax rates set to yield a modest surplus at high employment would, if left alone, tend both to dampen the inflationary pressures of a boom and to cushion any decline into recession. Constancy in the tax structure, which had been implicit in the earlier 1944 tax program, was now placed at the very heart of the CED's program for economic stability.

Tax rate stability had long been an issue of discussion within the CED, even after the initial, implicit approval given the concept in 1944. At that time, Research and Policy Committee chairman Ralph Flanders had admitted that the recommendation of constancy was made in passing, "in advance of a thorough study of the other tools of control, and with the knowledge that the results of that study may lead to putting more dependence on variable taxation." He specifically left open the possibility of discretionary tax policy "in spite of the great difficulties in administration." In fact, a CED study co-authored by the research staff and published in 1946 advocated a discretionary fiscal policy to meet changing economic conditions.[58]

Hoffman threw his considerable influence wholeheartedly on the side of stable rates, arguing for an automaticity which would leave as little as possible to the judgment of political leaders.[59] Ruml observed that "in principle it would be wonderful to be able to vary tax rates to meet the ups and down of business activity," but he remained doubtful about the technical, legislative, and administrative problems involved in such an advanced fiscal policy.[60] Ultimately, Hoffman's view prevailed, and virtually automatic controls were made the foundation of the CED's stabilizing budget policy. The use of discretionary devices was reserved for "an economic crisis of great magnitude."[61]

This brief debate resolved a dilemma which had long plagued businessmen who appreciated the potential of fiscal policy and especially deficit finance during periods of recession, but who feared that such deficit spending, once begun, could never be halted because of the electoral appeal of distributive politics. "There should be some automatic method," Folsom had written to Ralph Flanders as early as 1937, "of concluding the period of unbalanced budget and going into the period of debt reduction."[62] In providing for the automatic generation of deficits in hard times and surpluses in good, the CED's stabilizing budget offered a middle ground between the positions of those who would balance the budget annually regardless of economic fortunes and those who would vest in the federal government the power to alter revenue rates and expenditures to fit the conditions at hand or those predicted for the future.

The CED proposal excluded entirely the position of the stagnationists, who stressed increased government spending and deficit finance on a secular basis. It was, Herbert Stein observed proudly, a program which "would adapt the balanced-budget idea to the fact of economic instability" and "the compensatory budget idea to the fact that foresight is imperfect and fiscal action slow-moving." The strength—and the brilliance—of the program lay in its appeal "to persons who approach the budget question from differing points of view."[63] It was an attractive compromise.

The basic framework of the CED's response to the New Economics was completed in 1948 with the publication of *Monetary and Fiscal Policy for Greater Economic Stability.* Conceived in an atmosphere of increasing concern over inflation, this statement addressed the problem of economic stability from a different perspective than had the Committee's earlier, recession-centered statements, and added to the stabilizing budget policy a call for a flexible monetary policy.[64] The CED recommended that in times of inflation the Federal Reserve System pursue a contractionist monetary policy by tightening the reserve requirements of member banks, selling government securities on the open market, and increasing the discount rate. In periods of deflation, the opposite policies would be implemented in order to expand the money supply and increase bank reserves. Throughout, the stabilizing budget policy would be followed so as to exert a dampening effect in the case of inflation and a cushioning effect in the case of an economic slump; thus, monetary policy, the efficacy of which many Keynesians had come to doubt, would be wedded to conservative Keynesian fiscal policy.

Whereas the CED preferred automaticity in fiscal policy, it deemed flexibility "essential to wise monetary action."[65] A flexible monetary policy required, however, a fully independent Federal Reserve System. In 1948, the Fed was still committed, somewhat against its will, to the support of a favorable market for government securities. This relationship (which had hardened during the war because of the Treasury's undeniable need to borrow large amounts of money as cheaply as possible) meant that the actions of the Federal Reserve were determined more by the needs of the Treasury Department than by the Fed's own assessment of the needs of the economy.[66] The intervention of the CED in the dispute between the two agencies was perhaps the most dramatic aspect of the 1948 statement. The Committee unequivocally demanded that economic stability—and not the price of government security issues—be made the "primary objective" of monetary policy: "The Federal Reserve should feel free to reduce the support level [of government bonds] unless it finds a superior alternative way of bringing about a monetary restriction if and when that is required by the objective of economic stability."[67]

This contribution to what one economist later labeled "the rediscovery of money" completed the basic policy package which was to guide the CED through the decade of the 1950s.[68] The program had four components: (1) a prescription for fiscal policy built around stable tax rates set to yield a surplus in the cash-consolidated budget at a level of national income consistent with high employment; (2) the reservation of further deliberate antirecession or anti-inflation budgetary policy for serious and unusual circumstances; (3) emphasis on tax changes rather than expenditure changes when strong discretionary measures were indeed required; and (4) stress on a flexible monetary policy to be administered by a fully independent Federal Reserve System. It was a program which consciously rejected the idea of an annual budget balance and which was designed instead to generate deficit spending during a serious downturn. Without mentioning Keynes by name, the CED had developed a policy package which borrowed the most conservative of the policy prescriptions flowing from the Keynesian approach. It quickly became the major alternative both to the left-wing stagnationist formulation, which promised more or less continuous deficits in conjunction with highly redistributive taxation, and to the managed compensatory spending formulation, which, although less radical in its implications than the former, nonetheless recommended discretionary government power and depended in the main on the manipulation of spending rather than taxing. The American business community had at last domesticated Keynes.

IV

In announcing the CED's budget proposal in 1947, Beardsley Ruml played the historian and placed the program in historical perspective. He traced the government's role in the maintenance of high employment back to Secretary of Commerce Hoover's conference on unemployment in 1921. Most discerningly, he observed that the early formulations of Keynesian economics in the United States had exhibited a distinctly ideological coloration which reflected political philosophy as well as economic theory: "It became apparent that many of the advocates of a compensatory fiscal policy were much more interested in advancing the socialization of one factor or another in our economy." Ruml added that the balanced budget concept was also used as a rationalization by those whose real interests were the reduction of government spending and the limitation of government competition with private enterprise.[69] The Committee's own policy recommendations were believed to be untainted by such ideological influences. In reality, however, the CED had over the period 1942–1948 developed a set of policies as profoundly ideological and political as those formulated earlier by Alvin Hansen and the other stagnationists.

The CED's fiscal and monetary policy package sought to integrate the concepts of Keynesian economics into the group's corporatist vision of the American political economy. As research director Theodore Yntema reported in 1944:

Public policy as to ways and means for coping with business fluctuations has yet to be shaped, but it can easily take the form of specific business controls, of government ownership and operation, and/or of huge government expenditures. It is of vital concern to all who are interested in keeping a system of private enterprise and large personal freedom, that ways be found to counter the tendencies toward boom and depressions without resorting to great expansion of detailed state controls or . . . state employment. We hope our studies will be a significant contribution to this end.[70]

The CED's Research Committee attempted to devise over-all economic controls which would, in the words of chairman Ralph Flanders, allow "natural adjustments under the laws of supply and demand and under the incentives of the profit system, rather than efforts by direct regimentation."[71] It assumed from the beginning that successful operation of the economy required government use of fiscal policy to provide the economic stability without which private enterprise capitalism would collapse, politically if not economically. As Stein admitted, there were a number of alternative Keynesian programs. These included the one proposed by the stagnationists, which could probably maintain high employment but which was unacceptable largely because of its political and ideological implications.[72] Properly devised measures of fiscal and monetary policy would be impersonal and would leave to the private sector the basic decisions about resource allocation, production, prices, and wages. They would necessitate little expansion of the government bureaucracy and would minimize further concentration of economic and political power in Washington. Benton, with an ad man's flair for the epigram, concluded that the problem was to regulate the economic climate without rationing the raindrops.[73]

Accordingly, the Committee emphasized the revenue side of the budgetary ledger. This contrasted sharply with the prominence accorded spending in the Keynesian formulations of the 1930s, and the change was a crucial one. The stabilizing budget promised both reduced taxes and rate stability over time; by shifting emphasis away from expenditure-generated deficits, it promised also to minimize the growth of the public sector. Ruml explained, "It is because I want a free economy that I want to revise our ideas on taxes. If we can leave sufficient purchasing power in the hands of the people and let private business compete to get it we will have a very different situation than if we have purchasing power pumped out by the central government under the direction of a bureaucracy."[74]

The stabilizing budget was also consciously designed to salvage as much as possible of the fiscal discipline which made the annually balanced budget so attractive to conservatives. Under the CED's plan, once the budget was agreed upon and the tax rates set to yield a surplus at high employment, any further increase in expenditures would have to be accompanied by increased revenue rates. The only exceptions were: (1) some gradual increase in normal government expenditure that would be made possible by population growth and the rise of national income; (2) possibly large but clearly temporary disbursements of an extraordinary nature; and (3) emergency tax increases or reductions to meet an economic crisis. Thus, the Committee hoped, "the close link between expenditures and tax *rates* will be kept at all stages of the business cycle," and "the really frightening possibility" of "an endless ascent to higher and higher government spending, both in prosperity and depression" would be averted.[75]

Consistent with its desire to limit the scope of the public sector as much as possible while still providing for a government guarantee of aggregate economic performance, the CED also stressed the need for automaticity in fiscal policy. The poor forecasting record of the government economists who predicted mass unemployment at the end of World War II lent credence to a position in fact taken much earlier. In January 1943, the chairman of CED's newly formed Research Committee observed:

Imagination and inventiveness will be required . . . in so organizing the remaining governmental controls that they shall be so far as possible statutory, rather than of the type involving a wide range of administrative discretion. Controls of the latter sort will be inevitably subject to political abuse, and are more open to serious dangers from ignorance and incapacity in political appointees.[76]

There was, of course, one element of the CED package which strayed from the ideal of automaticity: monetary policy was to remain flexible. But this exception to the rule was thoroughly consistent with corporatist values. As Neil Jacoby, a long-time member of the CED's Research Advisory Board, has observed, "Money controls operate impersonally and without any of the direct interference with the details of private business which is so irksome and inefficient in a free economy."[77] Restrictive monetary policy—the phase of flexibility that most interested the CED—had a particular appeal because it offered a technique for fighting inflation while avoiding higher taxes and/or direct wage and price controls. Those who opposed restrictive monetary policy, on the other hand, often did so because of a liberal's distaste for the kind of income redistribution which resulted from higher interest rates, because of a desire for easy and cheap Treasury financing of the federal debt, and because of a belief that the threat of secular stagnation required that interest rates be kept low in the long run. The CED felt none of these concerns deeply.[78]

The CED's conjunction of modern fiscal and monetary policy with corporatist values provided, Benton argued, an American "answer to the European brands of socialism."[79] Closer to home, it supplied the business community with an answer to the left-wing formulations of Keynes which had dominated the fiscal policy debate under the New Deal and during World War II. By accepting that "government holds the key to maintaining the variations of the whole social organism within safe limits" and by liberating itself from the rigidity of the annually balanced budget, the CED provided the American business community with a formidable program to promote in the continuing national debate over the federal government's economic role.[80]

Chapter Six

The Ascendancy of Commercial Keynesianism

At the very least, the development of a sophisticated "commercial Keynesianism" by even a relatively small segment of American business in the years immediately after World War II calls into question the common belief that the New Economics was somehow imposed on a reluctant business community by antibusiness liberals. CED chairman Donald David was probably correct in asserting in 1957 that "at every major economic watershed of these past 15 years you will find a reservoir of CED research and recommendations." The Committee's prescription of automatic stabilizing action through the federal budget and a flexible monetary program constituted the heart of federal economic policy prior to the Kennedy-Johnson tax reduction of 1964. Writing on the tenth anniversary of the 1947 publication of the CED's stabilizing budget policy, economist Walter Heller (later Kennedy's chief economic adviser) observed that "a review of CED's tax policy for economic stability is a review of the dominant theme in postwar fiscal-policy thinking." Throughout much of the postwar period, there existed striking parallels between CED and government policy.[1]

Evaluating the precise impact of the CED's proposals on federal policy remains, however, a difficult task. The corporatists of the CED were not alone in advocating what

they did, but they appear to have played a significant role
in gaining acceptance for their brand of commercial Keynesianism among the several constituences involved. Addressing economists, government policymakers, and fellow businessmen, the Committee exerted influence in three distinct
ways: (1) through its contributions to economic thought;
(2) through the activities of its personnel; and (3) through
its relationships, as an institution, with the various agencies
active in formulating, selling, and implementing national
economic policy.

The CED helped to influence national affairs by developing concepts which shaped the parameters of the debate
over federal fiscal policy. Of special significance was the
Committee's sponsorship of the concept of "automatic stabilizers" and its emphasis on the "built-in flexibility" which
such stabilizers would provide. Although it is difficult to
determine with precision the exact origins of the "automatic
stabilizers" concept, the CED's 1946 study entitled *Jobs and
Markets* and the pioneering work of staff economist Albert
Hart seem to have played a crucial part in building "the
basic framework for future considerations of built-in
flexibility."[2]

The influence of the Committee, moreover, extended
beyond the mere development of ideas to the popularization
of such concepts among economists and laymen alike. From
the very beginning, the CED had a shrewd appreciation of
the value of public relations. "We got a lot of publicity,"
Marion Folsom later recalled laconically. The Committee
aimed particularly at the "opinion-influencing group" in
America society, especially those "equipped by education
and desire to make a real study of our economy."[3] The
organization's Information Committee included (in 1955)
the head of the Book of the Month Club, top executives from
both Young and Rubicam and the J. Walter Thompson
Agency, the editors of the *Atlanta Constitution* and *Look*

magazine, the publisher of the *Washington Post*, the board chairman of the Curtis Publishing Company, and the presidents of Time-Life and the Columbia Broadcasting System. With such support, the CED was able to keep its recommendations in the public mind. For example, its 1958 pamphlet entitled *Defense Against Inflation* was discussed within one month of its publication in 354 papers and magazines representing a total circulation of over 31 million.[4] Even so astute an economist as Paul McCracken of the University of Michigan (later a member of Eisenhower's Council of Economic Advisers) admitted that "the Committee for Economic Development, among others, has done a great deal to educate us on this point of built-in flexibility."[5] As a self-styled "merchant of ideas," the CED played a prominent role in the major postwar discussions regarding the government's role in the economy.[6]

In addition to its activities as an educational force, the Committee affected public policy through the personal activities of its most fertile "idea man," Beardsley Ruml. An important element in the CED's style of Keynesianism was a shift in emphasis from the expenditure to the revenue side of the budget. The stabilizing budget would use automatic variations in revenue to cushion minor fluctuations and rely on discretionary tax reduction rather than increased public spending to stimulate the economy in a depression. But before such a fiscal policy could be implemented, the rickety prewar tax structure of the United States had to be revamped.

The problem at the outset lay in the state of the personal income tax. First, it did not affect enough people, for only 4 million persons or families were subject to the federal income tax in 1939.[7] Second, there was a lag in tax payment which delayed the impact of any change either in taxable income or in the tax rate assessed. Ralph Flanders had considered the use of taxation "as an active, flexible means of controlling the business cycle" during the 1930s, but he concluded that the system was simply not equal to the task: "The income tax is delayed in its application, and conditions may well change between the time when a new policy . . . is set, and the time when the funds are actually collected, which will be going on fully two years later."[8] For example, taxes on income earned in calendar year 1940 were not paid until the following year, 1941.

Wartime changes in the tax system resolved both of these difficulties, however. The Revenue Act of 1942 brought nearly all working Americans into the income tax system; by 1944, 42.4 million persons or families were subject to the federal income tax.[9] But putting the tax on a pay-as-you-go basis proved to be more difficult. The problem of making tax payment current had been under discussion in the Treasury Department for some time, but no concrete proposals of scope and imagination were forthcoming. Ruml swept into this vacuum in 1942 with a pay-as-you-go plan which was to make his name a household word and which was to allow taxation to play a more important role in economic stabilization.

Ruml's pay-as-you-go crusade had three aims.[10] First, he wanted to end the hardships which the existing tax system sometimes imposed. The retirement of executives was often complicated by the fact that taxes based on last year's handsome salary had to be paid from this year's smaller pension. The sudden death of a highly paid executive could leave a relatively small estate saddled with a large tax bill. Prolonged illness or unemployment similarly left many persons with tax bills but little income. And of course the coming of war meant that taxes on civilian salaries would in many cases have to be paid out of rather meager army wages. Second, current payments would facilitate the collection of taxes, especially if coupled with a procedure for tax withholding at the source of income. Third, as Ruml later recalled:

The greatest advantage of all I think is . . . that we do not find ourselves in a lower period of business activity with higher taxes to pay. And exactly the same thing is true in reverse. As you go forward and have higher incomes you have higher taxes simultaneously and not the low taxes of this year which would have been inflationary.[11]

Ruml had long given thought to the potential of taxation as a tool for economic stabilization. He endeavored now to bring the structure of the tax system into line with his rapidly developing formulation of Keynesian policy.

Ruml submitted his plan to the Treasury on March 30, 1942.[12] The proposal called for tax payments made in 1942, which were calculated on 1941 income, to be redefined as tentative payments on current 1942 income. In March 1943, income for the previous year would be known with certainty and the taxpayer could make up any sum owed the government (or vice versa) because of the difference between estimated 1942 income and the actual 1942 income. In the process, taxes for 1941 would be forgiven; they would simply be skipped. Tax payment would thus be made current and withholding procedures could be implemented with little trouble.

When the Treasury reacted coolly to his proposal, Ruml brought it to the attention of Congress in July 1942 by appearing "as an individual" before the Senate Finance Committee. The plan received much publicity, and a bitter controversy ensued over the issue of forgiveness. For some, the very idea that a year's taxes could be skipped without the Treasury losing money was incomprehensible. Liberals argued that to forgive a year's taxes across the board would result in unfair benefits for the rich.[13] Ruml continued to argue for equality of treatment (i.e., total forgiveness) regardless of income level, but he revised his plan to incorporate several windfall provisions to prevent the most blatant profiteering.

In the end, the appeal of the proposal and the extraordinary publicity that it received proved irresistible. Capitalizing on Ruml's abilities as an articulate and indefatigable promoter and utilizing such clever catchphrases as "setting the tax clock ahead" and "daylight saving for the taxpayer," the supporters of the scheme made pay-as-you-go a popular issue. By late 1942, 81 percent of those questioned in a Gallup poll had heard of the Ruml plan.[14] Additional notoriety was achieved when Ruml was made the subject of the $64 question on "Take It or Leave It," a popular radio quiz show.

Roosevelt finally signed into law on June 9, 1943, the congressional compromise which put most wage and salary earners on a withholding basis beginning July 1 and which provided for the cancellation of 75 percent of one year's taxes (the lower of the 1942 or 1943 tax liabilities) or $50, whichever was higher. The unforgiven part of the tax would be paid in two installments, one due in 1944 and the second in 1945. As Representative Frank Carlson (R-Kans.) observed with some satisfaction, "It was at least 75 percent Ruml"; what Representative Bertrand Gearhart (R-Calif.) derisively labeled "the plan that slogans built" was a reality.[15] Ruml's campaign had been a significant element in the process of change. His crusade also helped make practical the CED's policy of reliance on the built-in flexibility of the economy's automatic stabilizers.

The Committee's views also entered the public policy dialogue through the influx of CED members and alumni into federal service, a movement which established an important liaison between the CED and the government. In the first fifteen years of the organization's existence, thirty-eight CED trustees held public office.[16] Ralph Flanders and Ruml served as the presidents of the Boston and New York Federal Reserve Banks. William Benton and Flanders went to the Senate, and Paul Hoffman became administrator of the Marshall Plan. Marion Folsom relinquished the chairmanship of the CED to serve in the Eisenhower administration, first as Under Secretary of the Treasury and later as Secretary of Health, Education, and Welfare. Both of Eisenhower's Secretaries of the Treasury, George Humphrey and Robert Anderson, were exposed—with varying degrees of acceptance—to CED doctrine during their tenure as trustees. Indeed, President Eisenhower and his brother Milton served for a time on the Committee's board. Nor were such contacts limited only to trustees. For example, Grover Ensley, who was recommended to Senator Flanders by research director Herbert Stein, became staff director of the congressional Joint Economic Committee.[17] Theodore Yntema, who was the CED's first director of research, later served as chief economist in the government's Economic Stabilization Agency, and ultimately returned to the Committee as a trustee when he became a vice-president of the Ford Motor Company. Economist Neil Jacoby, a long-time member of the CED's Research Advisory Board, served in Eisenhower's Council of Economic Advisers.

An example of the impact this sort of interchange could have is provided by the experience of CED alumnus Thomas McCabe, who had a role in implementing the flexible monetary policy proposed by the Committee in 1948. McCabe, the president of Scott Paper, was one of the founding trustees of the CED and a member of its original Research Committee (under Ralph Flanders). Selected by President Truman in 1948 to succeed Marriner Eccles as chairman of the Board of Governors of the Federal Reserve System, McCabe became an important figure in the Fed's attempt to free itself from the domination of the Treasury Department. The tension between the two agencies had been festering for years, with the Fed increasingly unhappy over its inability to pursue an independent course in economic stabilization. Finally, in 1951, the Fed forced a confrontation by asserting its right to sell federal securities at rates of interest other than those desired by the Treasury.[18]

The policy views which McCabe brought to this battle had been provided to a significant extent by his CED service. He explained to his CED associates in 1949:

I can testify from personal experience to the impact that the effort left upon me as a participant. . . . I have been wrestling with the same type and range of problems as a public official. I can also testify, consequently, to the impact of the CED upon our public policies and upon the thinking of those who formulate policies. It goes without saying, of course, that the preliminary contact with the CED has been invaluable to me.[19]

The Committee's repeated calls for the Federal Reserve to use to the maximum its statutory powers to maintain economic stability made a strong impression on McCabe.[20] Moreover, the CED's declarations generated support which helped McCabe succeed in the struggle to liberate monetary policy. He later recalled:

More and more public officials turn to CED for counsel and assistance, as I did when I was Chairman of the Board of Governors of the Federal Reserve System. I found CED gave me more aid in its statements on monetary and credit problems than any other group of business or financial people, especially in the very critical period prior to the Treasury-Federal Reserve accord, which was reached in 1951.[21]

Though not all alumni of the CED were so inspired by their experience or so well-positioned to affect events, the "old boy network" worked and, in the case of McCabe, exerted an important influence on public policy.

The Committee's connection with the federal government involved, in addition, an organizational interaction that went beyond the exchange of personnel. Often such contact was informal. Leon Keyserling, chairman of the Council of Economic Advisers, reported to Truman that "we here in the Council have been in constant contact with various members of the Committee for Economic Development, have received from them much evidence of understanding and support for our work, and look upon them as the most forward looking of the major business organizations. . . . These gentlemen, most of whom you undoubtedly know, drop in to see me when they get a chance, and in general are helpful although they disagree with us on some points."[22]

The Committee also enjoyed a close working relationship with the Federal Reserve System. From its inception during World War II, the CED found the Fed and its regional banks willing and active collaborators in various research activities. Federal Reserve economist Ralph Young, a member of the CED's Research Advisory Board, served as an expert adviser and critic in the preparation of several CED policy statements and actually represented the Committee at a meeting of the Conference of National Organizations in 1948. All the while, Young reported to his superiors regarding the views and activities of his CED colleagues. Such connections served all involved; information and influence flowed both ways.[23]

The CED often used its close relationships with other private and public groups to direct research into areas of mutual concern. In 1945, the Committee gave $50,000 to another private group, the National Bureau of Economic Research, to finance a study of the flow of money payments through the principal sectors of the American economy. The CED arranged for representatives of the Federal Reserve System to serve on the project's technical advisory committee and induced the Fed to provide office space for this private study. Once it was under way, the Federal Reserve System agreed in 1946 to take over the entire effort.[24]

The CED utilized its organizational ties in a similar

fashion when it became concerned over the probable economic impact of winding down the Korean War military spending. The Committee prodded the Commerce Department into surveying the immediate economic prospects. Chairman Marion Folsom prevailed upon Commerce Secretary Charles Sawyer, and in 1952 the Department launched a study designed "to inform the business community on factors affecting the level of civilian demand after the present defense program has reached its peak." The CED advised Sawyer in the selection of outside experts to guide the project, and members of its own research staff "participated in an advisory capacity" and reviewed successive drafts of the study.[25] Though the substance of the Commerce study was hardly reassuring, the CED had once again achieved an integration of private and public interests and organizations. In such instances the CED's corporatist ideology posited a mutuality of interests which played down the importance of determining who used whom; according to the corporatist outlook, private and public goals were the same. It was thus appropriate that during the Truman-Eisenhower interregnum, Eisenhower directed department and agency heads to maintain working relations with the CED. "This group has such connections with several government agencies," Administrative Assistant for Economic Affairs Gabriel Hauge noted, "and wants to keep them under the new administration; so does Ike."[26]

In addition to such direct and indirect influence and interaction, the CED shaped events by providing commercial Keynesianism with a champion of impeccable credentials. As John Kenneth Galbraith has observed, "In our tradition of economic debate, a proposition can often be more economically destroyed by association than by evidence. . . . The charge that an idea is radical, impractical, or long-haired is met by showing that a prominent businessman has favored it. Businessmen—successful ones at least—are by

definition never radical, impractical, or long-haired."[27]
Once embraced by the CED, occasional deficit finance became less frightening. Respectability by association gave to
the CED's Keynesianism a status and an influence never
enjoyed by the earlier stagnationist formulation. By such
means, the Committee was able within a few years after its
formation to alter the public debate over economic affairs
and to affect the content of public policy.

I

In the 1950s, the rise of commercial Keynesianism was
tested by the coming to power of a Republican administration. After twenty years of crying in the wilderness against
fiscal irresponsibility, many hardshell conservatives hoped
that the election of Dwight Eisenhower would bring a return
to the economic probity and balanced budgets of an earlier
day. Had not Ike, while president of Columbia University,
decried the liberal's welfare state as "a mule's sort of
heaven—a tight roof overhead, plenty of food, a minimum
of work and no worries or responsibilities"? And had not
the wooing of Senator Robert Taft and his conservative constituency been a prominent theme during the 1952 campaign, culminating in the so-called "surrender of Morning-
side Heights" at which Taft announced that he and the
candidate were in full agreement on domestic policy?[28]

Others saw in the General a more complex, flexible,
and moderate leader, however. Paul Hoffman described him
to Ralph Flanders as "a new kind of candidate" who would
take orders "neither from the N.A.M. nor the C.I.O.," and
agreed to chair the Advisory Committee of Citizens for Eisenhower.[29] In office, Eisenhower's views on fiscal policy
proved to be closer to those of groups like the CED than to
those of Taft's supporters or either of the groups mentioned

by Hoffman. He had, for example, a modern view of the role of government in the national economy. Another depression, he wrote to the vice-chairman of J. P. Morgan and Company in 1954, would be "a national tragedy." As president, he was "prepared to use every resource" to maintain economic stability. "There will always be differences of view as to the timing of certain governmental actions," he concluded, "but there can now be no disagreement among responsible citizens about the proper role of the Federal Government as a preventive agent in times of economic stress."[30]

Of course, Eisenhower was not an avowed Keynesian; he once told his cabinet that he would consider his presidency fulfilled could he but balance the budget.[31] But this goal was not an obsession. Budget balancing, he wrote,

is not in my mind the single or governing criterion of our economic and financial policy. Economic stability and growth is another and one of compelling importance at certain times. If conditions require, we shall not hesitate to subordinate the first of these criteria to the second.[32]

The concept of an annual budget balance, the President later agreed with Secretary of the Treasury Robert Anderson, was "by way of being a great cliche, anyway."[33]

In keeping with such views, Eisenhower brought with him to Washington economic advisers who were attuned to the emergent commercial Keynesianism. Gabriel Hauge, who had taught economics at Harvard and Princeton, accompanied the General during the campaign and became the chief economic adviser on the White House staff. A self-proclaimed "Eisenhower conservative," he believed that "government budget policy must be directed not only to the economical use of tax money and the balancing of outgo against income, it must also be geared to the goal of main-

taining the stable growth of the economy"; and he cited
approvingly William Benton's call for government to influence the economic weather without rationing the raindrops.[34] Hauge in turn recruited Arthur Burns from Columbia University and the National Bureau of Economic
Research to serve as the chairman of the Council of Economic Advisers. Burns initially impressed White House
chief of staff Sherman Adams as a prototypical New Deal
professor—"a glassy stare through thick lenses, peering out
from under a canopy of unruly hair parted in the middle,
a large pipe with a curved stem: the very incarnation of all
the externals that were such anathema to Republican businessmen and politicians."[35] In reality, Burns was an em-
pirical economist who was suspicious of grand theory in
general and of Keynes in particular. But his disagreement
was more theoretical than practical. "The Employment
Act," he observed, "reflects a revolutionary change in our
attitudes towards the business cycle." Indeed, in times of
economic adversity, the balanced budget was an enemy—
"in a time of declining business activity it is wiser to reduce
taxes than to raise them . . . [because] tax reductions can
effectively offset the decline in incomes that accompanies
a decline of production."[36] Such views were reinforced
when Neil Jacoby, a long-time adviser to the CED and an
original member of its Research Advisory Board, joined
Burns on the Council.

Not even George Humphrey, Eisenhower's first Secretary of the Treasury and the administration's most outspo-
ken advocate of fiscal probity, could remain completely immune from the influences of the Keynesian revolution.
Board chairman of the M. A. Hanna Company, Humphrey
brought to Washington an instinctive conservatism, and his
public statements often rang with calls for a balanced
budget. "I don't think you can spend yourself rich," he
announced at a press conference in Jaunary 1957. But Hum-

phrey's dislike of deficit spending would at crucial points be muted by political expediency and the advocacy of commercial Keynesianism by others within the administration. Ever the loyal party man, the Secretary would acquiesce in passive Keynesian policies when the price of budget balancing appeared too high. As Herbert Stein has observed, "No one could be more sincere and persuasive in reciting the litany of budget-balancing and sound finance at the drop of a hat. But when decisions with important economic and political consequences were to be made, [Humphrey] relied upon the simple pragmatism of modern economics."[37]

Eisenhower also took steps to strengthen the institutional base of economic expertise within the administration. When Congress, unhappy with the performance of the Council of Economic Advisers under its controversial chairman Leon Keyserling, limited its 1953 appropriation, the group in effect passed out of existence. Determined "to form an agency reflecting the economic thinking of . . . [the] Administration," the President reestablished the Council and increased the chairman's responsibilities as the operating head of the agency.[38] At the same time, he created the Advisory Board on Economic Growth and Stability to provide "the most careful planning against the results of depression and general retard [sic] of the economic activity of the country."[39] Composed of representatives of the Departments of the Treasury, Agriculture, Commerce, and Labor; the Federal Reserve System Board of Governors; the Bureau of the Budget; and the Council of Economic Advisers, the Board never became an important initiator or coordinator of policy, but it served Burns well for several years as a valuable source of interdepartmental intelligence.[40] The formation of the Board reflected Eisenhower's recognition of the need for some overall integration of economic problem-solving.

The administration's attitudes and bureaucratic innovations were quickly tested. Even before his inauguration, a CED delegation which included Meyer Kestnbaum, Jr., J. Cameron Thomson, Frazar Wilde, and Wesley Rennie met with the General and left a memorandum which warned:

Some time in the next four years there may be a recession of business activity and a tendency toward depression in the American economy. This tendency may result from the expected reduction of government spending, possibly accompanied by a drop in housing construction and business investment. It is not certain that there will be such a tendency, and if it comes it is not likely to be nearly as severe as 1929–32. Nevertheless, it is of extreme importance to begin preparations now against the possibility of a depression.[41]

In late summer, the recession which the CED had predicted became a reality. On September 25, 1953, Burns reported to the cabinet that the movement of key economic indicators foreshadowed "a possible economic downturn." Secretary of State John Foster Dulles added that a "near panic" sentiment existed among businessmen in New York. The President immediately asserted the need to avoid "another 1929" at all costs, a concern that would become a refrain as the administration sought to meet the first test of its economic modernity.[42]

At the outset of the slump the administration acted with restraint. Burns observed that the Council favored the use of "monetary policy and private business action, tax reductions rather than increased government expenditures, and practical government programs to the extent necessary with preference given to loans and loan guarantees rather than direct government construction."[43] Accordingly, the government's response to the recession was largely passive.[44] The administration depended on the cushioning action of the automatic stabilizers and on an expansive monetary policy. It allowed a previously scheduled, large reduction in the personal income tax and the mandated expiration of the excess profits tax to take effect in Jaunary 1954, and in April it approved a reduction in federal excise taxes—all in the face of an impending budget deficit. More actively, it pushed ahead with its major revision of the internal revenue code, which the President signed into law in August 1954 and which reduced revenue by about $1.4 billion in fiscal year 1955. Proceeding cautiously, Eisenhower and his advisers refused, however, to heed the call of some Democrats for more dramatic tax reductions to combat the slump.

The administration acted with even greater circumspection regarding spending. In February 1954, the President directed Burns to coordinate planning for a major expansion of public works activity, setting July 1 as the tentative target date for the implementation of such a program.[45] Two months later, Eisenhower noted in his diary that the government was at the "point of no return": "From here on I believe it will become clear that we are going one way or the other and I am convinced that the dangers of doing nothing are far greater than those of doing too much."[46] In May, the administration accelerated public works spending within the limits of existing appropriations, but its sense of urgency waned as the July 1 decision date for a major spending expansion approached. By early July, Sherman Adams could write to John L. Lewis that the downturn had ended; to policymakers, success obviated the necessity of acting more forcefully.[47]

The failure of the administration to cut taxes or spend more aggressively should not, however, obscure the salient features of its response to the first Republican recession in a generation. As was stated in a subsequent report by a Council of Economic Advisers whose Keynesian credentials were beyond dispute: "Significantly, in 1954, the bipartisan character of expansionary fiscal policies was established for the first time, as the Republican Administration . . . adopted measures that had previously been linked to the New Deal

and Keynesian economics."[48] Even the staunch Democrat
John Kenneth Galbraith congratulated the Council of Economic Advisers for its "considerable grace and ease in getting away from the cliches of a balanced budget and the
unspeakable evils of deficit financing."[49] The Republicans
had accepted a deficit and had refused to raise taxes in order
to balance the budget in a downturn; economic stability had
taken priority over bookkeeping neatness.

In short, Eisenhower had embraced the emergent commercial Keynesianism which the CED and others had helped
develop and popularize. The administration resisted the
advice of both the laissez-faire advocates who held the balanced budget as the *sine qua non* of political leadership and
the spenders who viewed the expansion of public sector
investment as the salvation of American capitalism. Later,
in 1959, Secretary of the Treasury Robert Anderson, a CED
alumnus, sought to explain the rationale underlying the administration's economic thinking:

We should, in my opinion, follow some variation of the stabilizing
budget proposal, in which budget policy, year in and year out,
would be geared to the attainment of a surplus under conditions
of strong economic activity. . . . On this basis, the automatic decline in revenues and increase in expenditures during a recession—reflecting in part the operation of the so-called built-in stabilizers—would generate a moderate budget deficit. In prosperous
periods, tax receipts would automatically rise and certain types
of spending would contract, producing a budget surplus.[50]

His comments to the congressional Joint Economic Committee could easily have been mistaken for a CED policy
statement.

II

As the recommendations of the CED and the behavior of the
administration converged, the Chamber of Commerce moved

to join the nascent Keynesian consensus. Even in the immediate postwar era, not everyone in the Chamber agreed with the organization's decision to embrace fiscal orthodoxy. The staff economists in the Economic Research Department and the expert-laden Committee on Economic Policy (COEP) remained particularly concerned over the Chamber's continued advocacy of an annually balanced budget. In January 1949, Schmidt told the Joint Committee on the Economic Report that government had become the nation's dominant industry. "If the Government itself were able to adopt a contra-cyclical policy that would make, probably, the most powerful contribution to economic stability . . . that could be made."[51]

The recession of 1948–1949 soon provided the fiscal modernists within the Chamber with an opportunity to express such views. In March 1949, the Department of Manufacture Committee warned of the probability of a severe downturn in the foreseeable future and recommended that the Chamber undertake an examination of possible government policies to deal with a serious depression.[52] When the Board referred the problem to the Committee on Economic Policy, the dissidents seized their opportunity.

The COEP attempted to bring the Chamber into accord with moderate compensatory economics. The committee's interim report observed that, in the event of a severe depression, the application of existing Chamber policy would be economically, politically, and socially harmful. The cost of an annually balanced budget and debt reduction during a major depression would be intolerable. The committee suggested that the existing policy declarations calling for such balanced budgets be allowed to lapse without publicity, and that they be replaced by a declaration which recognized that deficits would naturally arise as unemployment increased and revenues fell and that tax increases to balance the budget at such times were counterproductive.[53]

These recommendations ran into heavy opposition

when the COEP's interim report was referred by the Board to all of the other interested committees for comment. The Finance Department staff provided the businessmen of the Committee on Federal Finance (COFF) with two important criticisms: first, that existing policy was neither as orthodox nor as rigid as the COEP feared; second, that the proposed formal changes would increase the possibility that the Chamber might through such changes be maneuvered into supporting some scheme of activist compensatory fiscal policy. The COFF flatly stated that differences existed regarding the role of the budget in national economic policy. The Finance Department staff did recommend that some changes be made in the Chamber's budget policy declaration, so as not to preclude completely some deviation from the annually balanced budget in time of economic crisis.[54] Even this compromise was, however, unanimously rejected by the COFF's businessmen; after lengthy discussion, the committee urged retention without modification of the existing policy declaration. The initiative thus defeated, the Board of Directors in March 1950 ordered the COEP to continue its study.[55]

The COEP raised the issue anew in 1953, when it warned the Chamber's Policy Committee of an impending decline in business activity and again charged that the existing demand for an annually balanced budget was too rigid.[56] The modernists' proposals had remained in bureaucratic limbo throughout the dramatic economic expansion which accompanied the Korean War, but this time the proposed change was accepted with little apparent opposition. The policy declaration on the budget adopted at the 1953 annual meeting did not include the requirement that the budget be balanced "each year."[57] The change was a small one—only two words were dropped—but it was an important opening wedge.

Near victory, the COEP continued its struggle into 1954.

Once again, the fear of an impending recession prompted action. The arguments remained unchanged; the COEP claimed that the Chamber was still on record as favoring an annually balanced budget despite the danger that such a policy would cause considerable embarrassment in the event of a serious downturn and thereby call into question the Chamber's reputation for responsible leadership.[58] This time, the COEP's success was more complete, as a comparison of the old (1952) policy declaration with that passed at the 1954 convention indicates:

1952 Policy Declaration

A balanced budget, with definite provision for debt retirement, should be the normal procedure. Recognition of this basic policy calls for rejection of temporizing proposals such as that the budget be balanced or debt reduced only in years of an expanding and prosperous economy. The objective should be to achieve a balance of the budget each year at the lowest possible level which will suffice for indispensable public services and adequate reduction of the national debt.[59]

1954 Policy Declaration

A balanced budget, with definite provision for debt retirement, should be the normal procedure. The objective should be to achieve a balance at the lowest possible level which will suffice for indispensable public services and requirements of national safety and, particularly in periods of inflationary pressures, adequate reduction of the national debt. The long-term policy should be to reduce federal expenditures systematically so as to permit of equally systematic reduction in federal taxes.[60]

As an added touch, the 1954 annual meeting approved, also at the instigation of the COEP, a statement on economic stability which explicitly endorsed the commitment of the federal government to encourage "policies which will help industry to promote high levels of employment, production and purchasing power with due regard to its [government's] other obligations, essential considerations of national policy and the encouragement of economic progress." The statement emphasized the role of the Federal Reserve, "independent of the Executive Branch," in furthering this commitment. Most significantly, the Chamber was now formally on record as recognizing that the very size and scope of government fiscal operations "make it inevitable that fiscal policy will influence the national economy for good or ill." As a result, "Overall fiscal policy should be evaluated not only on the merits of particular appropriations and tax proposals, but also in terms of its impact upon the prosperity of the nation."[61]

The deed was done quietly if not quickly. Commenting on the annual meeting, the Chamber's *Washington Report* observed that "current policy . . . [was] slightly revised to make it clear that the Chamber's advocacy of a balanced budget allows for some flexibility."[62] The politics of large-scale organization dictated that the controversy surrounding the changes be hidden from view. In fact, the debate had been settled in committee, well before the membership gave formal approval to the changes at the convention in May 1954; on February 11, representatives of the Committees on Finance, Government Expenditures, and Government Taxation (all three affiliated with the Chamber's Finance Department) had finally acquiesced in the COEP's proposals. On the next day, Chamber economist Emerson Schmidt wrote, "As you know we have had considerable difficulty and embarrassment over our budget policy. . . . I am happy to say that the issue now seems to have been reasonably well resolved."[63] The Chamber had finally made a formal peace with John Maynard Keynes.

The peacemaking process had been a complicated one, and the preceding account raises many important questions. Why, for example, was the Committee on Economic Policy the leader in the drive to bring Chamber policy into the mainstream of economic thought? What motivated the modernists and the fiscal conservatives who opposed them so successfully for so long? And why did the COEP finally succeed? The answers to these questions lie in a complex nexus of organizational pressures and tendencies, external political and economic developments, and interpersonal relationships.

The COEP's relatively liberal position on fiscal matters resulted in part from the broad mandate that had been given the committee upon its formation. The COEP was established to analyze "the essential conditions for attaining high levels of stable production and employment."[64] It was not designed as a watchdog committee, restricted to one particular problem area, but rather was expected to monitor the national economy as a whole, focusing on long-run as well as on short-run phenomena. Its viewpoint fitted neatly with the "big picture" macroeconomic perspective of Keynesian theory.

Also important for understanding the role of the COEP is an appreciation of the special characteristics of the personnel who manned the committee over the years. Economic sophistication was the hallmark of the committee. There was, for example, noteworthy interchange with other organizations of a more pronounced Keynesian bent. Emerson Schmidt was a frequent observer at the early meetings of the Committee for Economic Development; J. Cameron Thomson and Harry Bullis, both prominent members of the COEP, were also trustees of the CED. The COEP worked closely with the professional economists of the Chamber's Economic Research Department. Schmidt served as secretary of the committee, and the staff of the Research Department provided a steady stream of background memoranda and reports. Moreover, the membership of the committee itself was heavily larded with business economists, academics, and business journalists. Soon after joining the Chamber, Schmidt had recommended increased participation by scholars in Chamber committee work; the COEP bore the fruit of this suggestion.[65] Particularly striking was the representation of such expertise on the COEP relative to those committees which opposed its efforts to modernize the Chamber's fiscal policy views (see the table). It is not surprising that such experts were, by virtue of intellectual disposition and academic training, both more likely than ordinary businessmen to have been exposed to the mysteries of Keynesian economics and less inclined to treat the New Economics as an ideological variant of bubonic plague.

The recession of 1949 galvanized this potential and transformed the COEP into a force for change within the Chamber. The recession was the first real test of the postwar economy and the first concrete challenge to the Chamber's postwar policies regarding the desirability of the balanced budget. The committee firmly believed that the business cycle could be tempered and thus reacted more vigorously

TABLE: Experts[a] on Chamber of Commerce Committees

Year	Committee on Economic Policy	Committee on Federal Finance	Committee on Government Expenditures[b]	Committee on Taxation[b]
		Number of Experts		
1945–46	6 of 26	1 of 24		
1946–47	10 of 27	1 of 19		
1947–48	10 of 27	1 of 18		
1948–49	12 of 25	2 of 23		
1953–54	9 of 29		3 of 31	0 of 34
1954–55	10 of 29		2 of 28	0 of 37

SOURCE: Chamber of Commerce, *Men Who Serve You* for the years in question.

[a] Experts being: (1) academics (both teachers and administrators); (2) business economists; and (3) business journalists.

[b] In 1953, the Committee on Federal Finance was divided into two separate committees, one dealing with expenditures and the other with revenues.

than other elements in the Chamber to the possibility of
failure in this regard. Although outgoing president Shreve
explained calmly that the recession was an "inevitable readjustment . . . to normal market conditions" and that when
the "current readjustment has run its course" business
would "find itself on a sounder and infinitely more satis-
fying foundation," the chairman of the COEP, Harry Bullis,
warned: "The specter of idle men is rising again. It is the
responsibility of business leadership to provide jobs and
maintain them. If we fail, government will shoulder the
load."[66] Prodded by the downturn into reassessing Chamber
policy, the COEP concluded that the alternatives to deficit
finance in the event of a serious depression involved unacceptable social and political risks.[67]

If such fears lent urgency to the COEP's attempt to alter
Chamber policy in 1949 and early 1950, fear of another sort
motivated those who opposed the change. As the Finance
Department staff admitted, one major reason for clinging to
the rhetoric of fiscal orthodoxy in the Chamber's policy
declarations was the fear that any deviation might be mis-
interpreted as support for liberal spending programs.[68] A
similar fear had prompted an earlier clash between the
COEP and the Finance Committee. When, in late 1948, the
former had called for Chamber support of a proposed national monetary and fiscal commission to investigate the
problems and possibilities of monetary and budgetary policy, the Finance Committee vetoed the request; it argued
that any searching evaluation of existing practices might
encourage further government intervention in the economy.[69] Fear of such intervention was not totally unfounded.
Truman's January 1949 State of the Union Message had,
after all, laid bare the Fair Deal's plans for an expanded
social welfare program. Even more to the point, both the
Spence Bill (the proposed "Economic Stability Act of 1949")
and the Murray-Patman Economic Expansion Bill promised

unprecedented peacetime government action in order to overcome adverse economic trends. Both measures died in committee, but they gave the business community an unpleasant start.[70]

The Korean War boom allowed considerations of recession policy to be postponed, but as the war wound down to its dreary conclusion, renewed fear of a recession caused the COEP to reopen its campaign.[71] When the Korean expansion slowed in 1953, the COEP began to worry and wonder: "As the defense program levels out or begins to decline will jobs, markets and production decrease? Are there enough unsatisfied demands to maintain an expanding economy?"[72] In January 1954, Schmidt told the Board that layoffs and unemployment were up, output down, and that the economy was indeed in something of a slide.[73] Once again the Chamber's devotion to the balanced budget threatened to collide with the reality of a genuine slump. The COEP reiterated its call for a policy declaration which would enable the Chamber to adapt effectively to changing conditions.[74]

The economy, the Chamber's fiscal modernists argued, was undergoing an important transition. The "great powerful somewhat artificial stimuli growing out of World War II and the reconstruction, as well as the Korean expansion" were finally played out. The superabundance of liquidity and hunger for civilian goods (especially housing and automobiles) which had characterized the immediate postwar years, the foreign demand financed by the Marshall Plan, the Korean rearmament—all such extraordinary forces of expansion were gone. Marriage and family formation rates had been steadily declining since 1946 (a result of the decreased birthrate of the Depression-ridden 1930s), and the Chamber predicted that the downward trend would not be reversed until the war-boom babies came of age in the 1960s. "We are," the Economic Research Department admitted glumly, "now 'on our own,' so to speak. In fact, we are in something of a fix."[75]

At this point, the COEP's dissatisfaction with Chamber policy was heightened by its exposure to the economic analysis of Dr. Clark Warburton, a relatively unknown economist in the Federal Deposit Insurance Corporation. Addressing the COEP in February 1953, Warburton proclaimed that the key to business fluctuations was change in the total money supply of the nation. Economic stability, he argued, required not merely stability in the money supply but rather steady growth. He feared that the new administration's fixation with the "sound dollar" might cause it to stabilize or even decrease the money supply, thereby inducing a "mild business depression."[76] Schmidt, who already believed that Warburton "was on the right track," remembers that the committee was "tremendously impressed" by the presentation.[77]

The COEP quickly put Warburton's analysis to use in support of the effort already long under way to alter the Chamber's stand on budget policy. Schmidt feared that a firm commitment to repay the national debt might cause a contraction in the money supply and thereby bring on a depression. Conversely, government action could prevent contraction of the money supply—and thereby avoid recession. In this schema, deficit spending could be used to maintain or expand the money supply and "thereby prevent deflationary forces from taking over."[78] In January 1954, Schmidt explained the practical implications of the Warburton analysis to the Chamber's Board of Directors: the government could borrow in such a way as to maintain the money supply. He added pointedly, however, that such thinking was contrary to the Chamber's demand for an annually balanced budget.[79] Thus a monetarist interpretation of business cycles was used to support a cause which originally had been advocated on fiscal grounds. Ideas were significant, it would seem, in direct proportion to their relevance to the goal already decided upon.

The question still remains, however: why did the COEP finally succeed in 1953–1954, after having failed earlier? Why did the fiscal conservatives finally acquiesce in the proposals for change? And, even granting the smooth manner in which the changes were pushed through, why were they accepted by the membership without a whisper of dissent?

In large part, the answer lies in the return of the opposition party to presidential power. The election of Eisenhower, Chamber president Richard Bowditch noted, offered the opportunity "to duplicate our good work with the Congress in our relations with the Executive Department."[80] At the very least, the Republican resurgence promised that fiscal flexibility would not be harnessed to "social welfare" schemes. The appointment of George Humphrey as Secretary of the Treasury appeared to guarantee the financial probity of the administration, and *Nation's Business* was impressed by the "general economy-mindedness" which permeated the new regime. By 1954, Chamber president Clem Johnston could observe that business' sense of political uncertainty had lessened considerably.[81] In the face of such an auspicious political climate, arguments for resolute insistence on a balanced budget—lest flexibility be exploited by those desiring to extend the welfare state—seemed less persuasive than they had under Democratic regimes.

Moreover, the Eisenhower administration came to power promising tax reduction. Overly rigid adherence to the long-run goal of a balanced budget conflicted with the immediate hopes of the business community for an easing of the tax burden. The Chamber's sense of priorities was made clear by a poll taken at the 1953 convention; only 25 percent of those questioned felt that tax reduction should be postponed until the budget was actually in balance.[82] Dogma could not be allowed to stand in the way of such practical considerations.

To this welter of factors must be added a final organizational, and paradoxically personal, element. The struggle to revise the Chamber's budget policy was in many ways a personal duel between Schmidt and John O'Connor, who headed the organization's Finance Department. O'Connor's retirement from the Chamber in 1952 removed the chief opponent of moderation and eased his fellow stand-patters into acquiescence in the proposed reforms.[83] Thus, a combination of developments large and small, political, economic, and personal, caused the Chamber at last to follow the lead of its own fiscal modernists.

Although there were, to be sure, occasional atavisms, the Chamber gradually and grudgingly moved into the Keynesian camp. As late as 1955, Chamber president Clem Johnston could still observe that the laws of supply and demand and of the survival of the fittest were immutable, "foredooming to failure all hopeful attempts to contravene them by legislation and by national planning." Five years later, past-president Johnston informed the Democratic National Committee that prudent government action could indeed minimize cyclical unemployment. And in 1959, the Chamber's Board of Directors tabled a proposal by one of the organization's committees that the Chamber call for a constitutional amendment mandating an annually balanced budget (except in time of war); instead, the board included in its Congressional Action Program its explicit opposition to such a move.[84]

Concluding that the annually balanced budget concept had little to recommend it beyond the appeal of its label, the Chamber in the latter half of the 1950s adopted an approach similar to the stabilizing budget formulation of the CED. Emphasis was placed on the built-in flexibility of the economy's automatic stabilizers and on a discretionary, flexible monetary policy: "A 'stabilizing budget' policy should aim to balance the budget over the course of the business cycle. In recession there might be substantial deficits; in normal times, with reasonably high levels of employment and income, the budget should be balanced or yield a surplus for debt retirement; in inflationary periods the surplus should be substantial."[85] After much inner turmoil, the Chamber embraced the diluted Keynesian creed.

III

The Keynesian consensus was not all-inclusive, however. Some segments of the business community refused to join the Eisenhower administration, and groups such as the Chamber and the CED, in accepting the primacy of the federal government's role in economic stabilization and in forsaking the orthodoxy of the annually balanced budget. The NAM, for example, continued to view compensatory economics with distaste. The Association's postwar position was epitomized in its study of *The American Individual Enterprise System*. Published in 1946, this two-volume treatise was the culmination of six years of work by an "Economic Principles Commission" which included among its members Ludwig von Mises, an expatriate Austrian already famous as an archfoe of "statism." The study admitted that "at least under certain conditions and for a limited period, it is possible for government, by spending money and inflating the currency or bank deposits, to increase the volume of business activity." But such prosperity was adjudged transitory and ultimately lethal, for deficit spending at the same time undermined the private enterprise system and in the long run threatened political democracy. The national interest was best served by leaving the "Individual Enterprise System" alone.[86]

Translated into policy recommendations, such an analysis left the NAM in the position of advocating an annually balanced budget regardless of economic conditions. When NAM representatives William Grede and Harley Lutz spoke on behalf of this position in testimony before the Douglas subcommittee of the Joint Committee on the Economic Report (November 1949), they discovered that the NAM's rigid position was becoming increasingly difficult to defend. Under relentless questioning by Senators Paul Douglas and Ralph Flanders—Would you increase taxes in a depression?—they were forced to retreat from an unequivocal yes into a haze of obfuscation, concluding plaintively that "we must develop a philosophy that our bills have to be paid."[87]

The Association found itself in an awkward situation. Advocacy of an annually balanced budget had become a difficult task, but the alternatives seemed far worse than momentary embarrassment at a congressional hearing. The CED's formulation of Keynesianism, it was feared, would ultimately lead to a regimented economy.[88] Reliance on the built-in flexibility of the stabilizing budget meant "that by saddling ourselves with a high budget and high progressive tax rates we tend to stabilize the economy." "But," NAM economist Ralph Robey pointed out, "it is equally true in about the same sense that a man who is tied hand and foot may be said to be stabilized in his activities."[89]

The dilemma was not easily resolved. By the mid-1950s the NAM had come to admit that deficits might be unavoidable in a depression. It continued to insist, however, they they be treated as temporary aberrations—to be tolerated, but never manipulated for economic purposes. "Sound budget policy," the Association still warned, "should never be sacrificed for the purpose of attempting control of either inflation or deflation through budget manipulation."[90]

Thus, organized business by 1960 presented a spectrum of varied accommodations to the Keynesian revolution. In continuing to oppose compensatory economic policy, the NAM undoubtedly spoke for many businessmen. But the activities of the CED and the increasing receptivity of the Chamber to fiscal modernism are evidence that still others in the business community had already discarded much of the pre–World War II framework of ideas. Commercial Keynesianism was clearly ascendant in both the private and the public sectors.

Chapter Seven

Business and the New Economics of the Kennedy Era

The realm of public policy, like the world of economic phenomena, is dynamic. Even as it was being consolidated, the postwar Keynesian consensus was undergoing important changes. The persistence of economic instability and mounting dissatisfaction with the nation's rate of economic growth even in the midst of Republican affluence caused some to question whether automaticity was sufficiently powerful an approach to national economic policy. Once again, organized business was in the forefront of this reconsideration, and as before the Committee for Economic Development played an important role as an advocate of change.

The movement of the CED toward an activist Keynesianism had its genesis in the organization's brief flirtation with discretionary fiscal policy in the immediate postwar period. Although the Committee formally opted for automaticity in its 1947 budget proposal, Stein observed in 1948 that the Committee (and especially its research staff) "would not wish to be dogmatic" on the subject. "Perhaps as we develop more experience and know-how flexible devices may be invented which will permit fiscal policy to make a still greater contribution to stability."[1]

It was changes in economic and political circumstances

rather than the invention of new flexible devices, however, which prompted the CED to give renewed consideration to the potential of discretionary action. The Committee's initial decision to minimize the fiscal-management role of government had been based in large part on its memory of Roosevelt's liberalism and its fear of Truman's activist tendencies. The combination of economic circumstance and the return of the Republican Party to presidential power facilitated reconsideration of the earlier decision. "It may be desirable now," Stein wrote in 1954, "to take a more moderate position—i.e., to recommend non-automatic budget action in less extreme situations than might have been contemplated when the postwar budget policies were first developed. The inflationary and activist bias of government *may* be less than it seemed six years ago."[2]

Thus reassured, the CED in March 1954 issued a policy statement which indicated a new receptivity to discretionary fiscal management. The paper reiterated the Committee's emphasis on automatic stabilization and asserted that built-in flexibility and monetary policy were sufficient for combating relatively minor fluctuations. New, however, was the careful consideration given deliberate measures to prevent or check a more serious recession. The statement considered the expansion of federal public works to be effective in the case of a serious economic decline characterized by a large drop in construction activity, but it placed major emphasis on the potency of discretionary tax reduction to combat recession. In case of "either . . . an existing recession of some severity or . . . a recession that is forecast with a high degree of certainty," the Committee recommended a temporary, general income-tax rate reduction to stimulate demand. "When used, the less flexible but more powerful instruments [i.e., tax reduction] should be used with vigor and determination. Their goal should be not merely to moderate an economic decline but to stop it and promote recovery."[3]

The statement had been motivated by a concern over the economic prospects for the post-Korea era, and the subcommittee responsible had begun its deliberations in April 1953, when the economy was still buoyant.[4] The CED's report was published, however, in the midst of the 1953–1954 recession. By March 1954, production had been falling and unemployment rising for over six months. Despite this, the statement did not go beyond recommending that the administration lay plans for discretionary measures in advance. In the end, the CED decided that the patient was not quite sick enough to warrant the treatment it had just devised.[5]

As the economy swung into a mid-decade boom the Committee temporarily shifted its attention from recessions to the problem of inflation.[6] But the question of how to stimulate a sagging economy returned with the onset of a third, more serious postwar recession in 1957. When the gross national product fell from $445.6 billion in the third quarter of 1957 to $425.8 billion in the first quarter of 1958, and unemployment rose from 3.1 million in February 1957 to 5.1 million in February 1958, the Committee responded by moving still further toward a program of discretionary action—a massive tax cut in the face of an already large deficit—but once again stopped just short of a positive, unequivocal call for action.[7]

In March 1958, the CED's Program Committee publicly recommended a temporary 20 percent across-the-board cut in the individual income tax provided "business activity continues to contract for another two months, after February, unless there is unmistakable evidence of quickly forthcoming improvement."[8] The $7.5 billion reduction was to be accompanied by an acceleration of federal spending, an expansionary monetary policy, and an increase in the national debt ceiling. Having spoken, the Committee then sat back to await developments. On May 1, Frazar Wilde, chairman of the Research and Policy Committee, presented the CED's proposals to the Joint Economic Committee but was no more definite in his recommendations.[9] As the economic indicators continued to drop, pressure mounted within the CED for a direct request for tax reduction; but on May 19, the Program Committee decided to let its earlier statement stand.[10] Ray Saulnier, chairman of Eisenhower's Council of Economic Advisers, subsequently recalled:

The point is that, at that time—and this applied to the Committee for Economic Development as well as to the Rockefeller Brothers group—the experts were extremely cagey about tax cutting. They were saying, "maybe it's good, maybe it's not good. You ought to think about it." But nothing really straightforward.[11]

As in 1954, the Committee went to the brink but did not step over.

The administration's hesitancy in 1958 matched that of the Committee. The staff and cabinet vigorously debated antirecession measures, and Eisenhower complained poignantly of the welter of conflicting advice he received on the matter.[12] To be sure, tax reduction was considered preferable to increases in public spending, and the Treasury Department worked on more than twenty alternative tax measures.[13] But the President decided to "hold the line as long as I possibly can."[14] The reasons for inaction were many: Eisenhower himself doubted that a tax reduction would greatly increase purchasing power.[15] He also feared the future deficits that might result from an erosion of the tax base in an era of continually increasing expenditures.[16] The administration, moreover, worried that it might not be able to control the tax-reduction process in Congress and so might be confronted with a more radical tax measure than it desired.[17] In the end, it too retreated from strong, active fiscal stimulation.

In the case of the CED, however, studied ambiguity did not obscure its heightened receptivity to the discretionary management of fiscal policy. Measures which in 1947 had been reserved for catastrophic emergencies were now recommended for less calamitous circumstances; the threshold for discretionary action had been lowered significantly. As Howard C. Peterson, chairman of the CED's Subcommittee on Fiscal, Monetary and Debt Management Policy, observed:

The difference between deficit and surplus is like the difference between below freezing and above freezing temperature. There is nothing immoral about deficits, any more than there is anything immoral about below-freezing temperatures. Deficits, like freezing weather, have appropriate and inappropriate times. What is important about deficits is to have them at the right time. Not merely to avoid a deficit, but to create one when it is helpful and stop it when harmful—that will be the sign of successful and intelligent policy.[18]

The stabilizing budget was based on the acceptance of deficits in recessions, discretionary fiscal policy on the conscious generation of deficits when the need arose. By 1958, the CED was somewhere between these two points of policy orientation but moving in the direction of discretion. When John F. Kennedy's New Frontier embraced Keynesianism with an enthusiasm and candor new to American politics and advocated a more activist version of the New Economics, it found a receptive audience in the CED and other important segments of American business.

I

Upon their return to presidential power in 1961, the Democrats brought with them a more activist approach to modern economic policy than had been exhibited by their predecessors.[19] Kennedy was not a rabid Keynesian at the time of his election, but he was the first president who was not a pre-Keynesian, whose ideas and attitudes had not been molded by the unchallenged orthodoxy of classical economics. "At first . . . allergic to modern economics" in the words of adviser Seymour Harris, he sought guidance from a group of distinguished economists of a distinctly Keynesian hue.[20] Ultimately, their analyses and recommendations prevailed.

At the outset, however, the economics of the New Frontier wavered—as FDR's had—between a penchant for spending and a desire to balance the budget. "You know," Kennedy remarked to Walter Heller, chairman of the Council of Economic Advisers, "I like spending money. What I want from you are good programs by which money can be spent effectively."[21] The administration's first recovery program—a response to the 1960–1961 recession—was a moderate spending effort which increased expenditures for fiscal year 1962 by about $3 billion.[22] But Kennedy still betrayed a strong fiscal conservatism, induced in part by his assessment of the political environment. He steadfastly refused to be prodded into supporting the massive public works programs which were proposed by congressional liberals and by Secretary of Labor Arthur Goldberg and his labor constituency. "I don't want to be tagged as a big spender early in the administration," he remarked at one point.[23] When the Berlin crisis erupted in the summer of 1961, only a determined fight by his economic advisers dissuaded him from raising taxes to cover the cost of the ensuing military build-up.[24] In Kennedy's mind the desire to evoke a sense of sacrifice and commitment from the American people outweighed the attachment to expansionist Keynesian economics.

Nonetheless, the flow of Keynesian advice from his economic advisers continued and helped to push the President toward an explicit avowal of the New Economics. By June 1962, he was certain enough of his newly confirmed faith to lecture the nation on the dangerous mythology which had developed concerning the proper scope of the government's economic role, deficit finance, and the significance of the national debt. "Obviously deficits are sometimes dangerous—and so are surpluses," he observed. "But honest assessment plainly requires a more sophisticated view than the old and automatic cliche that deficits automatically bring inflation."[25] The President was not yet ready, however, to embrace with enthusiasm the idea of a massive deficit-generating tax cut to stimulate the economy. His ultimate conversion did not take place until the business community had signaled that such a course would be acceptable. Once again, business sentiment played a crucial part in circumscribing the limits of economic choice in the political arena.

Kennedy had opposed tax reduction from the very beginning. "I understand the case for a tax cut," the President-elect told Heller in December 1960, "but it doesn't fit very well with my call for sacrifice."[26] Nor, he might have added, did it fit well with his penchant for public spending; and it was feared that neither public nor congressional opinion was receptive to reduction, especially a cut which would increase the budget deficit.[27] Accordingly, when economist Paul Samuelson prepared a preinaugural economic report for Kennedy, he was instructed to avoid recommending a tax cut because "it would be embarrassing and it would not take place."[28] The Heller Council of Economic Advisers favored a cut, but at first found the "reluctance to consider tax cuts because of the political realities" an insurmountable obstacle.[29]

In March 1962, the recovery from the 1960–1961 recession slowed, giving the tax cutters renewed hope for their recommendation. If the situation deteriorated, Heller advised the President, "a quick, sure way of adding to purchasing power all over the country would be a temporary reduction of personal income taxes."[30] The sudden collapse of the stock market on May 28 occasioned the first real breakthrough. In its "cold new look at the economic outlook after the deluge," the Council of Economic Advisers recommended an immediate, substantial tax cut—no less than $5 billion—to support the economy and bolster business confidence.[31] The case for tax reduction, it argued, rested on two points: (1) expenditure expansion would be slow; and (2) tax reduction was "the stimulant which will appeal to both business and labor and will bolster confidence."[32] On June 7, Kennedy announced that in January 1963 the administration would submit to Congress a tax reform bill incorporating a net tax reduction.[33]

The tax cutters, however, still had not won. They believed that the economy needed "a tax cut—better soon than late, better large than small." They considered reduction more important than tax reform.[34] But Kennedy feared that a large, immediate cut would fail of passage in Congress. The President and his advisers Theodore Sorensen and Douglas Dillon viewed the forthcoming reduction not as a bold Keynesian program of economic stimulation, but rather as a sweetener, a secondary device designed to ease the passage of the tax reforms which remained uppermost in their thinking.[35] Throughout the summer and fall of 1962, Sorensen recalled, Kennedy "remained unenthusiastic, if not skeptical, about tax reduction."[36]

Business support for tax cuts was apparently a key factor in causing the administration to reverse its priorities and emphasize substantial reduction rather than structural reform, a development to which the CED once more made a significant contribution. Especially important were the recommendations of the Commission on Money and Credit (CMC), a private group that had been formed in 1957 at the initiative of the CED. In 1948, the Committee had called for the creation of a national commission to undertake a comprehensive study of the government's monetary and budgetary operations. Eisenhower proposed a similar undertaking in 1957, but was rebuffed by Congress. The CED then acted to create a private group—the CMC—to meet the need. CED secretary Robert Lenhart drew up the bylaws of the new group, and Donald K. David, chairman of the CED and executive vice-president of the Ford Foundation, arranged for a Ford grant of $500,000 to finance the effort and selected the initial members. Frazar Wilde, chairman of the CED's Research and Policy Committee, was named to head the CMC, and its membership of 25 included 7 CED'ers. The Committee provided office space in its New York headquarters, conference facilities, and some staff support. Formally established in October 1957, the CMC was a wholly private organization, legally separate from the CED, but the role of the Committee in its formation had been crucial.[37]

The recommendations of the CMC were consistent with the CED's increasing support for discretionary fiscal policy. The Commission's fiscal report in 1961 suggested that Congress grant the President "limited conditional power to make temporary countercyclical adjustments in the first-bracket rate of the personal income tax."[38] The CMC's findings seem to have had a broad educational impact. The CED assumed responsibility for publishing and publicizing the CMC recommendations; over 35,000 hardcover and more than 110,000 paperbound copies of the CMC report were distributed. In addition, a week after the publication of the report a sixteen-page supplement on the findings was included in the Sunday edition of the *New York Times*.[39] Through such activities, the CED helped to move discretionary tax reduction to the center of the public dialogue on national economic policy. In 1962, Kennedy's economic report specifically addressed the CMC's major recommendations and proposed a similar grant of power to allow the President to make necessary adjustments in tax rates.[40]

In the summer of 1962, the Chamber of Commerce provided even more direct support for tax reduction. On June 29, president Ladd Plumley announced that the Chamber favored an immediate and substantial cut in order to avert a possible recession and to combat the stagnation which threatened the American economy. Specifically, the Chamber called for a lowering of the corporate income tax rate from 52 percent to 47 percent and a general reduction in personal income tax rates with emphasis on relief in the middle and upper income brackets. The cuts were estimated to total approximately $7.5 billion. Plumley called attention to the need for economy in government but admitted that the Chamber's recommendations, if enacted, would result in a budget deficit. It might conceivably be two or three years before the budget could be brought into balance.[41]

Senator Harry F. Byrd immediately accused the Chamber of heresy. The Virginia Democrat, Congress' most vigorous and steadfast advocate of the balanced budget and a past director of the Chamber, proclaimed himself "astonished and dismayed" by what he perceived to be a "complete reversal of the Chamber's traditional policy." A program of tax reduction which promised enlargement of the federal deficit was "fiscally irresponsible in the highest degree."[42] But the Chamber leadership stood firm. Plumley rejoined that the Chamber had also called for a $5 billion cut in government spending, but he did not deny that an immediate tax cut would increase the federal deficit. The first requirement, he emphasized, was a healthy economy, for only in such a setting could balanced budgets actually be attained.[43]

The advocates of tax reduction within the administration made certain that the President was apprised of business support for their position. Heller cabled the text of the

Chamber's June 29 tax cut recommendation that same day to Kennedy, who was in Mexico City. "Good economics makes strange bedfellows," he added enthusiastically.[44] In July, presidential assistant Arthur M. Schlesinger, Jr., wrote of the "singular advantage" Kennedy would enjoy in asking for a tax cut: "You would not have to conduct the fight on straight pro-business/anti-business lines. A large and influential part of the business community would give you enthusiastic support."[45] Heller kept up the pressure with a continuing flow of reports to the President on mounting pro-tax cut sentiment in the business community.[46] On December 1, the Cabinet Committee on Economic Growth (composed of Heller, Secretary of the Treasury Dillon, Acting Secretary of Commerce Edward Gudeman, Secretary of Labor Willard Wirtz, and Budget Director David Bell) recommended a net tax reduction of $7–12 billion as "promptly as possible."[47] But Kennedy still remained unconvinced.

One source of this uncertainty was John Kenneth Galbraith: Kennedy's Ambassador to India continued to argue that tax reduction was a reactionary form of Keynesianism in light of the unmet public needs which Galbraith himself had described so brilliantly four years earlier in The Affluent Society.[48] In an important way, the argument echoed the views expounded earlier by Alvin Hansen. "I am convinced," Hansen wrote to a colleague in 1945, "that economists have been grossly negligent in not really examining the deficiencies in our society. We could have full employment through private enterprise for a hundred years and it would not solve the gross deficiencies which we have in education and public health or in the slums and blighted areas of our cities."[49] In the ensuing years, the social priorities issue became a staple of left-wing Democratic politics. During the 1950s Leon Keyserling, considered by the Eisenhower Republicans to be "one of the intellectual architects of the opposition," made the argument with particular vigor, and Hansen himself continued to espouse a social welfare point of view.[50] "Quality and social priorities," he wrote in 1955, "at long last must concern us or we perish in the midst of plenty."[51]

By 1962, however, Galbraith's position as Hansen's ideological heir had left him without great influence in the administration. Even Hansen soon despaired of "the American people approving very much expansion of the public sector (à la Galbraith and my own approach)," and he ultimately supported a tax cut "on the practical ground that a half-loaf is better than no loaf."[52] Heller might agree that "our cities need renewal, our colleges and universities have no place for the flood of students about to inundate them, our mass transport system is in a sad state, our mental health facilities a disgrace, our parks and playgrounds inadequate, housing for many groups unsatisfactory"; but to have battled for increased public investment rather than tax reduction would have required an ideological commitment to social welfare liberalism which was lacking in Kennedy and the New Frontier.[53]

More troubling to the President than Galbraith's long-distance nagging was the fear that, despite the efforts of business leaders to reassure him, the business community as a whole would not accept a tax cut in the face of a substantial budget deficit. Heller noted, "I have never seen the President so anguished and uncertain about the correctness of his course in a domestic matter in the two years that I have served with him."[54]

Doubt soon gave way to decision. On December 14, Kennedy gave a major economic policy address to the Economic Club of New York and was warmly received. Carefully tailoring his talk for his business audience, he discussed his tax cut proposal in the most general, conservative terms possible: "The purpose of cutting taxes now is not to incur a budget deficit, but to achieve the more prosperous, expanding economy which can bring a budget surplus."[55] The deficit, he promised, would be minimized by limiting federal civilian spending for fiscal year 1964 to current levels. The speech, Sorensen later wrote, "sounded like Hoover, but . . . was actually Heller." Galbraith was still the advocate of increased spending rather than tax reduction; he called it "the most Republican speech since McKinley." But to the President, who telephoned Heller immediately to boast, it was "straight Keynes and Heller, and they loved it."[56]

Whatever the combination, NAM president Werner P. Gullander announced that he was "encouraged" by the President's approach. As the NAM's Government Economy Committee subsequently explained to those less receptive to the idea:

Ironically, although understandably, commitment to *traditional fiscal policy may be acting as a barrier to the preservation and strengthening of traditional economic policy*. In impeding tax rate reform under deficit budget circumstances, commitment to traditional fiscal policy is in real degree stalemating economic growth.

The NAM, it was emphasized, supported tax reduction "*even in face of* a current deficit which can be only partially moderated."[57]

Kennedy's enthusiasm over his performance and reception in New York was reinforced by the simultaneous publication on December 14 of a CED policy statement advocating "prompt, substantial, permanent reduction" of taxes as the path to increased "production, employment, investment and growth in the American economy."[58] The CED recommended a two-step approach: (1) a $6 billion net reduction (i.e., not offset by spending cuts) to be achieved by lowering the corporate income tax from 52 percent to 47 percent and the individual income tax rate by 8 percent across the board; and (2) a second cut to be enacted as soon as it could be ascertained that federal spending for fiscal year 1964 would be held to 1963 budget levels. This second installment would further lower the corporate tax to 42 percent and reduce individual rates another 6 percent (from the initial 1962 base). In addition, the maximum individual rate would be cut to 60 percent. The entire program would amount to a tax reduction of $11 billion.

Kennedy read the CED statement over the weekend of December 15–16 and, Heller later told Stein, the President "was much impressed with it and was hopeful that it would have wide distribution."[59] Fearful of calling into question its legal status as an organization that did not engage in lobbying, the CED hesitated to send unsolicited copies of the statement to members of Congress. Claude Desautels of the White House legislative liaison office bypassed their problem, however, by arranging to have Senate majority leader Mansfield and House Speaker McCormack request the required number of copies and then distribute them to all members of Congress.[60]

Heller quickly capitalized on this new situation. On December 16, he sought to nail down his victory with a memorandum to the President entitled "Recap of Issues on Tax Cuts (and the Galbraithian alternative)." The economic case for positive fiscal action remained basically unchanged; the political case for tax reduction was sketched with bold strokes:

> 1. Congress may be lukewarm, but powerful groups through-out the country are *ready for action*. When the Chicago Board of Commerce, the AFL-CIO, the CED, and the U.S. Chamber of Commerce are on the same side—when repeated editorials in *Business Week* are indistinguishable from those appearing in the *Washington Post*—the prospect for action cannot be wholly dim. Can 3000 members of the N.Y. Economic Club be wrong?

2. To be sure, the supporters of action do not agree on details. But there seems adequate room for compromise, and the Treasury proposals are superbly conceived to provide something for everyone, and in a way that is solidly defensible on economic grounds.[61]

Heller's argument proved persuasive. Tax reduction was finally moved to the center of the administration's economic policy; the details of the tax proposal were worked out during planning sessions at Palm Beach over the Christmas holiday. On January 24, 1963, President Kennedy submitted to Congress a program calling for a $13.6 billion tax cut, to be partially offset by reforms which would, taken together, increase revenues by $3.4 billion. In short, Kennedy was requesting a net tax reduction of $10.2 billion, scheduled to become fully effective by January 1, 1965.[62]

II

The reasons for the widespread business support for tax reduction—even in the face of an already-forecast budget deficit—were varied, but unmistakable. The easing of the burden of taxation had long been a primary goal of the American businessman.[63] Furthermore, the doctrine of the balanced budget had already been dramatically weakened by twenty years of business exposure to Keynesian economics; the annually balanced budget dogma had never been accepted by the CED, had lost its hold on the Chamber by the mid-1950s, and was rapidly losing favor with the NAM. Business organizations also recognized that because of the balance of payments deficit plaguing the administration, expansive monetary policy had become especially hazardous; to lower interest rates, especially short-term rates, invited a withdrawal of capital from the United States. As J. Cameron Thomson of the CED announced in the midst of the tax cut debate in 1963, "With the possibilities of monetary expansion limited by balance of payments considerations, a more expansive fiscal policy is especially desirable."[64]

Agreement with the administration regarding the general necessity for some sort of economic stimulation also contributed to business receptivity to tax reduction. Administration spokesmen advanced two arguments in support of a tax cut: at times, they recommended it as a way of avoiding an imminent recession; on other occasions, Heller and the Council of Economic Advisers argued that such action was needed to free the economy from the doldrums of a long-run stagnation.[65] In announcing the Chamber's support for reduction in June 1962, Plumley echoed the first line of argument and warned that a delay in cutting taxes might bring on an American recession which could easily spread to other Western-bloc nations.[66] But on balance, organized business found the argument for long-run economic expansion even more compelling. George Hagedorn, NAM economist, testified in August 1962 that "the problem before us is one of chronic suboptimum economic performance, rather than of a short-term cyclical downturn which may or may not be in the offing."[67] The CED spoke of the "inadequate vigor" of the economy and of the need to establish "an economic climate that will nourish dynamic growth."[68] Organized business shared fully the concern of the Kennedy administration for long-term economic growth.

The particular mode of expression used by the administration in mounting its argument further eased business acceptance. As Walter Heller has observed, "Reorienting policy targets and strategy to the economy's full and growing potential yielded not only new norms but new semantics for stabilization policy, especially in its fiscal aspects."[69] One key shift was the administration's deemphasis of the traditional administrative budget as the measure of fiscal integrity.[70] The CED, however, had been using the cash-consolidated budget as its benchmark for fiscal policy recommendations since 1947, and in January 1962 had adopted the national income and product accounts version of the budget favored by Kennedy's Council of Economic Advisers. Also in 1962, the Chamber began to advocate using the cash budget as an indicator of the actual impact on the economy of the federal sector.[71] Increasingly, business and government were speaking the same language.

The administration also invoked the concept of the high employment budget as a measure of the impact of federal policy.[72] The high employment surplus, as it was termed by the Council of Economic Advisers, provided a means of comparing alternative budget programs by canceling out the effects of economic fluctuations. The usual difficulty in making such comparisons lay in the fact that a recession could cause a highly restrictive budget to yield a deficit because of the automatic action of the built-in stabilizers, i.e., a decline in revenues and an increase in expenditures. This would make the budget appear more expansionist than it actually was. The high employment budget canceled out such influences by indicating how large a surplus or deficit any given budget policy would generate at an arbitrarily defined high-employment level of economic activity. One of Kennedy's chief advisers, James Tobin, has characterized this concept as "a revelation to many informed and intelligent semi-economists or non-economists, including especially the corps of Washington economic reporters."[73]

To at least one segment of organized business, however, the idea was familiar analytical fare. Paternity of the high employment budget idea can be traced to Beardley Ruml, who in his Littauer lecture at Hunter College in November 1943 called for a reduction of tax rates "to the point where they will balance the budget at some agreed level of high employment." The concept first appeared in print the following summer and under Ruml's influence was early incorporated into CED policy, becoming an important ingredient in the stabilizing budget formulation of 1947.[74]

Even the concepts of "fiscal drag" and "fiscal dividends" struck responsive chords among businessmen. Fiscal drag referred to the tendency of federal tax revenues to increase steadily in a growing economy. Unless offset by "fiscal dividends" in the form of increased expenditures or lowered taxes, this automatic rise in revenues would act to retard economic growth by siphoning ever-increasing sums from the spending stream. Thus, tax reduction, even in the face of a budget deficit, could be seen as a well-deserved stimulant. Once again, the administration had invoked an idea long familiar to organized business. In 1947, the CED had recognized the phenomenon of "the long-time growth of the tax base" and the possibility of periodic readjustments of tax rates "at reasonable intervals, say five years."[75] The NAM's "Maytag plan" of 1954 (so named for Fred Maytag II, chairman of the Association's Taxation Committee) had offered a long-range program of tax reduction based on a recognition of this very tendency. A self-proclaimed "direct frontal assault on . . . [a] tax system which was taken out of the book of Karl Marx," the Maytag plan was designed to

stake out a claim to the tax reduction opportunities which come from the increase in the tax base and the rise in tax receipts resulting from the growth of the economy. In other words, we would recapture the revenue coming from the operation of the growth factor and use it exclusively to reduce the discriminatory rates.[76]

The basics of the Maytag plan later appeared in the Herlong-Baker bills, which were first introduced in Congress in January 1959 (H.R. 3000 and H.R. 3001) and were staunchly supported by the NAM.[77] The bills called for a five-year, five-step program of reduction, with the rate-spread of individual income taxes being gradually lowered from 20–91 percent to 15–47 percent, while the corporate rate would be dropped from 52 to 47 percent. Neither the Maytag plan nor its legislative embodiments advocated rate reduction in the face of a budget deficit, but they were based on concepts which the administration used in arguing for just such a tax cut in 1963. The conceptual basis for the political economy of the New Frontier thus had deep roots in the world of organized business.[78]

III

After it finally emerged from the White House, the tax cut still had to run the gauntlet of congressional scrutiny, a process which took thirteen months; many of the specifics of the administration's proposal were stoutly contested on the Hill. The legislative battle was important in several ways. The measure which finally emerged was substantially different from that first proposed in January 1963. The reforms—opposed by conservatives in Congress and by many in the business community—were largely eliminated; only 24 percent (as measured in terms of revenue) of JFK's proposed revenue-raising reforms and 59 percent of the smaller amount of revenue-losing changes were enacted.[79]

Congressional conservatives exacted a real measure of expenditure restraint as the price for passage of the reform-shorn bill. Three days after Kennedy's assassination, Lyndon Johnson told his economic advisers that the budget for fiscal year 1965 would have to be trimmed in order to placate Senator Harry Byrd, chairman of the Senate Finance Committee, and other conservatives. Unless the administrative budget was cut from the recommended $101.5 billion to $100 billion, he told Heller, "you won't pee one drop."[80]

On January 21, 1964, the new President submitted a budget calling for $97.9 billion in expenditures, and two days later Byrd's Finance Committee approved the tax cut.

The legislative debate on the specifics of the Kennedy program shed further light on the nuances of business attitudes towards tax reduction. The business community was far from monolithic in its advocacy of the New Economics as embodied in this proposal. Most clearly Keynesian in outlook was the Business Committee for Tax Reduction in 1963, an organization formed at the suggestion of Secretary of the Treasury Dillon (who joined the CED as its vice-chairman after his government service) and endorsed by Kennedy. Headed by Henry Ford II and railroad executive Stuart Saunders, the group served as the action agency for the CED constituency during the tax cut battle; four of the six businessmen called upon by Dillon to mobilize support for the reduction were trustees of the CED, as were 23 of the 50 businessmen invited to the formal organization meeting in April 1963. The Business Committee was, in Heller's words, "a potent outfit," with a membership of approximately 2,800 and a budget which made it the third largest spender among registered lobbying groups in 1963.[81] It based its support of the tax cut on Keynesian reasoning; the deficit was viewed as "an investment in the future of the country" and the Committee advocated simultaneous control, rather than offsetting reduction, of federal expenditures.[82] This position was similar in intent and conception, if not in details, to the CED policy statement of the previous December. The voice was that of corporate Keynesianism rallying to the support of the administration.

The Chamber once again occupied the middle of the new spectrum. As before, the need to speak for a diverse membership holding a wide variety of views obscured the precise lineaments of the Chamber's position. It attacked the administration's "overemphasis" on the need to stimulate consumer spending and called for larger cuts in corporate taxes and in the income tax at the middle and upper levels.[83] It advocated tax reduction not so much because of a Keynesian desire to increase aggregate demand but rather in the more traditional belief that increased incentives would stimulate the economy by encouraging greater investment and production. But even while emphasizing the need for direct stimulation of investment, Chamber president Plumley recognized that lower-bracket reductions would be helpful in creating additional purchasing power.[84] In proposing that the administration's three-year schedule for phasing in the tax cut be telescoped into one or at the most two years, the Chamber actually advocated a larger first-year deficit than would occur under the Kennedy program! Turning the President's own language and criteria of judgment against him, the Chamber observed tartly that "there would seem to be considerable doubt whether a $3 billion reduction in calendar 1963 is 'a sufficiently large amount to do the job required' or any 'important insurance against recession.'"[85] In the end, the Chamber supported immediate passage of the House-approved version of the Kennedy program, without awaiting concrete evidence— or even a firm guarantee—of accompanying cuts in expenditures.[86]

The NAM, on the other hand, avoided explicit approval of or support for the administration's program. Instead, it argued for the Herlong-Baker approach to reduction, a policy which it had been supporting for four years. The Association did, it is true, want tax reduction badly enough to pursue it in the face of a budget deficit. But its emphasis solely on reduction to give a direct spur to investment (rather than to stimulate aggregate demand or even to effect some mixture of the two) indicated a traditional pursuit of lower taxes, albeit in the unusual circumstance of an impending budget deficit.[87]

These subtle distinctions in business attitudes should not obscure the fact that in the twenty-eight years between the publication of Keynes's *General Theory* and the final passage of the Revenue Act of 1964, the spectrum of business opinion had shifted dramatically. To be sure, the shift was as uneven as it was gradual; but the 1964 tax cut proved conclusively that the doctrine of the annually balanced budget, the linchpin of pre-Keynesian orthodoxy, no longer held together the disparate forces of organized business. Not all business organizations embraced the New Economics with equal fervor, but no major group called for a tax increase in 1964 to balance the budget; most importantly, the CED, the Chamber, and the NAM all accepted the conscious generation of a budget deficit in order to get the economy moving during a period of sub-optimum economic performance.

No longer was the debate between fiscal orthodoxy and Keynesian economics. It was, rather, a question of which version of the New Economics would prevail. The choice was between increased public spending, with its attendant enlargement of the public sector, and tax reduction, along with a larger deficit. Important elements within the business community had been acting for twenty years to shape this decision. In shifting its attention away from the Galbraithian alternative of increased public investment, the Kennedy administration followed a course long advocated by the nation's most prescient businessmen.

Business organizations, especially the CED, had played an important role in establishing tax reduction as a viable alternative to the stagnationist formulation of Keynesianism; and in presenting a united front in favor of a tax cut during the crucial months of 1962, representatives of the business community tipped the scales in favor of their own formulation. As it had done so many times in the past, the business community successfully worked to define the parameters of the debate. Business leaders helped lead a wavering President Kennedy to the tax cut. The Revenue Act of 1964 was not an aberrant conversion experience for either government or business, but was, instead, the culmination of a number of varied trends, long under way, in both the public and private spheres.

Chapter Eight

Retrospect and Prospect

"To regulate large corporations and high finance," Walter Lippmann observed in 1935, "to extend government enterprise into fields unoccupied by private enterprise, to use government enterprise as a threat to compel private monopoly to reduce its rates, to insure the weaker members of the community by collective action—none of these things is new in principle. They are all the continuation of a movement in American politics which goes back at least fifty years, and there is little if anything in the New Deal reforms which are not implicit in the New Nationalism of Theodore Roosevelt or the New Freedom of Woodrow Wilson. The recovery programme, on the other hand, is new and is radical. For here we have an assumption of responsibility for the operation of the whole national economy and the conviction that all the reserve power of government and all the resources it can command may and must be used to defend the standard of life of the people 'against forces beyond their control.'"[1]

By April 1938, the "recovery programme" alluded to by Lippmann had evolved into the nascent Keynesianism of Roosevelt's decision to rely on federal expenditures and deficits to generate recovery. In the area of national economic policy, this was indeed a watershed of the kind historians search for. To pinpoint and identify such a topographical feature, however, is not enough. Equally important to those who wish to map the landscape of modern America is a knowledge of how the water subsequently falls, of the contours and direction of the rivulets and streams which flow from the watershed of the past. Hence, we must trace the changes of the Depression decade through time and see how executive and legislative decisions were actually administered, how the definition of Keynesianism changed through the years.

I

The New Deal's acceptance of Keynesian economic policies was hesitant, halting, and shrouded in ambiguity. It is doubtful that Roosevelt ever made a connection between the spending solution and the reform impulse which lay at the bottom of his political pragmatism. Oliver Wendell Holmes, Jr., once observed of FDR that he had a second-class intellect but a first-rate temperament. Roosevelt did indeed find it difficult to absorb and act on ideas not deeply rooted in a traditional political context. But his real failure lay in his inability to fuse the workings of his intellect (which even if second-rate was probably better than that of many of his detractors and almost certainly superior to that of most of his chroniclers) with that vision of a reformed America which made him so appealing to liberals. He failed, in short, to perceive the reformist possibilities of Keynesianism. To be sure, he was hardly alone in this. No other politician in the American mainstream was committed to Keynesianism at the time, and indeed FDR's flexibility on fiscal matters was considerable given his age, his education, and the continued strength of the prevailing economic orthodoxy. Still, his failure in this regard left the definition of the political economy enveloped in a mist of improvisation and expediency.

Other liberals, Alvin Hansen foremost among them, had a clearer view of the reform potential of Keynesian doctrine, and their version of the New Economics combined a perception of economic stagnation with a vision of an America rebuilt to liberal specifications by means of public investment. Their program was never enacted but their efforts resulted in a formulation of Keynesianism which dominated the fiscal policy dialogue in the late 1930s and throughout the war and which underlay the full employment proposals offered by liberals at the war's end.

Elements of the business community played a significant part in redefining Keynesianism for the postwar world. The Chamber of Commerce led the way by helping to strip the original Murray-Patman Full Employment Bill of its reformist trappings. But while the Employment Act of 1946 institutionalized the government's Keynesian responsibilities and provided a mechanism—the Council of Economic Advisers—for continuous government management of the economy, the definition of the postwar political economy still awaited the formulation of an alternative version of Keynes. This body of ideas was provided by a combination of businessmen and scholars and given concrete expression in the policy proposals of the Committee for Economic Development. The CED's variant of Keynesianism promised economic stability with minimal enlargement of the civilian public sector, stressed automaticity, and depended on manipulation of government revenues, rather than increased spending, in an emergency. The CED infused Keynesian analysis and technique with corporatist values, and its prescription informed the economic policy of the Eisenhower administration more than did the rhetorical orthodoxy of Secretary of the Treasury George Humphrey or the occasional atavism of the theoretically untutored but politically and practically astute Eisenhower.

The result provided a modicum of stability in an economy supported, for better or worse, by huge federal outlays for military purposes. Though there were aspects of the Cold War mobilization of the 1950s which disturbed many Americans, including the General in the White House, some business observers believed that military spending disrupted the economic order less than other alternatives. As *Business Week* explained:

There's a tremendous social and economic difference between welfare pump priming and military pump priming. . . . Military spending doesn't really alter the structure of the economy. It goes through regular channels. As far as a business man is concerned, a munitions order from the government is much like an order from a private customer.

Social welfare spending, on the other hand, "makes new channels of its own. It creates new institutions. It redistributes income. It shifts demand from one industry to another. It changes the whole economic pattern."[2] Ironically, the arms race brought about a level of public expenditure far exceeding that envisioned by the stagnationists, but for purposes of national defense considered by many to be more legitimate and less threatening than the social programs advocated by liberals.

When, in the early 1960s, fiscal passivity appeared incapable of generating desired levels of growth and stability, it was supplanted by an activist reformulation of the CED's postwar Keynesian alternative. When businessmen supported the tax cut of 1964, they in reality recommended a program for which business, in a collective sense, was largely responsible. The popular view of John F. Kennedy pulling a benighted business community, kicking and screaming, into the modern age of political economy is clearly mistaken. Above all, the outcome indicated the pervasive influence which the postwar corporatist version of Keynesianism had on subsequent economic policy in the United States.

Such influence reflected both the essential conservatism of American political life and the dynamism of American business. The primacy of capitalist values in American culture—the product of both long-term historical forces and self-conscious cultivation—has contributed greatly to, and been reenforced by, a political mainstream unusual in its depth and stability but striking in its narrowness. The political conservatism of the world's first democratic nation-state has long fascinated outsiders and has been both celebrated and condemned by our own scholars.[3]

The political flexibility of the business community has not, however, attracted as much attention.[4] The dynamism of American business organizations and leaders in accommodating to the advent of Keynesian economics was manifested in three ways: (1) business' willingness to make use of expertise in its attempts to influence public policy; (2) the relative ease with which new organizational forms were adopted when adaptation to change was inhibited by the old; and (3) the emergence of a cadre of business leaders who combined a talent for organizational innovation with a keen appreciation of the uses of expert knowledge and who were able to incorporate their political ideology into cogent policy recommendations. The first of these reflected in part the increased receptivity of individual firms to the use of social scientists in general during the 1930s and 1940s. As their planning horizons gradually lengthened, large firms turned to business economists to provide the foreknowledge which flowed from scientific market analyses and projections.[5] During World War II, industrial social scientists from the fields of psychology, sociology, anthropology, and human relations finally gained widespread acceptance in the business world.[6]

Following the lead of individual firms, business organizations soon began to rely on experts in the consideration of questions of national economic policy, recognizing that the growing complexity of such issues had put the amateur at a distinct disadvantage. The influx of experts into government service under the New Deal acted as an additional goad, and during the war the Chamber of Commerce integrated economists into its staff structure. Organized business' new regard for expert knowledge was most clearly expressed in the formation in 1942 of the Committee for Economic Development, a group specifically designed to bring together businessmen and scholars in the pursuit of economic stability at a satisfactorily high level of employment.

Increasingly during the Roosevelt years, expert knowledge was brought to bear on the formation of public policy, and by the end of World War II a number of the organized contending forces in the political arena availed themselves of expertise in a continuous and systematic fashion. In national economic policy, the 1920s were perhaps the last amateur decade. Some observers have predicted that this trend will culminate in expertise becoming an independent source of influence and power in the policy process. Hope for such a development, for the regeneration of American society through the intervention of the university, has been entertained by so distinguished a reformer as John Kenneth Galbraith. But while expertise is neutral, it is not independent. It can be used as easily and effectively by those who wish to buttress the status quo as by those who want to change it. The hope of Galbraith and other social reformers that "it is possible that the educational and scientific estate requires only a strongly creative political hand to become a decisive instrument of political power" may be fulfilled by future events. The preceding chapters, however, corroborate Galbraith's less sanguine observation that "economics, as a discipline, has extensively and rather subtly accommodated itself to the goals of the industrial system."[7]

In viewing power and ideas as separate phenomena, Keynes erred. "I am sure," he wrote with characteristic self-confidence, "that the power of vested interests is vastly exaggerated compared with the gradual encroachment of ideas."[8] Encroachment, however, was not the one-way street implied by Keynes, with ideas acting upon power but somehow remaining inviolate. The adoption of Keynesian concepts did result in an enlargement of the government's responsibility for economic affairs. But on balance, these ideas did not conquer power; they were, instead, absorbed and molded to fit the needs of the business system.

A second factor facilitating the flexibility of business was its skill at organizational innovation. Structural change loosed the forces of modernization within the Chamber. When the organizational constraints on a broad-based, large-membership peak association such as the Chamber proved too inhibiting, the businessmen who established the CED turned to a new form of organization which in its cohesiveness and institutionalization of expertise was better suited to respond to the challenges of the fiscal revolution. When the CED's legal status as a non-lobbying group limited its effectiveness in the legislative struggle over tax reduction in 1963, elements of the CED constituency moved to an even tighter organizational format, using the Business Committee for Tax Reduction in 1963 better to influence events.

The impact of the CED on the evolution of Keynesian economic policies over the period 1942–1964 calls into question the traditional emphasis of scholars on peak associations like the Chamber and the National Association of Manufacturers.[9] Indeed, the formation of the CED represented the emergence of a new, distinctive type of lobbying group. In his classic study *Group Representation Be-*

fore Congress, E. Pendleton Herring distinguished between two models of lobbies: one a highly personalized, individualistic operation, more often than not reliant upon underhanded and corrupt methods of influence peddling; and the second a twentieth-century phenomenon based on bureaucratic organization, on the generation of propaganda for consumption both by members and by the public at large, and on the mobilization of grass-roots political support for particular policy positions. One of the greatest sources of strength of the latter type of lobby, Herring believed, was the size of the membership for which it could speak.[10]

The CED differed from both models, especially from the bureaucratic type as exemplified by the Chamber, the NAM, and the American Federation of Labor. While carefully maintaining a small, cohesive membership, it emphasized expertise and research rather than propaganda of the more obvious and traditional sort. The CED subordinated the generation of grass-roots political support to the more subtle goal of defining alternative solutions—informed by expert knowledge but firmly rooted in corporatist values—to a relatively limited number of pressing social, political, and economic problems. Such an approach caused it to have greater influence upon the leadership and bureaucracy of the executive branch than upon Congress, where the more traditional lobbies of Herring's schema still retained considerable influence. The development of this new type of interest group is of particular importance because since the Great Depression the arena of power has shifted perceptibly from the legislative to the executive branch.

A third manifestation of the flexibility of the business community was the emergence of a group of business leaders able to adapt to changes in their economic and political environments. Indeed, in the area of national macroeconomic policy, such businessmen did not merely respond to the intervention of government; increasingly as the

Keynesian revolution unfolded, they became a major force behind such initiatives. Eric Johnston, William Benton, Ralph Flanders, Marion Folsom, Paul Hoffman, and Beardsley Ruml were men who felt acutely the failure of business to exercise a positive influence on events in the 1930s. Significantly, although their message was most warmly received in the executive suites of the giant corporations, they were not themselves, with the exception of Folsom and Hoffman, big businessmen in the traditional sense. Business' accommodation to Keynesian economic policies can not be traced in simple fashion to the board rooms of big business. Large firms, after all, dominated the National Association of Manufacturers and acquiesced in that organization's long unwillingness to accept deviation from the fiscal orthodoxy of the pre-Depression era. It is perhaps time to qualify our simplistic division of the American business community into the polar opposites of reactionary small and medium-sized business on the one hand and enlightened, flexible big business on the other.[11]

II

The dynamism of American business illuminates an important trend in the relationship between state and society in modern America—the conscious effort to build a corporatist sociopolitical order that would avoid the dangers of both statist regimentation and laissez-faire waste and social tension. Ellis Hawley has described the ideal-type of this domestic corporatism as:

one whose basic units consist of officially recognized, non-competitive, role-ordered occupational or functional groupings . . . one with coordinating machinery designed to integrate these units into an interdependent whole and one where the state properly functions as coordinator, assistant, and midwife rather than director or regulator.[12]

Although American corporatists have not been able to realize their vision in this pure sense, their ideas have commingled with the value systems of liberals and conservatives and with the nation's democratic traditions to influence the modern American political economy.

Both business and government leaders made efforts to establish a corporatist order. During the first three decades of this century, the corporatist vision was manifested in the activities of the National Civic Federation, in the cooperation between government officials and business leaders in forming a national Chamber of Commerce, in the mobilization of American industry during World War I, and in the attempts by Herbert Hoover and his colleagues in the Department of Commerce in the 1920s to build an "associative state."[13] Less attention, however, has been given to the continuation of such activity following the New Deal's NRA experiment in the mid-1930s.[14]

In the responses of the business community to the fiscal revolution, we find evidence of a significant resurgence of the corporatist impulse which had been so notable in the period 1900–1935. The foremost exemplar of this tendency was the CED. The Committee took an organic view of American society and denied the legitimacy of class or group conflict, believing instead in the existence of a "general interest" which could be ascertained through the application of expert knowledge to the problems of modern life. Its macroeconomic policy recommendations were congruent with this overarching philosophy. Moreover, the CED was from the outset a semipublic organization, operating in that murky area of the institutional environment where private and public interests and activities merged. A similar, if less well articulated, corporatist orientation also characterized the Business Advisory Council and the Chamber of Commerce under the leadership of Eric Johnston.

There were important similarities between the pre-Depression and post-Depression generations of corporatists.

For both, the experience of a world war strengthened the belief that cooperation between the public and private spheres was both desirable and feasible; wartime mobilization served as an important catalyst and facilitator of organizational innovation. There was also a continuity of personnel. Many of those who kept the corporatist vision alive during the 1930s and thus prepared the way for the creation of the CED—men such as Gerard Swope, Walter Teagle, Henry Dennison, Morris Leeds, Marion Folsom, and Jesse Jones—were veterans of the World War I mobilization and of various associational activities of the 1920s.[15] The pre-Depression corporatists had even attempted to limit economic fluctuations and minimize unemployment by developing private bodies to regularize business production and investment.[16]

The CED's program for economic stabilization through federal fiscal and monetary policy differed from that advanced by Hoover and a number of business leaders, however, in giving to the state a larger role in the salvation of American capitalism. As founder William Benton explained to his CED colleagues:

The historic attitude of business has been to use government if it could, and abuse it if it couldn't. Philosophically, business was committed to the doctrine that, "that government is best which governs least." The emerging CED attitude has been that "government has a *positive* and *permanent* role in achieving the common objectives of high employment and production and high and rising standards of living for people in all walks of life." . . . The greatest single achievement of CED . . . may turn out to be the clarification it has been developing on the role of government in the economy. . . . This is our present answer to the European brands of socialism. Long may it thrive.[17]

Yet, the CED's departure in this regard was not as sudden as Benton's rhetoric made it appear. First-generation corporatists had posited the government's role as that of energizer and coordinator of private action, but the challenge of the Great Depression made it clear that a spectrum of opinion concerning the proper level of government activity had developed among domestic corporatists. Some, such as Henry Harriman of the Chamber of Commerce and Gerard Swope of General Electric, began to argue for government-sponsored cartelization of industry as both necessary and desirable, and the New Deal's NRA brought these suggestions to fruition. But not all who had been active in promoting the ideal of an associative state in the 1920s supported such developments; Hoover, for one, regarded them with distaste and branded them fascistic. The businessmen of the CED in effect attempted to find some middle ground between these two wings of corporatist thought.

The corporatists of the CED did function in a more complex and demanding political world than did the corporate organizers of the 1920s, however; they operated in a much denser organizational environment than did their predecessors. The experience of the Great Depression forced the state to assume new responsibilities and to act as the ultimate guarantor of prosperity. Thus, the post-1929 era saw the development and strengthening of secondary organizations in the public sector (such as the Council of Economic Advisers) designed to coordinate the activities of primary economic organizations.[18] The continued appeal of statist and traditionally conservative alternatives and the strengthening of potentially antagonistic countervailing interest groups and institutions, such as organized labor and John Kenneth Galbraith's technostructure, further complicated matters. Yet the experience of the CED indicates that the post-Depression corporatists did very well.

The success of the CED resulted in part from factors of technique and institutional location. The group's alliance with academe allowed it to generate sophisticated alternatives which seemed particularly applicable to the complex problems of a highly organized society. The CED's determination and ability to operate as a neither fully private nor official but rather somehow "quasi-public" institution was also crucial. Nestled on the boundary between the private and public spheres and facing as it were in both directions at once, it was well placed to act as a combination training, recruiting, and legitimizing agency.

The continuing appeal of corporatist ideology to those outside the business world also contributed to the effectiveness of the postwar corporatists. After World War II, both Democratic and Republican administrations expanded the system of private government embodied in advisory committees and the employment without compensation of businessmen that was one hallmark of a functional corporatism.[19] Its most articulate spokesmen gave the "new Republicanism" of the Eisenhower regime a distinctly corporatist hue.[20] Even the thought of so impeccable a New Deal liberal as Leon Keyserling reflected a curious intermingling of corporatist ideas, statist values, and a penchant for redistributive economics: "In our kind of society, the industrial concert guided by the public interest and with some guide lines from the Government . . . is really the only alternative to chaos on the one side and excessive centralization under definitive public law on the other side."[21] As postwar liberals came increasingly to see their political role as that of technocratic managers of the social order, they became amenable to corporatist solutions to their problems. Kennedy viewed issues of economic policy not as ideological questions but rather as problems in the management of an advanced industrial society. He was, as Arthur Schlesinger, Jr., has acutely observed, "possessed not by a blueprint but by a process," and his assessment that "most of the problems, or at least many of them, that we now face are technical problems, are administrative problems . . .

very sophisticated judgments which do not lend themselves to the great sort of 'passionate movements' which have stirred this country so often in the past," narrowed considerably the philosophical distance between the new corporatism and the liberalism of the New Frontier.[22] The attraction of the former bespoke the spiritual poverty of the latter. As Galbraith subsequently wrote to Hansen, "I associate you with a strongly humanistic view of Keynesian economics. But in the hands of other people it did become a mechanical instrument for increasing output or . . . reducing unemployment."[23]

The story of the absorption of the Keynesian Revolution by the business community illuminates a significant part of the history of America's recent past. But history moves on; the historian's tale, once told, is immediately dated. The definition of the modern American political economy did not suddenly end in 1964. Events of recent years have cast grave doubt on the efficacy of the Keynesian system—however defined. It is altogether possible that new, alternative schemes for the ordering of the nation's political economy will be advanced, proposals bred by the current spectacle of stagflation and by the numerous complexities of worldwide economic and political change. But the process of definition, if not the particulars, will I think remain the same. Political and social forces will continue to push and pull at the framework of economic ideas. In that sense, an appreciation of a crucial aspect of the political process in America may help us better understand the indeterminate future.

Notes

ABBREVIATIONS

BAC	Business Advisory Council
BOD	Board of Directors
CEA	Council of Economic Advisers
CED	Committee for Economic Development
CMC	Commission on Money and Credit
COCUS	Chamber of Commerce of the United States
COEP	Committee on Economic Policy
COFF	Committee on Federal Finance
GPO	Government Printing Office
NACOS	National Association of Commercial Organization Secretaries
NAM	National Association of Manufacturers
NRPB	National Resources Planning Board
NYT	New York Times
OF	Official File
PPF	President's Personal File
PSF	President's Secretary's File

Manuscript Locations

COCUS	Chamber of Commerce of the United States Archives, Washington, D.C.
COHC	Oral History Collection, Columbia University
DDEL	Dwight D. Eisenhower Presidential Library, Abilene, Kansas

FDRL   Franklin D. Roosevelt Presidential Library, Hyde Park, New York
FRS   Records of the Federal Reserve System, National Archives, Washington, D.C.
HSTL   Harry S. Truman Presidential Library, Independence, Missouri
JFKL   John F. Kennedy Presidential Library, Boston, Massachusetts

1. THE KEYNESIAN REVOLUTION: A PERSPECTIVE

1. George Peek, *Why Quit Our Own* (New York: Van Nostrand, 1936), p. 20.

2. Solomon Fabricant, *The Trend of Government Activity in the United States since 1900* (New York: National Bureau of Economic Research, 1952), pp. 146, 198; U.S., Bureau of the Census, *The Statistical History of the United States from Colonial Times to the Present* (Stamford, Conn.: Fairfield Publishers, 1965), pp. 710–11. Subsequent budget and unemployment statistics are from this last work unless otherwise noted.

3. Robert A. Lively, "The American System: A Review Article," *Business History Review* (March 1955), 29:81–96; Carter Goodrich, *Government Promotion of American Canals and Railroads, 1800–1890* (New York: Columbia University Press, 1960); Louis Hartz, *Economic Policy and Democratic Thought: Pennsylvania, 1776–1860* (Cambridge: Harvard University Press, 1948); and George Rogers Taylor, *The Transportation Revolution, 1815–1860* (New York: Rinehart, 1951), pp. 352–83; Fred Shannon, *The Farmer's Last Frontier: Agriculture, 1860–1897* (New York: Farrar, 1945), pp. 64–65.

4. Adolf A. Berle, Jr., "Reshaping the American Economy," *The Centennial Review* (Spring 1965), 9:209; Franklin D. Roosevelt, *The Public Papers and Addresses of Franklin D. Roosevelt*, comp. Samuel Rosenman, 13 vols. (New York: Random House, 1938–1950), 7:237. Perhaps the most perceptive contemporary view of the significance of the government's new role in the national economy is Walter Lippmann, "The Permanent New Deal," *Yale Review* (June 1935), 24:649–67.

5. Ellis Hawley, *The New Deal and the Problem of Monopoly* (Princeton: Princeton University Press, 1966).

6. Frank Freidel, *Franklin D. Roosevelt: The Triumph* (Boston: Little, Brown, 1956), pp. 226–27; Thomas Greer, *What Roosevelt Thought: The Social and Political Ideas of Franklin D. Roosevelt* (East Lansing: Michigan State University Press, 1958), pp. 51–52.

7. Rexford Tugwell, *The Democratic Roosevelt* (Baltimore: Penguin, 1957), p. 240.

8. Roosevelt, *Public Papers*, 1:663. See also ibid., pp. 795–812; and Freidel, *The Triumph*, pp. 361–64.

9. Roosevelt, *Public Papers*, 2:50. See also Frank Freidel, *Franklin D. Roosevelt: Launching the New Deal* (Boston: Little, Brown, 1973), pp. 237–54.

10. Quoted in Arthur Schlesinger, Jr., *The Age of Roosevelt: The Coming of the New Deal* (Boston: Houghton Mifflin, 1958), p. 290. For discussions of Douglas' role in the early days of the New Deal, see ibid., pp. 7–11, 15, 289–93; Tugwell, *Democratic Roosevelt*, p. 265; Frances Perkins, *The Roosevelt I Knew* (New York: Viking Press, 1946), pp. 197, 269–74; and James E. Sargent, "FDR and Lewis W. Douglas: Budget Balancing and the Early New Deal," *Prologue, The Journal of the National Archives* (Spring 1974), 6:33–43. Douglas' own views can be found in *There Is One Way Out* (Boston: Atlantic Monthly Co., 1935), and *The Liberal Tradition: A Free People and a Free Economy* (New York: Van Nostrand, 1935).

11. FDR to House, April 5, 1933, in Elliott Roosevelt, ed., *F.D.R.: His Personal Letters*, 4 vols. (New York: Duell, Sloan and Pearce, 1947–1950), 3:342. Johnson is quoted in Freidel, *Launching the New Deal*, p. 452.

12. James T. Patterson, *Congressional Conservatism and the New Deal* (Lexington: University of Kentucky Press, 1967), p. 5.

13. Marriner Eccles, *Beckoning Frontiers* (New York: Knopf, 1951), pp. 104–13; Freidel, *Launching the New Deal*, p. 58. See also Sidney Hyman, *Marriner S. Eccles: Private Entrepreneur and Public Servant* (Stanford: Graduate School of Business, Stanford University, 1976).

14. Alan Sweezy, "The Keynesians and Government Policy, 1933–1939," *American Economic Review* (May 1972), 62:118; Lauchlin Currie, "The Keynesian Revolution and Its Pioneers: Discussion," ibid., p. 140; Walter Salant to Seltzer, February 10, 1936, Box 1, Walter Salant MSS, HSTL.

15. Keynes's open letter to the President is reprinted in Max Freedman, ed., *Roosevelt and Frankfurter: Their Correspondence, 1928–1945* (Boston: Little, Brown, 1967), pp. 178–83. Similar advice had been passed on to Roosevelt by Frankfurter in November 1933, in the form of a confidential letter to the President from a group of Oxford economists. Ibid., pp. 167–73.

16. Keynes, for his part, related to Secretary Perkins that he had "supposed the President was more literate, economically speaking." Perkins, *Roosevelt I Knew*, pp. 225–26. Tugwell, on the other hand, reports that Keynes's attitude was that of an admiring observer rather than an instructor. *Democratic Roosevelt*, p. 375. It is wholly unrealistic, however, to assess their relationship as close and fruitful, as Freedman attempts to do in *Roosevelt and Frankfurter*, p. 13.

17. Roosevelt, *Public Papers*, 4:189. See also Herbert Stein, *The Fiscal Revolution in America* (Chicago: University of Chicago Press, 1969), pp. 57–60; and John Morton Blum, *From the Morgenthau Diaries: Years of Crisis, 1928–1938* (Boston: Houghton Mifflin, 1959), pp. 259–68.

18. FDR to Bankhead, October 16, 1937, in Roosevelt, *Personal Letters*, 3:717–18; Blum, *Years of Crisis*, pp. 391–92.

19. Roosevelt, *Public Papers*, 7:221–48; Blum, *Years of Crisis*, pp. 380–426; Henry Morgenthau, Jr., "The Morgenthau Diaries: The Struggle for a Program," *Collier's*, October 4, 1947, pp. 20–21, 45–49; Hawley, *Problem of Monopoly*, pp. 408–10; Tugwell, *Democratic Roosevelt*, pp. 441–49; Joseph Alsop and Robert Kintner, *Men Around the President* (New York: Doubleday, Doran, 1939), pp. 119–56. On the vehemence of the struggle, see "Notes on Meeting at Mr. Morgen-

thau's Apartment" (January 5, 1946), Box 391, Morgenthau Correspondence, FDRL. Regarding the program itself, see *Time*, April 25, 1938, pp. 9–10; and Patterson, *Congressional Conservatism*, pp. 234–35. On the rationale behind the decision, see Eccles, *Beckoning Frontiers*, p. 311; and John H. Williams, "Federal Budget: Economic Consequences of Deficit Financing: Deficit Spending," *American Economic Review* (suppl. February 1941), 31:52–53.

20. Seymour Harris, "Fiscal Policy," in Harris, ed., *American Economic History* (New York: McGraw-Hill, 1961), p. 145.

21. Roosevelt, *Public Papers*, 8:10, 47; FDR to Cabinet Members, January 21, 1939, in Box 96, Harry Hopkins MSS, FDRL. For other contemporary expressions of Keynesian influence on official thinking and policy, see Blum, *Years of Crisis*, p. 387; U.S., National Resources Planning Board, Public Works Committee, *The Economic Effects of the Federal Public Works Expenditures, 1933–1938*, by John Kenneth Galbraith and Gore Griffith Johnson, Jr. (Washington: GPO, 1940); and U.S., Department of Commerce, *Twenty-Seventh Annual Report of the Secretary of Commerce, 1939* (Washington: GPO, 1939), esp. pp. v–xiv; Walter Salant to R. W. Goldschmidt, March 17, 1939, Box 1, Salant MSS, HSTL; Salant and Goldschmidt to Jerome Frank, March 17, 1939, ibid.; Salant, "The Failure of Private Investment Recovery in the 1933–1937 Recovery," undated memo [1939], ibid.

22. Keynes, *The General Theory of Employment, Interest and Money* (London: Macmillan, 1936). The following paragraphs are based especially on pp. 15–17, 28–29, 55, 95–98, 257–71.

23. Ibid., p. 373; Joseph Schumpeter, "Keynes, the Economist," in Seymour Harris, ed., *The New Economics: Keynes' Influence on Theory and Public Policy* (New York: Knopf, 1947), p. 99; E. E. Hale, "Some Implications of Keynes' *General Theory of Employment, Interest, and Money*," *Review of Radical Political Economics* (Winter 1976), 8:40. Hale's article was written in 1949 and published posthumously.

24. For some, Keynes's malevolence was compounded by his duplicity. "Just what (except expediency) prevented Keynes from announcing himself a complete socialist I do not know. What he seemed to want was a government-managed economy that would *imitate* some of the features of capitalism." Henry Hazlitt, *The Failure of the "New Economics"* (Princeton: Van Nostrand, 1959), p. 376. See also Veritas Foundation, *Keynes at Harvard* (New York: Veritas Foundation, 1960), pp. 2–3, 5; Carl B. Turner, *An Analysis of Soviet Views of John Maynard Keynes* (Durham, N.C.: Duke University Press, 1969).

25. Keynes, *General Theory*, pp. 380–81. In 1933 Keynes wrote to Roosevelt: "You have made yourself the trustee for those in every country who seek to mend the evils of our condition by reasoned experiment within the framework of the existing social system. If you fail, rational choice will be gravely prejudiced throughout the world, leaving orthodoxy and revolution to fight it out." Quoted in Arthur Schlesinger, Jr., *The Age of Roosevelt: The Politics of Upheaval* (Boston: Houghton Mifflin, 1960), p. 656. Of communism, Keynes asked, "How can I adopt a creed which, preferring the mud to the fish, exalts the boorish proletariat above the bourgeois and the intelligentsia who, with whatever faults, are the quality in

life and surely carry the seeds of all human advancement." *The Collected Writings of John Maynard Keynes* (London: Macmillan, 1971–   ), 9:258.

26. Keynes, *General Theory*, pp. 374–78.

27. Seymour Harris' religious phraseology catches the tension beautifully: "Keynes indeed had the Revelation. His disciples are now [1947] divided into groups, each taking sustenance from the Keynesian larder. The struggle for the Apostolic Succession is on." *New Economics*, p. 5. One result of this was a penchant for exegesis that came close to rivaling that of pedantic Marxists. On the various "wings" of Keynesianism, see Harris, ibid., pp. 547–49; Gottfried Haberler, "The General Theory," in ibid., pp. 177–78; William Fellner, "Keynesian Economics After Twenty Years: What is Surviving," *American Economic Review* (May 1957), 42:67–76.

28. Gerhard Colm, "Fiscal Policy," in Harris, *New Economics*, p. 463; Benjamin Higgins, "Keynesian Economics and Public Investment Policy," in ibid., p. 477; Seymour Harris, ed., *Saving American Capitalism* (New York: Knopf, 1948), p. 9. The stagnationist approach is contrasted with that of the compensatory spenders in Alvin Hansen, *Full Recovery or Stagnation* (New York: W. W. Norton, 1938), pp. 301–2. On the stagnationist analysis in general, see Alan Sweezy, "Declining Investment Opportunity," in Harris, *New Economics*, pp. 425–35; Alvin Hansen, "The Stagnation Thesis," in American Economic Association, *Readings in Fiscal Policy* (Homewood, Ill.: Irwin, 1955), pp. 540–57; Benjamin Higgins, "Concepts and Criteria of Secular Stagnation," in *Income, Employment and Public Policy: Essays in Honor of Alvin H. Hansen* (New York: W. W. Norton, 1948), pp. 82–107; and Donald Winch, *Economics and Policy* (New York: Walker, 1969), pp. 246–51. For a very negative assessment, see George W. Terborgh, *The Bogey of Economic Maturity* (Chicago: Machinery and Allied Products Institute, 1945). Hansen's rejoinder is in "Some Notes on Terborgh's 'The Bogey of Economic Maturity,'" *Review of Economics and Statistics* (February 1946), 28:13–17; and Hansen to David McCord Wright, July 30, 1945, Box 2, HUG (FP)-3.10, Alvin Hansen MSS, Harvard University. The examples above do not exhaust the possibilities; there were numerous other questions of political import raised by the Keynesian system. For example, the question of discretionary, as opposed to automatic, fiscal policy is one often resolved on grounds of political ideology, not economic theory.

29. Hansen, *Full Recovery*, pp. 290, 302. On Hansen's general contributions, see "Alvin H. Hansen—The American Keynes," in William Breit and Roger Ransom, *The Academic Scribblers: American Economists in Collision* (New York: Holt, Rinehart and Winston, 1971), pp. 85–110.

30. Alvin Hansen, "Economic Progress and Declining Population Growth," *American Economic Review* (March 1939), 29:1–15.

31. For his concern, see ibid., 14–15. For his advocacy of a strong social investment program, see his *Fiscal Policy and Business Cycles* (New York: W. W. Norton, 1941), pp. 440–43; "Social Planning for Tomorrow," in Hansen, et al., *The United States After War* (Ithaca, N.Y.: Cornell University Press, 1945), pp. 25–27; "Stability and Expansion," in Paul Homan and Fritz Machlup, eds., *Financing American Prosperity: A Symposium of Economists* (New York: Twentieth Century

Fund, 1945), pp. 227–38; and U.S., National Resources Planning Board, *After the War—Full Employment*, by Alvin Hansen (Washington: GPO, 1942), pp. 4–5.

32. Hansen, *Fiscal Policy*, p. 84. Though Hansen in this case placed himself to the left of the New Deal, some critics perceived him to be its very embodiment: "His book *Fiscal Policy and Business Cycles* is the academic apology par excellence for the inner New Deal and all its works. It may well become the economic bible for that substantial company of intellectuals, following Keynes and recklessly collectivist, whose influence grows no less rapidly in academic circles than in Washington." Henry C. Simons, "Hansen on Fiscal Policy," *Journal of Political Economy* (April 1942), 50:162. To Representative Walter Ploeser (R-Mo.) the Harvard political economist was, somewhat more simply, the leader of "the Hansen school of revolutionists in this country." *Congressional Record* (1943), 89:6106.

33. Richard Gilbert, et al., *An Economic Program for American Democracy* (New York: Vanguard, 1938). Authorship of the book was attributed to seven economists associated with Harvard and Tufts University. One of the group, Paul M. Sweezy, later emerged as America's premier Marxist economist. Three other economists—Emile Despres, Walter Salant, and Alan Sweezy—were active in the writing of the book but were working for the government by the time of publication and opted for anonymity. Sweezy, "Keynesians and Government Policy," p. 122.

34. James Roosevelt to FDR, February 2, 1939; FDR to James Roosevelt, February, 1939; and accompanying note in Roosevelt, *Personal Letters*, 4:857–58. The stagnationist thesis had also by this time come to influence Morgenthau's advisers in the Treasury Department. See Harry Dexter White to Beardsley Ruml, June 1, 1939, in Series 2, Box 1, Ruml MSS, University of Chicago. Also, Henry A. Wallace to FDR, November 26, 1938, OF 2527, FDRL.

35. John Morton Blum, *From the Morgenthau Diaries: Years of Urgency, 1938–1941* (Boston: Houghton Mifflin, 1964), p. 41; Stein, *Fiscal Revolution*, pp. 120–23; Patterson, *Congressional Conservatism*, pp. 288–324.

36. *New Republic*, July 29, 1940, p. 158.

37. E. Cary Brown, "Fiscal Policy in the 'Thirties: A Reappraisal," *American Economic Review* (December 1956), 46:863, 866–87; Broadus Mitchell, *Depression Decade* (New York: Rinehart, 1947), pp. 371–72, 376–77; A. E. Holmans, *United States Fiscal Policy, 1945–1959* (London: Oxford University Press, 1961), pp. 30–44; Paul Samuelson, "American Economics," in Ralph Freeman, ed., *Postwar Economic Trends in the United States* (New York: Harper and Brothers, 1960), pp. 44–46; Robert Lekachman, *The Age of Keynes* (New York: Vintage Books, 1966), pp. 149–75; Byrd L. Jones, "The Role of Keynesians in Wartime Policy and Postwar Planning, 1940–1946," *American Economic Review* (May 1972), 62:125–33; Robert Nathan, "The Keynesian Revolution and Its Pioneers: Discussion," ibid., pp. 138–39; Stein, *Fiscal Revolution*, pp. 169–96; John Morton Blum, "Portrait of the Diarist," in Blum, ed., *The Price of Vision: The Diary of Henry A. Wallace, 1942–1946* (Boston: Houghton Mifflin, 1973), p. 33.

38. Roosevelt, *Public Papers*, 7:602.

39. Ibid., 8:493; John Flynn, *As We Go Marching* (Garden City, N.Y.: Doubleday, Doran, 1944), p. 235. On the NRPB, see Allan Gruchy, "The Economics of the

National Resources Committee," *American Economic Review* (March 1939), 29:60–73; Charles E. Merriam, "The National Resources Planning Board; A Chapter in American Planning Experience," *American Political Science Review* (December 1944), 38:1075–88; Philip Warken, "A History of the National Resources Planning Board, 1933–1943" (Ph.D. diss., Ohio State University, 1969); Byrd Jones, "A Plan for Planning in the New Deal," *Social Science Quarterly* (December 1969), 50:525–34; and Otis Graham, Jr., *Toward a Planned Society* (New York: Oxford University Press, 1976), pp. 52–58. The influence of Keynesianism is seen clearly in U.S., National Resources Planning Board, *National Resources Development: Report for 1943* (2 pts.; Washington: GPO, 1943); U.S., NRPB, *After the War—Full Employment*; U.S., NRPB, *After the War—Toward Security* (Washington: GPO, 1942); U.S., NRPB, *Postwar Planning* (Washington: GPO, 1942); U.S., NRPB, *Development of Resources and Stabilization of Employment in the United States* (Washington: GPO, 1941); U.S., NRPB, *The Structure of the American Economy: Part 2, Toward Full Use of Resources* (Washington: GPO, 1940), esp. pp. 27–45; and U.S., NRPB, *Economic Effects of Public Works Expenditures*. For a comparison of the Harvard-Tufts program and the March 1943 NRPB report on *Security, Work and Relief Policies*, see Lekachman, *Age of Keynes*, p. 157. For liberal reaction to the work of the Board, see "Chapter for America," *New Republic*, April 19, 1943, pp. 523–42. Regarding the economic bill of rights, see U.S., NRPB, *National Resources Development, Report for 1942* (Washington: GPO, 1942), pp. 3–4.

40. *Employment Act of 1946, Statutes at Large* (1946), 60:23–26. A superb history of the Act is Stephen Bailey, *Congress Makes a Law* (New York: Vintage Books, 1950). On the general significance of the Act, see National Planning Association, *The Employment Act Past and Future: A Tenth Anniversary Symposium*, ed. Gerhard Colm (Washington: National Planning Association, 1956); U.S., Congress, Joint Economic Committee, *Twentieth Anniversary of the Employment Act of 1946: An Economic Symposium, Hearing before the Joint Economic Committee*, 89th Cong., 2d sess., 1966; "The Employment Act in the Economic Thinking of Our Times: A Symposium," *American Economic Review* (May 1957), 47:96–144; and Karl Schriftgiesser, "Keeping Watch on the Economy," *Saturday Review*, January 8, 1966, pp. 65–69. On the Council of Economic Advisers, see E. Ray Canterbery, *The President's Council of Economic Advisers* (New York: Exposition Press, 1961); and Edward S. Flash, Jr., *Economic Advice and Presidential Leadership: The Council of Economic Advisers* (New York: Columbia University Press, 1965).

41. Alvin Hansen, "Keynes After Thirty Years (With Special Reference to the United States)," *Weltwirtschaftliches Archiv* (1966), 97:2160; Lekachman, *Age of Keynes*, pp. 125–37; John Kenneth Galbraith, "How Keynes Came to America," in Galbraith, *Economics, Peace and Laughter* (Boston: Houghton Mifflin, 1971), p. 51: and Dudley Dillard, "The Influence of Keynesian Economics on Contemporary Thought," *American Economic Review* (May 1957), 47:77–78.

42. (New York: McGraw-Hill, 1948). On the impact of Samuelson's text, see *NYT*, February 5, 1970, p. 41; November 1, 1970, 7:2.

43. Arthur Smithies, "The American Economic Association Committee Report

on Economic Instability," *American Economic Review* (May 1951), 41:181. The report is reprinted in American Economic Association, *Readings in Fiscal Policy*, pp. 405–40.

44. Wilfred Lewis, Jr., *Federal Fiscal Policy in the Postwar Recessions* (Washington: The Brookings Institution, 1962), p. 23; Holmans, *Fiscal Policy*, pp. 301–3; Lewis Kimmel, *Federal Budget and Fiscal Policy, 1789–1958* (Washington: The Brookings Institution, 1959), pp. 240–57, 289–94.

45. See, for example, Truman's statement upon signing the Employment Act in U.S., President, *Public Papers of the Presidents of the United States: Harry S. Truman, 1946* (Washington: National Archives and Records Service, 1953–   ), p. 125; Council of Economic Advisers, "Strength and Stability: The Overall Economic Record of the Last Two Decades," February 25, 1952, Box 1, James Loeb Files, HSTL; Council of Economic Advisers, "The Administration Program for Economic Expansion," May 17, 1954, Box 3, Whitman File, Cabinet Series, DDEL; and Kennedy's "Special Message to Congress: Program for Economic Recovery and Growth," February 2, 1961, in U.S., President, *Public Papers, Kennedy, 1961*, pp. 41–53.

46. Burns speech, June 16, 1955, Box 10, Whitman File, Administrative Series, DDEL.

47. Clinton Rossiter, *The American Presidency* (rev. ed.; New York: New American Library, 1960), pp. 25–26.

48. U.S., President, *The Midyear Economic Report of the President to the Congress, July 11, 1949* (Washington: GPO, 1949), p. 8. See also U.S., President, *The Economic Situation at Midyear 1949: A Report to the President by the Council of Economic Advisers* (Washington: GPO, 1949), p. 12. As Herbert Stein notes: "The experience of 1954 demonstrated what had not been clear to everyone even in the fall of 1953—that the question about tax policy in a recession would be not whether to raise taxes but whether or how much to lower them." *Fiscal Revolution*, p. 306. For a discussion of the Revenue Act of 1932, see Jordan Schwarz, *The Interregnum of Despair: Hoover, Congress, and the Depression* (Urbana: University of Illinois Press, 1970), pp. 106–41.

49. Lewis, *Postwar Recessions*, pp. 15–19. Some treatments tend to equate the postwar revolution in national economic policy with the Kennedy administration. Lekachman, *Age of Keynes*, p. 271; James Tobin, *The Intellectual Revolution in U.S. Economic Policy-Making* (London: Longmans, 1966), pp. 1–4; Arthur Okun, *The Political Economy of Prosperity* (Washington: The Brookings Institution, 1970), pp. 44–46; Bruce Miroff, *Pragmatic Illusions: The Presidential Politics of John F. Kennedy* (New York: David McKay, 1976), pp. 167, 203–22. Correctives to this oversimplification are Holmans, *Fiscal Policy*, p. 303; and Walter Salant, "Some Intellectual Contributions of the Truman Council of Economic Advisers to Policy-making," *History of Political Economy* (Spring 1973), 5:36–49. The most sophisticated view of the entire process—"an evolution with several critical points and gradual movement between them"—is in Stein, *Fiscal Revolution*.

50. Lekachman, *Age of Keynes*, p. 275; *Public Papers, Kennedy, 1962*, p. 474. Similarly, major historical studies also insist on the "neutrality" of the New Deal's

Keynesian solution. See Hawley, *Problem of Monopoly*, pp. 407, 455, 485. But as Joan Robinson has written: "By making it impossible to believe any longer in an automatic reconciliation of conflicting interests into a harmonious whole, the *General Theory* brought out into the open the problem of choice and judgment that the neo-classicals had managed to smother. The ideology to end ideologies broke down. Economics once more became Political Economy." *Economic Philosophy* (Chicago: Aldine, 1962), p. 76.

51. "The selection process stemming from the influence of ideology and power structures works like a sieve to screen out undesirable thoughts." Warren S. Gramm, "Natural Selection in Economic Thought: Ideology, Power, and the Keynesian Counterrevolution," *Journal of Economic Issues* (March 1973), 7:10.

52. Lekachman, *Age of Keynes*, p. 287.

53. "Toward Full Use of Our Resources," *Fortune*, November 1942, p. 170. When Keynes visited the United States in 1941, he found his American disciples more expansionist and less worried about inflation than himself. Walter Salant Oral History Memoir; and Salant to Joseph Dorfman, June 8, 1971, Box 1, Salant MSS, both in HSTL. See also Hansen to Ralph Flanders, April 20, 1938, Box 1, HUG(FP)-3.10, Hansen MSS.

54. The statistic is based on data from U.S., Bureau of the Census, *Statistical History*, pp. 139, 158, 718, 742(E). Alan Sweezy, "Keynesians and Government Policy," pp. 122–23; Michael Reich, "Does the U.S. Economy Require Military Spending?" *American Economic Review* (May 1972), 62:297–98; Alvin Hansen, *Economic Issues of the 1960's* (New York: McGraw-Hill, 1960), pp. 209–10. On the sluggishness of business fixed investment in the postwar economy, see Bert Hickman, *Investment Demand and U.S. Economic Growth* (Washington: The Brookings Institution, 1965), ch. 1.

55. Gabriel Kolko, *Wealth and Power in America: An Analysis of Social Class and Income Distribution* (New York: Praeger, 1962), pp. 9–29; Robert J. Lampman, *The Share of Top Wealth-Holders in National Wealth* (Princeton: Princeton University Press, 1962), pp. 24–25. Kolko's emphasis on the increased importance of income-in-kind (e.g., stock options and similar devices) for the most wealthy is supported by the findings of Wilbur Lewellen, *Executive Compensation in Large Industrial Corporations* (New York: Columbia University Press, 1968), pp. 8–9. A more sanguine view is taken in U.S., Bureau of the Census, *Income Distribution in the United States*, by Herman Miller (Washington: GPO, 1966). Miller finds a "marked drop" in income inequality during World War II (p. 19). As he notes, however, this change took place largely among families in the top and middle brackets (p. 3); the bottom 40 percent of the population was barely touched by wartime redistribution.

56. John Kenneth Galbraith, *The Affluent Society* (Boston: Houghton Mifflin, 1958), pp. 251–69, 322–33. Michael Harrington, *The Other America: Poverty in the United States* (Baltimore: Penguin Books, 1962), estimated 40 to 50 million impoverished Americans. U.S., Congress, Joint Committee on the Economic Report, *Characteristics of the Low-Income Population and Related Federal Programs*, 84th Cong., 1st sess., 1955, estimated 32 million. Frank Kristof, *Urban Housing Needs*

Through the 1980's: An Analysis and Projection: Prepared for the Consideration of the National Commission of Urban Problems, Research Report No. 10 (Washington: GPO, 1968), p. 89. Harrington estimated that approximately 25 percent of American housing units were substandard. *The Other America*, p. 137. See also Joseph Fried, *Housing Crisis U.S.A.* (New York: Praeger, 1971).

57. George Stigler, "The Politics of Political Economists," *Quarterly Journal of Economics* (November 1959), 73:522–32.

58. Robinson, *Economic Philosophy*, p. 1. See also John Kenneth Galbraith, *Economics and the Public Purpose* (Boston: Houghton Mifflin, 1973), pp. 3–9, 227.

59. The categories outlined above are based in part on Craufurd D. Goodwin's suggestive essay, "Economic Theory and Society: A Plea for Process Analysis," *American Economic Review* (May 1972), 62:409–15.

2. NEGATIVISTIC OPPOSITION TO THE NEW DEAL

1. Membership from COCUS, *Annual Report, 1929*, p. 49, in the Chamber of Commerce of the United States Archives, Washington, D.C. (hereafter COCUS); Coolidge quoted in Galen Fisher, "The Chamber of Commerce of the United States" (M.A. thesis, University of California, 1950), p. 5; budget figures from Harwood Lawrence Childs, *Labor and Capital in National Politics* (Columbus: Ohio State University Press, 1930), pp. 34, 37. On the Chamber's ideological stance in the 1920s, see James Prothro, *The Dollar Decade* (Baton Rouge: Louisiana State University Press, 1954). An excellent study of the formation and early history of the Chamber is Galen Fisher, "The Chamber of Commerce of the United States and the Laissez-Faire Rationale, 1912–1919" (Ph.D. diss., University of California, 1960). See also Julius Barnes, "Government and Business," *Harvard Business Review* (July 1932), 10:411–19; John Beukema, "From Ballyhoo to Civic Service in a Single Generation," *Nation's Business*, July 1939, pp. 14–16, 56–57; and Robert Wiebe, *Businessmen and Reform: A Study of the Progressive Movement* (Chicago: Quadrangle, 1962), pp. 33–41.

2. Albert Romasco, *The Poverty of Abundance* (New York: Oxford University Press, 1965), pp. 29, 44–51; Herbert Hoover, *The Memoirs of Herbert Hoover: The Great Depression, 1929–1941* (New York: Macmillan, 1952), pp. 44–45; Julius Barnes, "The New Philosophy of Stabilization," *Nation's Business*, May 20, 1930 (extra edition), pp. 19–20.

3. Harris Gaylord Warren, *Herbert Hoover and the Great Depression* (New York: W. W. Norton, 1959), p. 160; Arthur Schlesinger, Jr., *The Age of Roosevelt: The Crisis of the Old Order, 1919–1933* (Boston: Houghton Mifflin, 1957), p. 232.

4. "Report of the Committee on Federal Expenditures to the Board of Directors, 122nd BOD Meeting, November 20–21, 1931: Working Paper #17," in Committee on Federal Expenditures Papers, 1931–1932, COCUS; "Committee on Federal Taxation, Report No. 18 to the Board of Directors, 122nd BOD Meeting, November

20–21, 1931," in Committee on Federal Taxation Papers, 1931–1932, COCUS; "Staff Memo, 'Federation Taxation,' Discussed at 17th Meeting of the Committee on Federal Taxation, December 22, 1931," in Committee on Federal Taxation Papers, 1931–1932, COCUS.

5. Special Bulletin on Referendum No. 60, April 22, 1932, in *Referenda Nos. 54–68, 1929–1934*, COCUS. See also Silas Strawn, "How Business Views the Budget Crisis," *Nation's Business*, June 1932, pp. 37–38, 74–76. The Chamber often used its referendum procedure as a political weapon. Galen Fisher finds that "as applied by the Chamber, the referendum system seems to have been used more often as a means of giving effect to policies already deemed wise by the leaders than of ascertaining the exact opinion of the membership." Indeed, the Chamber itself in its 1917 *Annual Report* noted that "the strongest argument for a democratic rather than a mere representative action in referendum questions lies in the fact that Congress . . . is particularly solicitous in learning how widespread the participation in the voting has been." Fisher, "Chamber of Commerce" (1950), p. 65.

6. "Business Information—Special Fields: Trends in Business Reading in 1932," *Business Literature* (Business Branch, Public Library of Newark, N.J.) (January 1933), 5:2.

7. *NYT*, January 5, 1933, p. 31. Business representatives were not alone in their concern for a balanced budget. See also the joint American Federation of Labor–Chamber of Commerce letter, Henry Harriman and William Green to FDR, February 10, 1933, in PPF 1483, FDRL.

8. U.S., Congress, House, Committee on Ways and Means, *Revenue Revision, 1932, Hearings*, 72d Cong., 1st sess., 1932, p. 215.

9. Special Bulletin on Referendum No. 58, January 16, 1932, in *Referenda Nos. 54–68, 1929–1934*, COCUS. See also Silas Strawn to Secretary of Commerce Thomas Lamont, 92001/2 pt. 3, General Correspondence, General Records of the Department of Commerce (Record Group 40), National Archives (hereafter Commerce Files); and Henry Harriman, "The Stabilization of Business and Employment," *American Economic Review* (Suppl., March 1932), 225:63–74.

10. Schlesinger, *Old Order*, p. 235; Hoover, *Memoirs: Depression*, pp. 334–35; Warren, *Hoover*, p. 266; Eugene Lyons, *Herbert Hoover: A Biography* (Garden City, N.Y.: Doubleday, 1964), p. 294. Harriman later admitted his "misdeed" in public and without apparent regret. Minutes of the 23rd Annual Meeting, May 2, 1935, p. 447, COCUS.

11. FDR to Harriman, January 26, 1933, PPF 3572, FDRL.

12. Quoted in Schlesinger, *Old Order*, p. 416; Morris Edwards, "Roosevelt Talked Business With Me," *Nation's Business*, December 1932, p. 14. On the business community's perception of, and reaction to, the 1932 campaign see Linda Keller Brown's excellent study, "Challenge and Response: The American Business Community and the New Deal, 1932–1934" (Ph.D. diss., University of Pennsylvania, 1972).

13. *Nation's Business*, April 1933, p. 5. That portion of Thorpe's column which is quoted was written on March 1.

14. There is some debate over the precise responsibility of the Chamber for

the NIRA. John T. Flynn in an early effort ("Whose Child is the NRA?" *Harper's Magazine*, September 1934, pp. 385–94) and Raymond Moley (*Today*, April 14, 1934, pp. 12–13; May 5, 1934, p. 14) trace the paternity of the NRA directly to the Chamber, and historians of the New Deal have tended to follow this lead. William Leuchtenburg, *Franklin D. Roosevelt and the New Deal* (New York: Harper and Row, 1963), p. 56; Schlesinger, *Coming of the New Deal*, pp. 88–89, 97–98; Hawley, *Problem of Monopoly*, p. 42; and Basil Rauch, *The History of the New Deal, 1933–1938* (New York: Creative Age Press, 1944), pp. 76–79, all attribute to the Chamber a crucial role. Herbert Hoover thought the NRA an "idea . . . born of certain American Big Business." *Addresses Upon the American Road, 1933–1938* (New York: Charles Scribner's Sons, 1938), p. 221. Donald Richberg, on the other hand, specifically disputes what he labels the "entertaining fable" which ascribes the Recovery Act to the Chamber. *The Rainbow* (Garden City, N.Y.: Doubleday, Doran, 1936), p. 106. Louis Galambos, *Competition and Cooperation* (Baltimore: Johns Hopkins University Press, 1966), a finely drawn account of business participation in the drafting of the legislation, argues that too much credit has been given the Chamber and not enough to the representatives of the Cotton Textile Institute. The evidence, however, compels Galambos to concede to the Chamber a "special" role (p. 200). See also Robert Himmelberg's excellent study, *The Origins of the National Recovery Administration* (New York: Fordham University Press, 1976), esp. pp. 125, 204; and Henry I. Harriman, "Now It Can Be Told," statement of July 3, 1933, in Presidential Speech File, 1932–1935, COCUS.

15. Raymond Moley, *After Seven Years* (New York: Harper and Brothers, 1939), p. 185; Moley, *The First New Deal* (New York: Harcourt, Brace and World, 1966), pp. 285–86, 289; Rexford Tugwell, Notes from a New Deal Diary, January 14 and February 12, 1933, FDRL. Harriman was a very busy man at a very busy time. He also helped develop the New Deal's domestic allotment plan and was the originator of the idea of financing the AAA by means of a processing tax. Moley, *First New Deal*, p. 249; Rexford Tugwell, *The Brains Trust* (New York: Viking Press, 1968), p. 209; Elliot Rosen, *Hoover, Roosevelt, and the Brains Trust* (New York: Columbia University Press, 1977), pp. 183–84, 337–40. On the Chamber's general policy of cooperation with government at this time, one reliable contemporary observer reported: "That cooperation does not date—and I might let you in on a little secret—from just the 4th of March last. It began way back in 1932, when I was still in Albany." "Address by President Franklin D. Roosevelt" in Minutes of the 21st Annual Meeting, May 4, 1933, p. 100, COCUS.

16. The memo, dated April 18, 1933, is described in Harriman to FDR, May 1, 1933, in OF 105, FDRL. See also Henry Harriman, "Is Industrial Recovery Dependent Upon a Suspension of Anti-Trust Laws?" *Congressional Digest*, June 1933, p. 176.

17. Roosevelt, *Public Papers*, 2:156–57. For a slightly, but significantly, different version, which emphasizes the intimate cooperation between FDR and Harriman, see "Business Agrees to Regulate Itself," *Nation's Business*, June 1933, p. 15. Gerard Swope was also a featured speaker at the convention. Of a total of 49 speakers, fully 27 advocated a greater degree of government intervention; only 9

evidenced a lingering adherence to the doctrine of laissez faire. Freidel, *Launching the New Deal*, p. 429.

18. *NYT*, May 5, 1933, p. 1. See also "Business Agrees to Regulate Itself," *Nation's Business*, June 1933, pp. 13–18. The enthusiasm of FDR's auditors was quickly translated into a resolution which the meeting approved on May 5. It called for federal legislation to enable trade associations, with government approval, "to promulgate fair rules for industrial production and distribution, to improve the status of labor, the industries of the Nation, and the public welfare." Minutes of the 21st Annual Meeting, May 5, 1933, p. 127, COCUS.

19. Roosevelt, *Public Papers*, 2:202; FDR to Harriman, May 22, 1933, OF 105, FDRL.

20. *NYT*, May 21, 1933, p. 2; June 17, 1933, p. 2.

21. Ibid., May 21, 1933, p. 2; June 18, 1933, p. 2; Minutes, Board of Directors, June 22, 1933, COCUS.

22. Morris Edwards, "The Truce on the Sherman Law," *Nation's Business*, July 1933, p. 16. Harriman confided to Secretary of Commerce Roper, "The President's legislative program was enacted with remarkable celerity, and on the whole, it was well thought out and wise. Some of it was admittedly experimental, and undoubtedly, some mistakes were made in details. It could not have been otherwise, considering the magnitude of the program, and the shortness of the time." Harriman to Roper, July 20, 1933, 80553/21 pt. 1, Commerce Files. See also *NYT*, September 3, 1933, p. 13; and *Nation's Business*, August 1933, pp. 16–19, 59.

23. "The Federal Fiscal Situation: Staff Memo Presented to Joint Meeting of the Committees on Federal Taxation and Federal Expenditures, May 2, 1933"; and "Federal Fiscal Situation: Report of the Committees on Federal Taxation and Federal Expenditures to the Board of Directors, 132nd BOD Meeting, May 1–5, 1933," both in the Committee on Federal Taxation Papers, 1931–1932, COCUS; *Nation's Business*, May 1933, p. 27.

24. "Report of the Committee on Federal Taxation to the Board of Directors, 136th BOD Meeting, November 17–18, 1933," in the Committee on Federal Taxation Papers, 1933–1934, COCUS.

25. Cyril Upham, "Uncle Sam's New Pocketbook," *Nation's Business*, September 1933, p. 23. See also Harriman, speech, May 3, 1933, Presidential Speech File, 1932–1935, COCUS.

26. John Kelly and Paul McCrea, "The NRA and the Small City," *Nation's Business*, October 1933, pp. 30–32, 75–76; Memo, Roper to FDR, September 18, 1933, in OF 3, FDRL. See also "A Report of a Study Tour of Business Conditions in Fourteen Large Cities" by Edward A. Filene, March 1, 1934, in PPF 2116, FDRL; Hawley, *Problem of Monopoly*, pp. 56–62, 83–84, 134-35; Schlesinger, *Coming of the New Deal*, pp. 125–26.

27. Hawley, *Problem of Monopoly*, pp. 122, 205–20; *Business Week*, March 30, 1935, p. 36; Leverett S. Lyon, et al., *The National Recovery Administration: An Analysis and Appraisal* (Washington: The Brookings Institution, 1935), pp. 817–29; Harold Ickes, *The Secret Diary of Harold L. Ickes: The First Thousand Days, 1933–1936* (New York: Simon and Schuster, 1953), p. 95; Wilson Compton,

"Putting a Code to Work," *Nation's Business*, January 1934, p. 41; *NYT*, May 3, 1934, p. 4.

28. Irving Bernstein, *Turbulent Years: A History of the American Worker, 1933–1941* (Boston: Houghton Mifflin, 1969), p. 173; Joseph Rayback, *A History of American Labor* (rev. ed.; New York: Free Press, 1966), p. 37; Walter Kohler, "Interpreting Section 7(a) With Bricks," *Nation's Business*, November 1934, pp. 20–21. The quote is not from the article itself but rather from the bold-face lead provided by the magazine's editorial staff. See also Ernest T. Weir, "Theories and Facts About Labor Relations," *Nation's Business*, August 1934 pp. 24–26, 63. In *Business in American Life: A History* (New York: McGraw-Hill, 1972), p. 265, Thomas Cochran points out the beneficial effect the NRA had on the strength of company unions.

29. *NYT*, September 4, 1933, pp. 1, 6.

30. The proposed National Chamber "would be in a position of responsibility and could be held accountable by the public. It could speak and act for commerce and industry on legislative problems, on questions of finance and transportation and work out, nationally, better methods of promoting and maintaining good and continuous relations with employees." Swope sent a copy of his plan to Louis Howe, noting, "You will see that it is really not very radical, not very original, possibly too obvious and too conservative." Liberals, on the other hand, saw in it the path to "big business dictatorship." "Opening Statement, Meeting of the Business Advisory and Planning Council for the Department of Commerce, by Chairman Gerard Swope, November 1, 1933"; Swope to Howe, November 2, 1933, both in OF 3-Q, FDRL; *The Nation*, November 15, 1933, p. 554.

31. *Business Week*, November 4, 1933, p. 11; *NYT*, November 20, 1933, pp. 1, 3; November 21, 1933, pp. 2, 29; Harriman to Roper, November 18, 1933, 92001/2 pt. 3, Commerce Files.

32. *NYT*, May 1, 1934, p. 17.

33. A copy of FDR's message (May 3, 1934) is in PPF 1483, FDRL.

34. Minutes of the 22nd Annual Meeting, May 2, 1934, p. 644, COCUS; Harriman to FDR, May 10, 1934, PPF 1483, FDRL.

35. *Time*, September 24, 1934, p. 57. On the Liberty League, see Frederick Rudolph, "The American Liberty League, 1934–1940," *American Historical Review* (October 1950), 56:19–33; and George Wolfskill, *The Revolt of the Conservatives* (Boston: Houghton Mifflin, 1962). Brown, "Challenge and Response," pp. 225–73, presents the Securities Exchange Act as the turning point in business–New Deal relations. The present study, however, finds the NRA to be the critical element in the Chamber's relations with the administration. For a similar finding regarding another business organization, see Alfred Kelley, "A History of the Illinois Manufacturers' Association" (Ph.D. diss., University of Chicago, 1938), pp. 254–57.

36. Minutes, Board of Directors, September 21, 1934, COCUS; *NYT*, September 23, 1934, p. 1.

37. Harriman to FDR, September 24, 1934, in OF 105, FDRL; Special Bulletin on Referendum No. 68, January 10, 1935, in *Referenda Nos. 54–68, 1929–1934*, COCUS; *NYT*, November 10, 1934, p. 2; and December 28, 1934, p. 30; Harriman

to Roper, December 28, 1934, 94694 pt. 19, Commerce Files. Schlesinger, *Coming of the New Deal*, p. 166, incorrectly interprets this referendum as a vote "for continuance of the NRA by nearly four to one." He has been rightly corrected by William Wilson, "How the Chamber of Commerce Viewed the NRA: A Reexamination," *Mid-America* (April 1962), 44:95–108. Wilson's reappraisal, however, fails to do justice to either the significance or the complexity of his topic. He portrays a rather linear response: opposition from the outset degenerates into absolute repudiation at the end, with little or no soul searching in between.

38. Minutes, Board of Directors, September 21, 1934, COCUS; Harriman to FDR, September 21, 1934, OF 105, FDRL. FDR told the press that to answer such a questionnaire from a private organization would set an unacceptable precedent. *NYT*, September 27, 1934, p. 5. The Chamber twice reiterated its demand for a public response, without success. Ibid., September 30, 1934, p. 32; and October 28, 1934, 2:14.

39. The draft and covering memo are in OF 105, FDRL.

40. Harriman to FDR, September 28, 1934; Early to Harriman, September 28, 1934, both in ibid.

41. *NYT*, November 18, 1934, pp. 1–2. The concept of "cooperation" had shifted in meaning from "active collaboration" (as in the case of the NIRA) to "passive truce." See Arthur Krock's analysis, ibid., 4:1; and Rinehart Swenson, "The Chamber of Commerce and the New Deal," *The Annals of the American Academy of Political and Social Science* (May 1935), 179:137. See also Minutes, Board of Directors, November 16, 1934, COCUS; telegram, Harriman to FDR (aboard Presidential Special arriving Chattanooga), November 16, 1934, OF 105, FDRL; *NYT*, November 17, 1934, pp. 1–2.

42. Minutes, Board of Directors, January 18, 1935, COCUS.

43. Minutes of the 23rd Annual Meeting, April 30, 1935, p. 46, COCUS. For generally complete coverage of the convention, see *NYT*, May 1–5, 1935; *Evening Star* (Washington), April 28–May 5, 1935; *Newsweek*, May 11, 1935, pp. 5–6; *Business Week*, May 4, 1935, pp. 9–10; and May 11, 1935, pp. 8–9. For the Chamber's view, see Warren Bishop, "Business Drafts a Program," *Nation's Business*, June 1935, pp. 15–17, 76–79.

44. Minutes of the 23rd Annual Meeting, May 2, 1935, pp. 139–50. A spirited floor fight over policy was both unusual and, regardless of the outcome, seriously debilitating to the Chamber. David Truman's classic attempt at interest group theory, *The Governmental Process: Political Interests and Public Opinion* (2d ed.; New York: Knopf, 1971), p. 139, posits the existence in almost all interest groups of an "active minority" which controls both policy and the execution thereof. In the Chamber the active minority consists of the President, the Board of Directors, the Executive Committee (drawn for the most part from the Board and empowered to act in its stead when the Board is not in session), and the professional staff. The goals of such an active minority are three: the maximization of group cohesion, the maintenance of the minority's power, and the achievement of group goals (p. 164). Of these, cohesion is the most crucial (p. 167), and disunity can best be minimized if the active minority controls policy determination (p. 199). Chamber

policy is made by one of two methods: referenda sent to the organization membership and resolutions passed by annual conventions. Both are designed to meet "democratic" expectations as to nicety of procedure while focusing control of policy in the active minority (pp. 197–98, 208). In this context, the rejection and amendment of resolutions on the floor of the convention in 1935 was, indeed, a rebellion.

45. Minutes of the 23rd Annual Meeting, May 2, 1935, pp. 155–59, COCUS; *Newsweek*, May 11, 1935, p. 6. On the opposition of the Illinois Manufacturers' Association to the New Deal, see Kelly, "Illinois Manufacturers' Association"; and R. E. Wantz (president of the IMA) to Roper, September 18, 1934, PPF 1820 Speech Material ("Business vs. New Deal" folder), FDRL. Houston's role in the fight against the social security resolution is rather mysterious and casts doubt upon the spontaneity of the opposition. In September 1934, he had been one of the organizers of a closed-door conference of 150 industrialists, most of whom came from the durable goods industries, at Hot Springs, Virginia. The program developed by the conference supposedly aimed at the dismantlement of the New Deal and was vehement in its opposition to any federal social security program. NYT, September 16, 1934, pp. 1, 31; Schlesinger, *Coming of the New Deal*, pp. 497–98.

46. "Consolidation of Government Financial Position (Government Expenditures): Statement of F. H. Clausen to the BOD, 142nd Meeting, September 21–22, 1934," in Committee on Federal Finance (hereafter COFF) Papers, 1934–1935, COCUS.

47. COFF Minutes, January 12, 1935; "The 1936 Budget: Report of the Committee on Federal Finance to the BOD, January 18, 1935," both in COFF Papers, 1934–1935, COCUS.

48. NYT, July 12, 1935, p. 8. The Committee's drafts became shriller as the year wore on. Compare the documents in note 47 above with "Federal Expenditures (tentative draft): 27th Meeting, February 9, 1935," COFF Papers, 1934–1935; and "Federal Taxes and Expenditures, the Need for Revision and Reduction: Report of the COFF to the BOD, November 7, 1935," COFF Papers, 1935–1936, vol. 1, COCUS.

49. Special Bulletin on Referendum Seventy (Federal Taxes and Expenditures), February 28, 1936, in *Referenda, Amendment of By-Laws and Nos. 69, 70, and 72, 1935–1937*, COCUS.

50. "The Federal Budget and Recovery: Report of the COFF to the BOD, 143rd Meeting, November 16–17, 1934," COFF Papers, 1934–1935, COCUS; Harper Sibley's speech to the American Bankers Association, November 14, 1935, PPF 1820 ("Business vs. New Deal" folder), FDRL.

51. Regarding the initial sense of crisis, see "Staff Memo on Federal Expenditures: 6th Meeting of the Committee on Federal Expenditures, November 10, 1933" in Committee on Federal Expenditures, 1933–1934, COCUS; and William Leuchtenburg, "The New Deal and the Analogue of War," in John Braeman, et al., eds., *Change and Continuity in Twentieth-Century America* (Columbus: Ohio State University Press, 1964), pp. 104–9. On the undercurrent of optimism regarding

recovery at the 1935 convention, see *Evening Star* (Washington), April 30, 1935, p. 4; and *Literary Digest*, May 11, 1935, p. 5. This is discussed retrospectively in the "Report of National Councillor Robert A. Anderson (President of the American Chamber of Commerce of Cuba) on the 1936 Chamber Convention," copy forwarded by Walter Donnelly, Commercial Attaché, Havana, to Secretary Roper, June 1, 1936, in 92110/2, pt. 4, Commerce Files.

52. Address to American Bankers Association, November 14, 1935, in PPF 1820 ("Business vs. New Deal" folder), FDRL.

53. At a Board meeting in September 1935, Harriman lobbied for Chamber support of new NRA-style legislation. In November, the Chamber announced that any such legislation "would impede the continuance of economic gains." *NYT*, September 22, 1935, p. 6; November 17, 1935, p. 5.

54. Compare, for example, Harriman's address in National Association of Commercial Organization Secretaries (NACOS), Proceedings of the 20th Annual Meeting, October 21–24, 1934, p. 148, COCUS, with Sibley, "Business Looking Ahead," *Nation's Business*, June 1937, p. 37. On Sibley's political orientation, see *Sunday Star* (Washington), April 28, 1935, p. 1 (B); *Evening Star* (Washington), April 29, 1935, p. 8; May 1, 1935, pp. 2, 5; and *Business Week*, May 4, 1935, p. 9. Harriman's liberalism remained strong. He endorsed Harry Hopkins—the *bête noire* of the business community—for Secretary of Commerce in 1938, Senator Robert Wagner for reelection in 1938 (despite the National Labor Relations Act), and FDR for a third term in 1940. Harriman to FDR, December 21, 1938, in OF 3-A (Hopkins), FDRL; J. Joseph Huthmacher, *Senator Robert F. Wagner and the Rise of Urban Liberalism* (New York: Atheneum, 1968), p. 254; Harriman to FDR, October 17, 1940, PPF 3572, FDRL.

55. Quoted in Moley, *After Seven Years*, p. 290. For a review of the literature concerning the concept of two New Deals, see William H. Wilson, "The Two New Deals: A Valid Concept?" *The Historian* (February 1966), 28:268–88; and Otis Graham, Jr., "Historians and the New Deals: 1944–1960," *The Social Studies* (April 1963), 54:133–40. James MacGregor Burns, *Roosevelt: The Lion and the Fox* (New York: Harcourt, Brace and World, 1956), pp. 225–26, sees the leftward turn of the New Deal as a response to attacks by business. It is more likely, in my opinion, that business moved right, for a variety of reasons, at about the same time the New Deal moved left, for a somewhat different assortment of motives. The motion of each merely served to confirm and reenforce the movement—already under way—of the other.

56. Merle Thorpe, "A Stranger in Its Own House," *Nation's Business*, November 1937, p. 13. See also Thorpe, "Trust in Need of a Press Agent," ibid., August 1937, p. 13; and Howard Wood, "Business Must 'Sell Itself,'" ibid., January 1938, pp. 27–28, 88–89.

57. "Business Takes Its Own Part," *Nation's Business*, March 1938, p. 72. On the broad movement in the late 1930s to "sell" American business and the free enterprise system, see S. H. Walker and Paul Sklar, *Business Finds Its Voice: Management's Effort to Sell the Business Idea to the Public* (New York: Harper

and Brothers, 1938); and Richard Tedlow, "The National Association of Manufacturers and Public Relations during the New Deal," *Business History Review* (Spring 1976), 50:25–45.

58. "Report of National Councillor Robert A. Anderson (President of the Chamber of Commerce of Cuba)" in 92001/2 pt. 4, Commerce Files. Roosevelt agreed fully with this analysis. Apparently forgetting the NRA experience, he expressed the opinion that such negativism had always characterized the Chamber: "Almost every piece of legislation has met merely with its opposition without the presentation of any reasonable alternative." FDR to Oliver Ober, August 24, 1937, in PPF 1483, FDRL.

59. COCUS, *Board of Directors: Annual Report, 1935*, p. 29. See also the Gallup surveys of October 20, 1935; December 15, 1935; April 22, 1936; December 5, 1937; January 6, 1939; and March 6, 1940, in George H. Gallup, ed., *The Gallup Poll: Public Opinion 1935–1971*, 3 vols. (New York: Random House, 1972), 1:1, 5, 18, 77, 134, 212. Of course, those who opposed welfare-state economics in the abstract often supported the individual programs that fell under that rubric. For discussion of this phenomenon, see Lloyd A. Free and Hadley Cantril, *The Political Beliefs of Americans: A Study of Public Opinion* (New Brunswick, N.J.: Rutgers University Press, 1967), pp. 1–40.

60. For examples of the way fiscal issues were combined with other concerns, see Merle Thorpe, "Taxes, Our No. 1 Problem," *Nation's Business*, August 1938, p. 13; Thorpe, "Sweet Land of Gimme," ibid., September 1939, p. 13; Thorpe, "Liquidation of Enterprise," ibid., March 1939, p. 13; "Two Hours and Twelve Minutes a Day," ibid., January 1939, p. 13; ibid., June 1939, p. 103; George H. Davis, speech, February 17, 1939, in Presidential Speech File, 1937–1939, COCUS; and W. Gibson Carey, speech, January 18, 1940, in Presidential Speech File, 1939–1940, COCUS.

61. On the spending decision in general, see Stein, *Fiscal Revolution*, pp. 91–120; Eccles, *Beckoning Frontiers*, pp. 287-323; Blum, *Years of Crisis*, pp. 380-426; Burns, *Lion and the Fox*, pp. 324-36; Hawley, *Problem of Monopoly*, pp. 383–410; Leuchtenburg, *Franklin D. Roosevelt*, pp. 244–51, 256–57; Alsop and Kintner, *Men Around the President*, pp. 119–56; Tugwell, *Democratic Roosevelt*, pp. 441–49; and Henry Morgenthau, Jr., "The Morgenthau Diaries: The Struggle for a Program," *Collier's*, October 4, 1947, pp. 20–21, 45–49. Advocates of renewed spending included Harry Hopkins, Aubrey Williams, Marriner Eccles, Mordecai Ezekiel, Louis Bean, Lauchlin Currie, Isador Lubin, Jerome Frank, Henry Wallace, Tommy Corcoran, Ben Cohen, Leon Henderson, Robert Jackson, and Harold Ickes.

62. FDR's Message to Congress and explanatory Fireside Chat, April 14, 1938, in *Public Papers*, 7:221–48.

63. "Public Spending," *Washington Review* [a COCUS biweekly], May 23, 1938, p. 2. The new rationale for spending was made even clearer in FDR's 1939 annual and budget messages. The COFF noted dejectedly that whereas previous deficits had been treated by the administration as faults requiring some apology, in these messages no excuses had been made. Deficit spending had been presented as a positive policy. "Budget for 1940: Working Paper for Committee Use, 42d

Meeting, January 13, 1939" in COFF Papers, 1938–1939, COCUS. See also Arthur Ballantine, "Can We Go on Mortgaging the Future?" *Nation's Business*, April 1939, p. 16; and the remarks of Senator Harry F. Byrd in Minutes of the 27th Annual Meeting, May 2, 1939, p. 260, COCUS.

64. Quoted in *NYT*, September 12, 1937, p. 28.

65. Quoted in Herman Krooss, *Executive Opinion* (Garden City, N.Y.: Doubleday, 1970), p. 17; *NYT*, May 9, 1939, pp. 1–2; Merle Thorpe, "Thoughts on Dull Reading and Pessimism," *Nation's Business*, June 1939, p. 13.

66. "Federal Debt and Expenditures (or Government Credit): Report of the COFF to the BOD, September 20, 1938, Working Paper #1" in COFF Papers, 1938–1939, COCUS. See also *Nation's Business*, January 1939, p. 11; and the resolution on public expenditures in Minutes of the 27th Annual Meeting, May 4, 1939, p. 150, COCUS.

67. "New Spending," *Washington Review*, April 25, 1938, pp. 1–2; "Public Spending," ibid., May 23, 1938, pp. 1–2; "What Business Needs," ibid., May 9, 1938, pp. 21–24.

68. Minutes of the 26th Annual Meeting, May 2, 1938, p. 35, COCUS. See also George Davis, speeches of December 15, 1938, and January 3, 1939, in Presidential Speech File, 1937–1939, COCUS; Turner Catledge, "Congress Turns to Business," *Nation's Business*, January 1938, pp. 15–17, 82–85; Ray Tucker, "Congress Rediscovers Its Backbone," ibid., July 1938, pp. 15–17, 61–62; John Brookes, Jr., "Politics—A First Order of Business," ibid., November 1938, pp. 15–16, 61; and R. L. Van Boskirk, "Congress Will Check Up on Past Legislation," ibid., January 1939, pp. 20–22, 62–63. On conservative regard for the Supreme Court, see Prothro, *Dollar Decade*, pp. 192–96; and Morton Keller, *In Defense of Yesterday: James M. Beck and the Politics of Conservatism, 1861-1936* (New York: Coward-McCann, 1958), p. 267.

69. Congressional approval was needed for roughly $3.5 billion of the total spending requested by Roosevelt in April. In June, Congress authorized $3.75 billion in spending. Patterson, *Congressional Conservatism*, pp. 234–42.

70. FDR to Senator James Byrnes (D-S.C.), June 21, 1939, *Public Papers*, 8:372–75; *Time*, July 3, 1939, p. 7; Blum, *Years of Urgency*, pp. 36–42.

71. On the reservations of the spenders, see Harold Ickes, *The Secret Diary of Harold L. Ickes: The Inside Struggle, 1936-1939* (New York: Simon and Schuster, 1954), pp. 657–58; Patterson, *Congressional Conservatism*, pp. 318–19; and Marriner Eccles in U.S., Congress, Senate, Committee on Banking and Currency, *Works Financing Act of 1939, Hearings* on S. 2759, 76th Cong., 1st sess., 1939, p. 180. Morgenthau's view is found ibid., pp. 120–21; and U.S., Congress, House, Committee on Banking and Currency, *Construction and Financing of Self Liquidating Projects, Hearings* on H.R. 2120, 76th Cong., 1st sess., 1939, p. 81.

72. Stein, *Fiscal Revolution*, pp. 120-22; Patterson, *Congressional Conservatism*, pp. 319–21; and Lee Tilman, "The American Business Community and the Death of the New Deal" (Ph.D. diss. University of Arizona, 1966), pp. 468–82.

73. Samuel Grafton, "Propaganda From the Right," *American Mercury*, March 1935, p. 264. Studies of the NAM include Albert Steigerwalt, *The National As-*

sociation of Manufacturers, 1895–1914: A Study in Business Leadership (Ann Arbor: University of Michigan Press, 1964); Alfred Cleveland, "Some Political Aspects of Organized Industry" (Ph.D. diss., Harvard University, 1947); Richard Gable, "A Political Analysis of an Employers Association: The National Association of Manufacturers" (Ph.D. diss., University of Chicago, 1951); and John Stalker, "The National Association of Manufacturers: A Study in Ideology" (Ph.D. diss., University of Wisconsin, 1951). Regarding the NAM and organized labor, see Albion G. Taylor, *Labor Policies of the National Association of Manufacturers* (Urbana: University of Illinois Press, 1927); Irving Bernstein, *The Lean Years: A History of the American Worker, 1920–1933* (Boston: Houghton Mifflin, 1960), p. 156; and "Significant Highlights of the Organization and History of the NAM, 1895–1948" (April 1, 1948), drawer 107 (yellow), storage, National Association of Manufacturers Archives, Eleutherian Mills Historical Library, Wilmington, Delaware (hereafter NAM MSS).

74. Statistic from NAM, *The NAM and Its Leaders* (New York: NAM, 1947), p. 7. Quote from "The Very Human History of NAM: An Address by Wallace F. Bennett . . . January 21, 1949," drawer 107 (yellow), storage, NAM MSS.

75. "Suggested Outline for NAM, February, 1934," drawer 131 (yellow), storage, NAM MSS.

76. Membership figures from Robert Brady, *Business as a System of Power* (New York: Columbia University Press, 1943), p. 201; and NAM, *Annual Report, 1953*, p. 24. On big business support, see U.S., Congress, Senate, Committee on Education and Labor, *Violations of Free Speech and Rights of Labor*, Hearings before a subcommittee pursuant to S. Res. 266 (74th Cong.), 75th Cong., 3d sess., 1938, pt. 17, pp. 7386–87.

77. Cleveland, "NAM: Spokesman for Industry?" *Harvard Business Review* (May 1948), 26:357; NAM, *The Platform of American Industry . . . 1935* (New York: NAM, 1936), p. 3.

78. Robert Lund (NAM president) to FDR, December 9, 1933, PPF 8246, FDRL; "Statements in Respect to Pump Priming, 1934–1938" (December 30, 1938), drawer 133 (yellow), storage, NAM MSS.

79. *NAM News-Letter*, April 30, 1938, p. 1.

80. Quoted in Patterson, *Congressional Conservatism*, pp. 325–26.

81. I am using the word "expert" to refer to a person who works primarily on a restricted range of problems and who brings to bear on such problems a body of specialized theory, information, and skill.

82. Filene to the President and Directors of the Chamber, May 23, 1936, copy in OF 105, FDRL; *NYT*, May 25, 1936, p. 3. For Filene's definitely atypical but often insightful views, see Edward A. Filene, *Speaking of Change* (Freeport, N.Y.: By Former Associates of Edward A. Filene, 1939).

83. See Richard Kirkendall, "Franklin D. Roosevelt and the Service Intellectual," *Mississippi Valley Historical Review* (December 1962), 49:456–71; Kirkendall, *Social Scientists and Farm Politics in the Age of Roosevelt* (Columbia: University of Missouri Press, 1966); Tugwell, *Brains Trust*; Richard Hofstadter, *Anti-Intellectualism in American Life* (New York: Knopf, 1963), pp. 214–21; Carroll

W. Pursell, "The Administration of Science in the Department of Agriculture, 1933–1940," *Agricultural History* (July 1968), 42:231–40; Barry Karl, "Presidential Planning and Social Science Research: Mr. Hoover's Experts," *Perspectives in American History* (1969), 3:347–409; and Karl, *Executive Reorganization and Reform in the New Deal* (Cambridge: Harvard University Press, 1963).

84. Alsop and Kintner, *Men Around the President*, p. 172. See also pp. 167–200. A listing of Keynesian economists serving the government in one way or another before the war includes: Richard Gilbert, V. L. Bassie, Roderick Riley, Robert Nathan, Emile Despres, John Kenneth Galbraith, Gerhard Colm, Walter and William Salant, Griffith Johnson, Alan Sweezy, Arthur Gayer, Malcolm Bryan, George Eddy, Albert Hart, Martin Krost, Harry Dexter White, Gardiner Means, Thomas Blaisdell, and Louis Bean. Lauchlin Currie, "The Keynesian Revolution and Its Pioneers: Discussion," *American Economic Review* (May 1972), 62:141.

85. Quoted in Kirkendall, "Roosevelt and the Service Intellectual," p. 458.

86. K. G. Crawford, "From Pump-priming to Pumping: Permanent Government Spending," *Nation*, May 27, 1939, pp. 606–7; "What Causes a Business Downturn?" *New Republic*, February 2, 1938, pp. 382–84; Richard Lee Strout, "Hansen of Harvard," *New Republic*, December 29, 1941, pp. 888–90; Alonzo Hamby, *Beyond the New Deal: Harry S. Truman and American Liberalism* (New York: Columbia University Press, 1973), pp. 10–11; Hamby, "Sixty Million Jobs and the People's Revolution: The Liberals, the New Deal, and World War II," *The Historian* (August 1968), 30:585–86.

87. U.S., Congress, Temporary National Economic Committee, *Investigation of Concentration of Economic Power, Hearings* pursuant to Public Resolution No. 113 (part 9: Savings and Investment), 76th Cong., 1st sess., 1939, pp. 3495–3520, 3538–59, 3837–59; Currie, "Keynesian Revolution: Discussion," p. 141. Chase was an important popularizer of the stagnationist prescription. See for example, "If You Were President," *New Republic*, July 15, 1940, pp. 73–76. His lesson on semantics was embodied in a 1938 memo entitled "Investment Banking Study, TNEC, Preliminary Suggestions for Standardizing Terminology or First Aid to the Layman," Box 9, Stuart Chase MSS, Library of Congress.

88. *Fortune*, March 1939, p. 124.

89. Ibid., pp. 60, 118–24; Henry S. Dennison, et al., *Towards Full Employment* (New York: Whittlesey House, 1938); and Eccles, *Beckoning Frontiers*, p. 310.

90. James Weinstein, *The Corporate Ideal in the Liberal State* (Boston: Beacon Press, 1968).

3. PATTERNS OF POSITIVE BUSINESS RESPONSE

1. Moley, *After Seven Years*, pp. 289–90, 292–93, 298, 330–32, 337–39, 343; Ernest Lindley, *Half Way With Roosevelt* (New York: Viking Press, 1936), pp. 7, 413-15, 417-19, 422-23; Marquis Childs, *They Hate Roosevelt* (New York: Harper and Brothers, 1936); Childs, "They Still Hate Roosevelt," *New Republic*, September

14, 1938, pp. 147-49; Frederick Lewis Allen, *Since Yesterday, 1929-1939* (New York: Harper and Brothers, 1940), pp. 184-88; Tugwell, *Democratic Roosevelt*, pp. 242–43, 372, 377–78, 452, 507–8, 537; Schlesinger, *Coming of the New Deal*, pp. 444, 456–64, 471–88, 501–3, 567–69; Dexter Perkins, *The New Age of Franklin Roosevelt, 1932–1945* (Chicago: University of Chicago Press, 1957), pp. 39–40; Burns, *Lion and the Fox*, pp. 205–8, 225–26, 238–41, 245–46; Leuchtenburg, *Roosevelt and the New Deal*, pp. 176-77, 183-84, 339; Ellis Hawley, "The New Deal and Business," in John Braeman, Robert Bremner, and David Brody, *The New Deal: The National Level* (Columbus: Ohio State University Press, 1975), pp. 65–66, 70–72, 76; Hawley, *Problem of Monopoly*, pp. 151–58, 387–88; George Wolfskill and John Hudson, *All but the People* (New York: Macmillan, 1969), pp. 144–71; Wolfskill, "The New Deal Critics: Did They Miss the Point?" in Harold Hollingsworth and William Holmes, eds., *Essays on the New Deal* (Austin: University of Texas Press), pp. 51–53; Paul Conkin, *The New Deal* (New York: Crowell, 1967), pp. 34, 67, 74–78, 96–98.

2. NYT, May 4, 1935, p. 2; November 6, 1935, p. 24; November 11, 1935, p. 1; November 15, 1935, p. 18; November 22, 1935, p. 4; R. T. Stuart to FDR, May 6, 1935, in PPF 2478; Cason Callaway to Marvin McIntyre, March 26, 1937, in PPF 1345; and the correspondence supporting the President in OF 105, all in FDRL.

3. April 18, 1936, p. 7. On the healthy development of the auto industry under the New Deal, see Lawrence H. Seltzer, "Federal Budget: Economic Consequences of Deficit Financing: Direct Versus Fiscal and Institutional Factors," *American Economic Review* (Suppl. February 1941), 31:104.

4. NACOS, Proceedings of the 24th Annual Meeting, October 23–26, 1938, p. 91, in COCUS.

5. NACOS, Proceedings of the 23rd Annual Meeting, October 24–27, 1937, pp. 205-8, in COCUS.

6. Letter of May 24, 1939, 92001/2 pt., 4, U.S., General Records of the Department of Commerce, General Correspondence (Record Group 40), National Archives (hereafter Commerce Files). See also the remarks of Christy Thomas (Executive Vice President, Seattle Chamber of Commerce) in NACOS, Proceedings of the 22nd Annual Meeting, November 8–11, 1936, pp. 45–47, in COCUS.

7. Interview with Ralph Bradford (chief executive officer of COCUS, 1942–1950), July 10, 1974; Bradford to James Kemper, June 6, 1940, in the Ralph Bradford MSS (privately held, Ocala, Florida).

8. Minutes of the 28th Annual Meeting, April 29, 1940, p. 14, COCUS. See also the remarks of W. Gibson Carey, ibid., p. 11.

9. John J. O'Leary, quoted in William Feather, "Build America," *Nation's Business*, June 1940, p. 36.

10. Daniel Roper, *Fifty Years of Public Life* (Durham, N.C.: Duke University Press, 1941), p. 284.

11. Nathan Boone Williams to Roper, March 29, 1933; Pyke Johnson, et al. to Roper, April 5, 1933; "Memorandum on Conference with David Lawrence, April 13, 1933"; Carl Bahr to John Dickinson, May 2, 1933, all in 94765, Commerce Files; NYT, May 6, 1933, p. 7.

12. *NYT*, June 8, 1933, p. 31; and June 22, 1933, pp. 1, 4; Roper to H. H. Callan, June 6, 1933; Roper to Fred Kent, June 9, 1933, both in 94765, Commerce Files; Gerard Swope to Grace Tully, March 30, 1949, Box 11, File IV-A-4, Papers of the Franklin D. Roosevelt Memorial Foundation, FDRL. On the general history of the BAC, see Kim McQuaid, "The Business Advisory Council of the Department of Commerce, 1933–1961," in Paul Uselding, ed., *Research in Economic History, 1976* (Greenwich, Conn.: JAI Press, 1976), pp. 171–97; and Edward Berkowitz and McQuaid, "Businessman and Bureaucrat: The Evolution of the American Social Welfare System, 1900–1940," *Journal of Economic History* (March 1978), 38:120–42.

13. Roper to Harold C. Smith, June 1, 1934, in 94765, Commerce Files; "Memorandum in Re: Services of Business Advisory and Planning Council, August 9, 1934" in OF 3-Q, FDRL. The overrepresentation of big business in the BAC is obvious from a perusal of the membership lists provided in Roper, *Fifty Years*, pp. 404–7; and the 1944 BAC Membership Booklet in Box 110, Hopkins MSS, FDRL.

14. Roper, "Government Getting Closer to Business," *NYT*, February 3, 1935, 4:10; and Roper to Frank C. Walker, May 7, 1934, in 94765, Commerce Files.

15. *NYT*, March 17, 1934, p. 32; BAC to Roper, March 6, 1934, in 94765, Commerce Files. For complaints regarding other New Deal measures, see the Council's reports on the Wagner Act (April 10, 1935), the Banking Act of 1935 (April 29, 1935), and the administration's tax proposals (August 13, 1935), all in OF 3-Q, FDRL.

16. *NYT*, May 3, 1935, pp. 1, 5; May 4, 1935, p. 1; FDR Press Conference of May 3, 1935, in *Complete Presidential Press Conferences of Franklin D. Roosevelt* (New York: Da Capo Press, 1972), 5:262–67.

17. The reports are in OF 3-Q, FDRL. See also *NYT*, May 12, 1935, p. 10; and June 29, 1935, p. 2; *Evening Star* (Washington), May 4, 1935, p. 2; and May 5, 1935, p. 2.

18. *NYT*, May 24, 1935, p. 2; June 27, 1935, p. 5; June 29, 1935, p. 2; July 4, 1935, p. 29; July 11, 1935, p. 5; August 8, 1935, p. 11; "Advisors' Problem," *Business Week*, July 6, 1935, p. 29; Roper to BAC members, July 5, 1935, OF 3-Q, FDRL.

19. Regarding general criticism, see Robert E. Wood to Marvin McIntyre, July 18, 1935, and August 8, 1935, in PPF 1365; Wood to Roper, January 3, 1938, OF 3-Q; Fred Kent to FDR, December 10, 1937, PPF 744; Wood to Hopkins, April 29, 1939, Box 100, Hopkins MSS, all in FDRL; *NYT*, January 24, 1938, p. 6.

20. "Report of the Monetary Committee of the BAC, as Approved April 8, 1937." See also W. A. Harriman to Roper, May 20, 1937; and Gerard Swope to Harriman, May 6, 1937, all in OF 3-Q, FDRL.

21. Press statement, W. A. Harriman, January 19, 1938, in Box 110, Hopkins MSS, FDRL. See also Harriman to Roper, November 8, 1937, in Box 22, Ralph Flanders MSS, Syracuse University.

22. *NYT*, December 2, 1937, p. 5; Walter White to Marvin McIntyre, February 26, 1938, OF 3-Q, FDRL; Henry Harriman to FDR, April 20, 1938, ibid. See also Turner Catledge's report in *NYT*, May 8, 1938, p. 3.

23. *NYT*, June 2, 1938, p. 1; and June 3, 1938, p. 16.

24. FDR to Lincoln Filene, March 11, 1936, PFF 3364; Kent to FDR, December 10, 1937, PPF 744; and FDR to Kent, April 19, 1938, PPF 744, all in FDRL.

25. Marion Folsom, "Millions of Workers Still Lack Adequate Benefits," in Clarence Walton, ed., *Business and Social Progress: Views of Two Generations of Executives* (New York: Praeger, 1970), p. 98; Folsom Memoir (Social Security Project), pp. 80–81, COHC; BAC, "Report of Committee on Social Legislation regarding Old Age Security Sections of Bill HR 7260, April 30, 1935," in OF 3-Q, FDRL; Arthur Altmeyer, *The Formative Years of Social Security* (Madison: University of Wisconsin Press, 1966), p. 33; Charles McKinley and Robert W. Frase, *Launching Social Security: A Capture-and-Record Account, 1935–1937* (Madison: University of Wisconsin Press, 1970), p. 490.

26. Swope to FDR, August 16, 1938, PPF 2943, FDRL. See also Swope's radio address on economic security legislation, March 21, 1935, ibid.

27. Leeds, "A National Economic Council" in Program, Third General Meeting, BAC, March 5, 1934, in 94765, Commerce Files; Dennison, "Planning," ibid. See also "List of Agenda Topics for Commerce Advisory Committee, Suggested at Group Meeting, June 4, 1933," ibid.; Leeds to Dennison, June 21, 1934; Ralph Flanders to Dennison, June 22, 1934, both in Box 25, Flanders MSS; and Kim McQuaid, "Henry S. Dennison and the 'Science' of Industrial Reform, 1900-1950," *American Journal of Economics and Sociology* (January 1977), 36:79–98.

28. "BAC Interim Report of the Committee on Business Legislation, January 6, 1938," Box 50, Flanders MSS. See also Hawley, *Problem of Monopoly* pp. 164–65, 396–97; *NYT*, July 13, 1933, p. 25; July 1, 1935, p. 2; December 5, 1935, p. 14; the BAC resolutions of January 17 and March 13, 1935, regarding NRA renewal; George Sloan to Roper, March 5, 1937; Roper to FDR, June 10, 1935, all in OF 3-Q, FDRL; Fred Kent to FDR, May 2, 1938, PPF 744, FDRL.

29. Flanders, "Experience with the CED," speech of July 21, 1948, Box 134, Flanders MSS; Roper, Statement to the BAC, November 29, 1936, in 94765, Commerce Files. As Wetmore Hodges observed, "The greatest value in the Council lies in building up a continuity of daily relationships." Hodges to Marvin McIntyre, December 10, 1935, OF 3083, FDRL. Both the chairman and vice-chairman of the War Production Board, Donald Nelson and William Batt, were recruited from the BAC.

30. Flanders to Leeds, May 19, 1938, Box 56; March 6, 1937, Box 32, both in Flanders MSS.

31. Flanders, "Autobiographical Sketch" (late 1945 or early 1946), Box 129, Flanders MSS. Dennison's views are found in John Bakeless, ed., *Report of the Round Tables and General Conferences at the Twelfth Session*, Institute of Politics, Williams College (New Haven: Yale University Press, 1932), pp. 62–68, 72–74; and "Suggestions for a Popular Presentation of Planning," Box 25, Flanders MSS.

32. Flanders, "Business Looks at the N.R.A.," *Atlantic Monthly*, November 1933, p. 634. For correspondence with various experts, see the Leeds file, Box 32; Leeds file, Box 56; and Dennison File, Box 25, all in Flanders MSS. Regarding Galbraith's role, see Galbraith, "How Keynes Came to America," pp. 51–52; Flan-

ders to Dennison, et al., June 8, 1937, in Box 32, Flanders MSS; and Galbraith to Dennison, June 30, 1937, Box 27, ibid.

33. Dennison, et al., *Toward Full Employment*, pp. 60–62, 184–98, 287–97.

34. Ibid., pp. 18–30.

35. Ibid., pp. 26–27, 31–51, 120–33.

36. Flanders to Will Clayton, July 27, 1937, Box 51, Flanders MSS. See also Flanders to Alf Landon, May 31, 1938, Box 55, ibid.

37. Flanders to Virgil Jordan, September 16, 1936, Box 35; Leeds to Flanders, February 7, 1938, Box 56; Leeds to Dennison and Flanders, May 16, 1938, Box 56; Flanders to Leeds, December 31, 1938, Box 56, all in Flanders MSS.

38. Frank to Leeds, May 6, 1938, Box 56; Eccles to Leeds, May 26, 1937, Box 32; Eccles to Leeds, January 17, 1939, Box 56, all in Flanders MSS; Wallace to FDR, July 14, 1937, OF 79 (Misc), FDRL. See also FDR to Hopkins, August 5, 1937; and Aubrey Williams to FDR, August 10, 1937, ibid.

39. Flanders to Leeds, April 21, 1938; Leeds to Filene and Flanders, December 22, 1938, both in Box 56, Flanders MSS. Regarding book sales, see Leeds to Filene, November 2, 1938, ibid.

40. Teagle to Leeds, September 1, 1937, Box 32, ibid.; "The First Fortune Round Table: The Effects of Government Spending upon Private Enterprise," *Fortune*, March 1939, pp. 60, 118, 120, 123. See also J. David Stern to FDR, November 13, 1937, PPF 1039, FDRL; and Robert Wood to FDR, May 12, 1939, Box 100, Hopkins MSS, FDRL.

41. Unless otherwise noted, the sketch of Ruml that follows is based upon: E. B. Garnett, "Beardsley Ruml Has Never Worked Except with His Mind," *Kansas City Star*, December 5, 1948, pp. 19–20 (c); *Current Biography Yearbook, 1943* (New York: H. H. Wilson, 1944), pp. 647–50; C. Hartley Grattan, "Beardsley Ruml and His Ideas," *Harpers*, May 1952, pp. 78-86; "Beardsley Ruml," *Fortune*, March 1945, pp. 135–38, 170–80; "Ruml," *Life*, April 12, 1943, pp. 35–38; Alva Johnston, "The National Idea Man," *New Yorker*, February 10, 1945, pp. 28–35; February 17, 1945, pp. 26–34; and February 24, 1945, pp. 30–39.

42. Brownlow to C. Hartley Grattan, May 13, 1952, in Series 1, Box 1, Ruml MSS.

43. Barry Karl, *Charles E. Merriam and the Study of Politics* (Chicago: University of Chicago Press, 1974), p. 159.

44. Ruml, "The Position of the Social Sciences" (edited in 1956, apparently written at some earlier date) in Series 2, Box 9, Ruml MSS; *The Laura Spelman Rockefeller Memorial: Final Report*, esp. pp. 10–17; "Memorial Policy in Social Science: Extracts from Various Memoranda and Dockets"; untitled personal memorandum, dated 1929, all in Series 1, Box 5, ibid.; Ruml, "Recent Trends in Social Science" (December 17, 1929), Series 2, Box 1, ibid. Ruml's important role in the development of the social sciences in America is discussed in Karl, *Merriam*, pp. 132–39, 228–29.

45. Karl, *Executive Reorganization*, pp. 113-23.

46. Ruml to Teodoro Moscoso, Jr., April 3, 1950, Series 1, Box 5, Ruml MSS.

47. Tugwell, *Brains Trust*, p. 208; Tugwell to FDR, August 26, 1937, PPF 564,

FDRL; Harold Ickes, *The Secret Diary of Harold L. Ickes: The Inside Struggle, 1936–1939* (New York: Simon and Schuster, 1954), pp. 114–15; Morris Cooke to McIntyre, January 13, 1938, OF 177, FDRL; "Memorandum of E. N. Conversation with Leon Henderson for B. R. Memoirs," Series 1, Box 2, Ruml MSS.

48. Ruml, "Business Outlook, October 28, 1937," Series 2, Box 1, Ruml MSS.

49. Untitled memorandum, dated February 5, 1938, ibid.

50. Quoted in Blum, *Years of Crisis*, p. 397. This account of the spending decision is based upon: Jonathan Grossman, "The Budget and the Bonus Fight" (MS, August 1946), Box 392, Morgenthau Correspondence, FDRL; Paul Appleby Memoir, COHC; Leon Henderson, "I Came to Know F.D.R. First . . ." memo, July 28, 1948, File IV-A-4, Box 6, Papers of the Roosevelt Memorial Foundation, FDRL; "Leon Henderson in the Lyons Den," August 13, 1943, Box 36, Leon Henderson MSS, FDRL; "Memorandum of E. N. Conversation with Leon Henderson for B. R. Memoirs," Series 1, Box 2; Ruml to Jacob Viner, February 25, 1958, Series 1, Box 4; Ruml to Arthur Burns, February 25, 1958, ibid., all in Ruml MSS; Henderson to Hopkins, October 12, 1937, and March 23, 1938, Box 54; Aubrey Williams to Hopkins, n. d. (December, 1937 or early 1938), Box 100; Henderson to Hopkins, November 9, 1942, Box 97, all in Hopkins MSS, FDRL; Eccles, *Beckoning Frontiers*, p. 311; and Stein, *Fiscal Revolution*, pp. 109-14.

51. Ruml, "Warm Springs Memorandum, April 1, 1938," Series 2, Box 1, Ruml MSS. See also the "Miami Memorandum, April 6, 1938," ibid.

52. Henry Wallace's observation, quoted in Morgenthau Diary, Book 118, p. 176, FDRL. Morgenthau complained to his associates, "They have just stampeded him during the week I was away. . . . They stampeded him like cattle." Quoted in Blum, *Years of Crisis*, p. 421.

53. Roosevelt, *Public Papers*, 7:243–45.

54. Benton to Donald David, December 24, 1957, Benton MSS, privately held, New York (hereafter Benton MSS, NYC). An excellent biography is Sidney Hyman, *The Lives of William Benton* (Chicago: University of Chicago Press, 1969).

55. Benton, "Statement of Historical Background of the CED, October 26, 1943," Reel 32, CED Archives, Washington, D.C.; Benton to Ed Noble, October 24, 1939; Willard Thorp to Benton, November 16, 1939, both in 102611, Commerce Files.

56. Harold Lasswell, "American Policy Commission Memo," June 3, 1941, Marion Folsom MSS, University of Rochester. See also memo, Lasswell to Hutchins, May 12, 1941, Box 22; Benton to Hoffman, March 24, 1941, and May 7, 1941, Box 20, all in Benton MSS, University of Chicago (hereafter Benton MSS, Chicago).

57. Benton to Francis, October 30, 1941; Benton to Hutchins, November 17, 1941, both in Box 28; Benton to James Young, January 14, 1942, Box 32; Benton to Ruml, January 28, 1942, Box 30, all in Benton MSS (Chicago).

4. PRECIOUS ROOM FOR MANEUVER

1. Roosevelt, *Public Papers*, 13:42.

2. John Morton Blum, *V Was for Victory: Politics and American Culture During World War II* (New York: Harcourt Brace Jovanovich, 1976), pp. 110–16.

3. Quoted in Richard Lingeman, *Don't You Know There's a War On?* (New York: Putnam's, 1970), p. 71. The statistics are from ibid., pp. 67-70; and Richard Polenberg, *War and Society: The United States, 1941–1945* (Philadelphia: Lippincott, 1972), p. 139.

4. Polenberg, *War and Society*, pp. 158–59.

5. Regarding the treatment of veterans, see Davis R. B. Ross, *Preparing for Ulysses* (New York: Columbia University Press, 1969).

6. John Robert Moore, "The Conservative Coalition in the United States Senate, 1942–1945," *Journal of Southern History* (August 1967), 33:373; FDR quoted in Polenberg, *War and Society*, p. 199. In actuality, the President's party was nominally in control with 222 seats in the House and 57 in the Senate. See also Donald R. McCoy, "Republican Opposition in Wartime, 1941–1945," *Mid-America* (July 1967), 49:180–81; and F. M. Riddick, "Congress versus the President in 1944," *South Atlantic Quarterly* (July 1945), 44:308–15. The degeneration of relations between Congress and the administration is a major theme in Allen Drury, *A Senate Journal, 1943–1945* (New York: McGraw-Hill, 1963).

7. Polenberg, *War and Society*, pp. 77–78; Blum, *V Was for Victory*, pp. 140–46; Hawley, *Problem of Monopoly*, p. 442; and Donald Nelson, *Arsenal of Democracy* (New York: Harcourt, Brace, 1946), pp. 98–99.

8. U.S., Civilian Production Administration, *Dollar-A-Year and Without Compensation Personnel Policies of the War Production Board and Predecessor Agencies*, by George Auxier and James McAleer (Washington: GPO, 1947); Merle Thorpe, "They're Whistling Business Out of the Doghouse," *Nation's Business*, August 1940, p. 13.

9. "Remarks of Jesse Jones and R. R. Deupree, BAC, January 30, 1942," Folsom MSS. See also Walter White to Thomas Holden, January 27, 1941; Minutes, General Council Meeting, BAC, November 15–16, 1941; Folsom, "Postwar Economy: Pundit Club, December 2, 1941," all in Folsom MSS; Folsom Memoir (Eisenhower Project); and Folsom Memoir (Social Security Project), both in COHC.

10. Jones speech, CED Meeting, April 14, 1943, Box 226, Jesse Jones MSS, Library of Congress; Jones to S. Clay Williams, June 25, 1942, Box 172, ibid. Jones' role as the New Deal's archconservative is examined in Richard Fenno, Jr., "President-Cabinet Relations: A Pattern and a Case Study," *American Political Science Review* (June 1958), 52:388–405.

11. Carroll Wilson, "Business Post-War Planning," Folsom MSS.

12. George Sloan to Walter White, February 4, 1942; Walter White to Thomas Holden, February 3, 1942; Bert White to Folsom, February 4, 1942, and February 7, 1942; Walter White to Folsom, February 19, 1942, all in Folsom MSS.

13. "Report of the Committee on Economic Policy . . . , Approved April 9, 1942," Folsom MSS; Folsom to Walter White, March 26, 1942, ibid.; "Formation of the Institute of Business Enterprise," drawer 81 (yellow),storage, NAM MSS.

14. Benton to Folsom, April 30, 1942, Benton MSS (NYC). See also Benton to Folsom, May 21, 1942, ibid.; and the Folsom Memoir (Eisenhower Project), COHC.

15. Benton, "Statement of Historical Background of the CED, October 26, 1943," Reel 32, CED Archives.

16. Paul Hoffman, address to CED Trustees, May 11, 1949, Box 102, Flanders MSS. There is much material regarding the field development program of the CED in the Lou Holland MSS, HSTL.

17. CED, Executive Committee Minutes, February 8, 1943, Folsom MSS. On Jones' selection of the trustees, see Karl Schriftgiesser, *Business Comes of Age* (New York: Harper and Brothers, 1960), pp. 24–25.

18. Eighteen trustees constituted the original board, but two of these were replaced in December 1942, making a total of twenty who saw service in 1942. On the BAC-CED connection, see also Flanders to Lucien Warner, January 19, 1943, Box 50, Benton MSS (Chicago).

19. See, for example, Weinstein, *Corporate Ideal*; Charles Hirshfield, "National Progressivism and World War I," *Mid-America* (July 1963), 45:139–56; Robert Himmelberg, "The War Industries Board and the Antitrust Question in November 1918," *Journal of American History* (June 1965), 52:59–74; Murray Rothbard, "War Collectivism in World War I," in Ronald Radosh and Rothbard, eds., *A New History of Leviathan: Essays on the Rise of the American Corporate State* (New York: E. P. Dutton, 1972),pp. 66–110; Ellis Hawley, "Herbert Hoover, the Commerce Secretariat, and the Vision of an 'Associative State,' 1921–1928," *Journal of American History*, (June 1974), 61:116–40; Hawley, "Herbert Hoover and American Corporatism, 1929–1933," in Martin Fausold and George Mazuzan, eds., *The Hoover Presidency: A Reappraisal* (Albany: State University of New York Press, 1974), pp. 101-19; Hawley, *The Great War and the Search for a Modern Order* (New York: St. Martin's Press, 1979); David Burner, *Herbert Hoover: A Public Life* (New York: Knopf, 1979), pp. 159–89; Himmelberg, *National Recovery Administration*; Richard Hume Werking, "Bureaucrats, Businessmen, and Foreign Trade: The Origins of the United States Chamber of Commerce," *Business History Review* (Autumn 1978), 52:321–41; Kim McQuaid, "Corporate Liberalism in the American Business Community, 1920–1940," ibid., pp. 342–68; McQuaid, "Young, Swope and General Electric's 'New Capitalism': A Study in Corporate Liberalism, 1920–1933," *American Journal of Economics and Sociology* (July 1977), 36:323-34; McQuaid, "The Frustration of Corporate Revival during the Early New Deal," *The Historian* (August 1979),41:682–704. The best overview is Hawley, "The Discovery and Study of a 'Corporate Liberalism,'" *Business History Review* (Autumn 1978), 52:309–20. Analogous developments in Europe are discussed in Charles Maier, *Recasting Bourgeois Europe* (Princeton: Princeton University Press, 1975).

20. On the general nature of American corporatism, see Daniel Fusfeld, "Rise of the Corporate State in America," *Journal of Economic Issues* (March 1972), 6:1–22; Arthur S. Miller, *The Modern Corporate State: Private Governments and the American Constitution* (Westport, Conn.: Greenwood Press, 1976); Grant McConnell, *Private Power and American Democracy* (New York: Knopf, 1966); Theodore Lowi, *The End of Liberalism* (New York: W. W. Norton, 1969); David Noble, *America by Design: Science, Technology, and the Rise of Corporate Capitalism* (New York: Knopf, 1977); and Philippe Schmitter, "Still the Century of Corporatism," *Review of Politics* (January 1974), 36:85–131. I have found particularly helpful two unpublished papers by Ellis Hawley: "Techno-Corporatist For-

mulas in the Liberal State, 1920–1960: A Neglected Aspect of America's Search for a New Order" (1974); and "The New Corporatism and the Liberal Democracies, 1918–1925: The Case of the United States" (1977).

21. Hoffman in CED, Minutes, Board of Trustees, April 18, 1947, Folsom MSS; Stein to CED Trustees, January 10, 1962, ibid. Interestingly, Stein went on to observe that the CED's pursuit of truth and the general interest furthered the class interest of businessmen; thus, objectivity and self-interest merged.

22. *C.E.D. News*, February–March, 1945, p. 7. See also Sumner Slichter to Folsom, October 3, 1949, Folsom MSS; and Paul Hoffman, "The Great Challenge to Capitalism," *New York Times Magazine*, September 8, 1946, p. 65.

23. Theodore Yntema, "How CED Research Works," *C.E.D. News*, December 1944–January 1945, p. 6.

24. "CED, Joint Meeting of the Research Committee and Research Advisory Board, April 7–8, 1945," Box 131, Flanders MSS. See also Benton to J. C. Hormel, June 1, 1945, Box 52, Benton MSS (Chicago); Robert Calkins to Robert Brady, December 27, 1943, Box 52, ibid.; Gardiner Means to Brady, January 8, 1944, Box 51, ibid.

25. Benton to John K. Galbraith, September 29, 1944, Benton MSS (NYC); Flanders speech of June 6, 1942, Box 126, Flanders MSS; "CED Tax Report: Summary of Conclusions and Recommendations," Box 128, ibid.; "CED Research Committee and Advisory Board Meeting, April 10, 1944," ibid.; Gardiner Means to Robert Brady, January 8, 1944, Box 51, Benton MSS (Chicago); Benton, "The Economics of a Free Society: A Declaration of American Economic Policy," *Fortune*, October 1943, p. 165. This article was in reality a declaration of principles for the CED; it was the product not so much of one man, but rather (as a result of extensive consultation and redrafting) of the CED's leadership as a whole.

26. "Public Debt and Deficit Spending: A Report Prepared by the Statistical Department, NAM" (September 1940), Subject File 100-NN, drawer 51; "Summary of Discussion at Joint Meeting of Subcommittees on Distribution of Income and Economic Aspects of Defense to Consider Proposed Study on the Future of Private Enterprise, May 13, 1941," drawer 74 (yellow), storage, both in NAM MSS.

27. "Public Debt and Deficit Spending" (September 1940), Subject File 100-NN, drawer 51, NAM MSS.

28. Press release, address by Sargent, May 12, 1943, drawer 81 (yellow), storage; Ray to Sargent, October 20, 1942, drawer 82 (yellow), storage, both in NAM MSS.

29. On the reorganization, begun in 1945, see "Renovation in N.A.M.," *Fortune*, July 1948, pp. 72–75, 165–69; "Report of Special NAM-NIIC Committee, April 25, 1945" (the Wampler Report), Subject File 100-Q, drawer 17, NAM MSS; Memo on Recommendations contained in the Wampler Report . . . February 11, 1949, ibid.; "Operations of the NAM, April 13, 1954," drawer 131 (yellow), storage, ibid.

30. The need for such a journal—"Our policies sometimes are based on instinct and prejudice instead of unassailable economic logic"—was expressed in an early draft of a statement to the NAM board by president R. R. Wason but was

omitted from his actual statement of January 23, 1946. Materials in drawer 37 (yellow), storage, NAM MSS.

31. Johnston was nominated by a six-member committee which included three past presidents from the era of negativistic opposition. Nomination was tantamount to election, a formality undertaken at the annual convention. Minutes, Board of Directors, April 30, 1942, COCUS; interview with Ralph Bradford, July 10, 1974.

32. Minutes, Board of Directors, April 29, 1937, COCUS; Ralph Bradford, "Chamber of Commerce of the USA: A Memoir," Bradford MSS; letter, Bradford to author, February 15, 1974; interview with Bradford, July 10, 1974; *Business Week*, August 8, 1942, pp. 19–20.

33. "Statement by Delmar G. Starkey on Behalf of the Committee Headed by Christy Thomas of Seattle Which Appeared Before the Board, Friday, June 19, 1942," in Bradford MSS. See also Minutes, Board of Directors, June 19, 1942, COCUS; and "Proceedings, Board of Directors, June 19, 1942," in Bradford MSS.

34. It is difficult to ascertain what demographic factors, if any, predisposed one to insurgency against the Chamber's *ancien régime*. Just what united the rebels, besides obvious dissatisfaction with the impotency of the organization, is not clear. There appears, however, to have been a strong overtone of regionalism at the leadership level of the uprising. Of the total of eleven complainants on the two committees which appeared before the Board in June, only one was an Easterner. Johnston had long been an advocate of Western interests, and had led a fight in 1933 for more adequate representation of Western industry in Chamber councils. It is perhaps of some significance that the 1942 annual meeting was held in Chicago instead of Washington. Minutes, Board of Directors, June 19, 1942, COCUS; Minutes of the 21st Annual Meeting, May 5, 1933, pp. 123–26, COCUS. The regional identification is touched upon in *Business Week*, August 8, 1942, p. 19. See also Johnston's pointed remarks concerning the Chamber's "first discovery of the West" on the occasion of the organization's first West Coast convention. Minutes of the 20th Annual Meeting, May 1, 1932, pp. 766–67, COCUS.

35. Minutes, Board of Directors, June 19, 1942; July 7, 1942, COCUS.

36. Ralph Bradford, address to the 1943 convention, reprinted in Bradford, *Along the Way* (Washington: Judd and Detweiler, 1949),p. 173.

37. Remarks to COCUS Legislative Dinner, January 23, 1945, in Presidential Speech File, 1942–1946, COCUS.

38. "Notes Prepared and Used by Ralph Bradford in a Presentation to Committee on Reorganization of the National Chamber, about June 1942," in Bradford MSS; Eric Johnston, in Minutes of the 34th Annual Meeting, May 2, 1946, p. 161, COCUS; Johnston's "America Unlimited" address, April 27, 1943, in Presidential Speech File, 1942–1946, COCUS; Johnston, "Business Faces a Changing World," *American Mercury*, December 1942, p. 658.

39. Ralph Bradford in NACOS, Proceedings of the 28th Annual Meeting, October 18–21, 1942, p. 88, COCUS.

40. Minutes of the 31st Annual Meeting, April 27, 1943, pp. 22–23, COCUS. See also Minutes of the 34th Annual Meeting, May 2, 1946, pp. 158–64, COCUS; Eric Johnston, *America Unlimited* (Garden City, N.Y.: Doubleday, 1944), pp.

87–98; Johnston, "Three Kinds of Capitalism: Which Offers a Poor Boy the Best Chance?" *Readers Digest*, September 1943, p. 127; Johnston's speech of April 27, 1944, in Presidential Speech File, 1942–1946, COCUS; and Johnston's testimony on April 19, 1944, in U.S., Congress, House, Special Committee on Post-War Economic Policy and Planning, *Post-War Economic Policy and Planning, Hearings pursuant to H. Res. 408, 78th Cong., 2d sess., 1944*, pt. 1, p. 235. One possible explanation for the acceptance by Johnston (who was from Spokane) and his Western supporters of a more positive government role might lie in the favorable treatment accorded the West by New Deal spending programs. One recent study has concluded that "in general, the western states seemed most willing to extend an open hand to Washington, while New England and southern states were most antagonistic to federal programs." Western states received a significantly larger per capita share of New Deal loans and expenditures over the period 1933–1939 ($504.86) than did the South ($305.55) or the Northeast ($300.78). Don C. Reading, "New Deal Activity and the States, 1933 to 1939," *Journal of Economic History* (December 1973), 33:805, 795. See also Leonard J. Arrington, "The New Deal in the West: A Preliminary Statistical Inquiry," *Pacific Historical Review* (August 1969), 38:311–16. Defense spending after 1939 probably continued this trend. California, for example, contracted for 13 percent of the nation's defense spending between June 1 and Christmas, 1940. Geoffrey Perrett, *Days of Sadness, Years of Triumph: The American People, 1939–1945* (New York: Coward, McCann and Geoghegan, 1973), p. 71. See also Merlo J. Pusey, "Revolution at Home," *South Atlantic Quarterly* (July 1943), 42:216–18.

41. Johnston, *American Unlimited*, pp. 175–76, 187.

42. "Referendum: Amendment of By-Laws, January 20, 1943," in *Referenda, Amendment of By-Laws and Nos. 73, 74, 75, 76 and 78, 1939–1944*, COCUS.

43. Roosevelt is quoted in *NYT*, August 23, 1963, p. 23. See also Minutes, Board of Directors, July 17, 1942, COCUS; *NYT*, July 24, 1942, p. 7; and September 17, 1942, p. 46; FDR to Johnston, October 8, 1942, OF 5148-B, FDRL. In his first year in office (May 1942–May 1943), Johnston met with FDR seven times. The two previous Chamber presidents had failed to meet with Roosevelt at all. President's Appointments Index, FDRL. For the administration's very favorable first impression of Johnston, see McIntyre to FDR, May 19, 1942, in OF 105, FDRL; Blum, *Price of Vision*, p. 169. Johnston's arrival upon the national scene caused some to see him as a possible dark horse contender for the 1944 Republican nomination. George Soule, "Eric Johnston, Knight-Errant of Main Street," *New Republic*, December 13, 1943, p. 841. See also Gallup, *Gallup Poll*, 1:422, 425, 427–28, 431–33.

44. The quote is taken from a blurb in Eric Johnston, "A Talk to Britons," *Reader's Digest*, October 1943, p. 2; *Nation's Business*, August 1946, p. 8. Under Johnston's leadership, organizational membership (affiliated chambers and trade associations) increased from 1,635 (1942) to 2,643 (1947). Over the same period, corporate and individual memberships increased from 10,466 to 17,925.

45. Minutes of the 31st Annual Meeting, April 28, 1943, p. 50, COCUS.

46. "Referendum: Amendment of By-Laws, January 20, 1943" in *Referenda, Amendment of By-Laws and Nos. 73, 74, 75, 76, and 78, 1939–1944)*, COCUS. See

also Minutes, Board of Directors, July 17, 1942 and September 18–19, 1942, COCUS; *Business Week*, March 20, 1943, p. 14.

47. Minutes, Board of Directors, September 19, 1941, COCUS; Ralph Bradford, "Manager's Report, October 30, 1942," in Bradford MSS; Bradford, "Managers Report to the Board, December 11, 1942," ibid.; interview with Dr. Emerson P. Schmidt, July 29, 1974; letter, Schmidt to author, August 15, 1974. The Chamber had previously had one economist on its staff, but this earlier expert was a specialist in taxation and had not taken, nor was he given, the entire field of economics as his purview. Schmidt was soon joined by economist Ernst Swanson; the Department, once on its feet, usually enjoyed the services of from three to six economists.

48. Minutes of the 30th Annual Meeting, April 29, 1942, p. 312, COCUS.

49. Johnston's remarks (draft by Schmidt) in "Economists and the Economy," *Journal of Political Economy* (June 1944), 52:160–63; Schmidt, "Why We Must Plan," *Nation's Business*, April 1943, p. 41. The meeting in question established the Conference of Business Economists, a group which continues to meet regularly. Letter, Schmidt to author, August 15, 1974.

50. COCUS, *The Chamber of Commerce at Work: 31st Annual Report to the Members* (Washington: COCUS, 1943), p. 16.

51. COCUS, *Help Yourself to Better Government: How to Start and Operate a National Affairs Committee* (Washington: COCUS, 1945), p. 31.

52. NACOS, Proceedings of the 29th Annual Meeting, October 24–27, 1943, pp. 91–92; "Announcement of Creation of Department of Governmental Affairs," Campaign Book No. 1, January 14, 1943 to August 18, 1943, COCUS. In 1943, James Ingebretsen, the first director of the Department of Government Affairs, reported that over 300 members of Congress subscribed to the *Legislative Daily*. Minutes of the 31st Annual Meeting, April 29, 1943, p. 455, COCUS.

53. George Terborgh, *Economic Maturity*, p. 13. See also the remarks of Emmett F. Connely and H. W. Prentis, Jr., in Minutes of the 28th Annual Meeting, May 1, 1940, pp. 142–43, 167, COCUS; Millard Tydings, "Ideologies in the Budget," *Nation's Business*, October 1941, pp. 31–33; Eric Johnston, "We're Not Washed Up," *Reader's Digest*, November 1943, pp. 11–16; Johnston, speeches of May 19, 1943, and September 19, 1943, in Presidential Speech File, 1942–1946, COCUS.

54. Chase, "Is the New Deal Lost?" undated, Box 1, Chase MSS; Hansen to John K. Jessup, August 6, 1943, Box 1, HUG (FP)-3.10, Hansen MSS.

55. The social component of Hansen's thought is expressed particularly in Hansen, "Frontiers of Public Welfare Program," undated, Box 2, HUG (FP)-3.42, Hansen MSS; Hansen, "A Full Employment Program," updated, ibid.; and Hansen, "Postwar Employment Program," September 18, 1944, Box 1, Colm MSS, HSTL.

56. U.S., Congress, House, Special Committee on Post-War Economic Policy and Planning, *Post-War Economic Policy and Planning, Hearings* pursuant to H. Res. 408, 78th Cong., 2d sess., 1944, pt. 1, p. 157; Ernst W. Swanson and Emerson P. Schmidt, *Economic Stagnation or Progress: A Critique of Recent Doctrines on the Mature Economy, Oversavings, and Deficit Spending* (New York: McGraw-Hill, 1946), pp. vi, 7 (n.1), 10, 186–87.

57. Hamby, *Beyond the New Deal*, pp. 10-12; Hamby, "Sixty Million Jobs and the People's Revolution: The Liberals, the New Deal, and World War II," *The Historian* (August 1968), 30:585–87; and Richard Lee Strout, "Hansen of Harvard," *New Republic*, December 29, 1941, pp. 888–90.

58. U.S., National Resources Planning Board, *National Resources Development: Report for 1943*. For an analysis of the stagnationist underpinnings of the report, see Bruce Bliven, Max Lerner, and George Soule, "Charter for America," *New Republic*, April 19, 1943, pp. 537–38. On the report in general, see also Polenberg, *War and Society*, p. 84; Hamby, *Beyond the New Deal*, pp. 11–12; and Norman D. Markowitz, *The Rise and Fall of the People's Century: Henry A. Wallace and American Liberalism, 1941–1948* (New York: Free Press, 1973), pp. 61–62.

59. Review of Wallace, *Sixty Million Jobs* (New York: Simon and Schuster, 1945), in *New Republic*, September 17, 1945, p. 353.

60. For a good treatment of this episode, see Markowitz, *People's Century*, pp. 128–35. For indications that conservative fears were well founded, see Blum, *Price of Vision*, pp. 418, 420.

61. Quoted in Blum, *Years of Urgency*, pp. 41–42; Roosevelt, *Public Papers*, 12:99–100; ibid., 13:41, 372, 376; Wallace to FDR, October 29, 1944, in Blum, *Price of Vision*, p. 389; Roosevelt, *Public Papers*, 13:480–82.

62. See, for example, "Fortune Management Poll," *Fortune*, February 1945, p. 270; Krooss, *Executive Opinion*, p. 217.

63. "The Fortune Survey," *Fortune*, January 1945, p. 260; ibid., August 1945, p. 257; Gallup, *Gallup Poll*, 1:410 (October 3, 1943), 414 (October 30, 1943), 496 (April 1, 1945), 521 (August 25, 1945), 534 (October 22, 1945); U.S., Library of Congress, Legislative Reference Service, *Bibliography of Full Employment*, Report to the Senate Committee on Banking and Currency (Washington: GPO, 1945).

64. The first prize of $25,000 was awarded to Herbert Stein, who later became Chairman of the Council of Economic Advisers under President Nixon. Second prize ($10,000) went to Leon Keyserling, who occupied the same position under President Truman. The winning essays are found in Pabst Brewing Company, *The Winning Plans in the Pabst Postwar Employment Awards* (Milwaukee, Wisc.: Pabst Brewing Co., 1944). An analysis of all entries is found in Lyle Fitch and Horace Taylor, eds., *Planning for Jobs: Proposals Submitted in the Pabst Postwar Employment Awards* (Philadelphia: Blakiston, 1946). See also Thomas C. Cochran, *The Pabst Brewing Company: The History of an American Business* (New York: New York University Press, 1948), p. 396.

65. The text of the original bill may be found in Bailey, *Congress*, pp. 243–48. The discussion of the Employment Act which follows leans very heavily on Bailey's account. Though we differ on several important details, Bailey's book deserves the highest accolade; it is, quite simply, first-rate history. Another account is U.S., Congress, Senate, Committee on Banking and Currency. *The Employment Act of 1946, Final Report . . . by the Chairman, July, 1946*, Senate Committee Print No. 5, 79th Cong., 2d sess., 1946. Scholars interested in the origins of the bill should consult Boxes 2 and 3, Edwin G. Nourse MSS, HSTL; and Box 1, Colm MSS, HSTL.

66. Herbert Corey, "Three Helpmates of Destiny," *Nation's Business*, September 1946, p. 56. Hansen had begun lobbying for a full employment program even before American entry into the war. See Hansen to Wallace, May 6, 1941, Box 2; Hansen to Thomas Blaisdell, May 14, 1941, Box 1; and Hansen's memo, "Post-Defense Full Employment," May 14, 1941, Box 1, all in HUG (FP)-3.10, Hansen MSS.

67. See Gilbert, et al., *Economic Program*. Bailey notes that Gilbert's views were represented in the drafting of Murray's proposal. *Congress*, p. 45. The stagnationist underpinnings of S.380 are especially clear in the drafts which preceded the Murray bill. See ibid., pp. 47–48, 58. Regarding the spending bias of the Murray bill, see the oral history memoirs of Walter Salant (p. 12) and Leon Keyserling (p. 27), HSTL. For a defense of the spending emphasis, see Bertram Gross to Gerhard Colm, September 11, 1945, Box 1, Colm MSS, HSTL.

68. U.S., Congress, House, Committee on Expenditures in the Executive Departments, *Full Employment Act of 1945, Hearings* on H.R. 2202, 79th Cong., 1st sess., 1945, pp. 439–44, 445–98, 1128–29; Bailey, *Congress*, pp. 141–42.

69. Johnston, *America Unlimited*, p. 140. See also Johnston's speech of December 16, 1943, in Presidential Speech File, 1942–1946, COCUS; and "Where Are Postwar Jobs Coming From?" October 3, 1943 (transcript of radio interview), ibid. This concern was genuine. Some commentators have attributed business antagonism over full employment proposals to a desire to maintain a reserve army of unemployed available to work at low wages. Sidney S. Alexander, "Opposition to Deficit Spending for the Prevention of Unemployment," in *Income, Employment and Policy*, pp. 109–91. A hint of this logic appears in economist Gustav Stolper's contention that "we need reserves in manpower as well as in machine capacity. Cyclical fluctuations are the engines of economic progress." "Employment in War, Why Not in Peace," *Nation's Business*, April 1943, p. 68. This view was not typical of either the Chamber or business in general.

70. *Time*, October 4, 1943, pp. 80–84; *Business Week*, January 29, 1944, pp. 30–32; Clarence Woodbury, "Is *Your* Town Ready with Postwar Jobs?" *Reader's Digest*, January 1944, pp. 99–100; "We Will, You Bet We Will," *Nation's Business*, November 1943, pp. 94–95; Ralph Bradford, "Postwar or Postponed?" ibid., February 1944, pp. 46, 48; Johnston, "Where Are Postwar Jobs Coming From?" October 3, 1943, in Presidential Speech File, 1942–1946, COCUS.

71. "Transcript of General Staff Meeting—Washington Headquarters" (cover letter, Ralph Bradford to all employees, July 18, 1945) in Presidential Speech File, 1942–1946, COCUS.

72. Schmidt, *Can Government Guarantee Full Employment? Post-War Readjustments Bulletin No. 13* (Washington: COCUS, 1945), p. 10. For discussion of the British proposals, see Winch, *Economics and Policy*, pp. 269–74; and William Beveridge, *Full Employment in a Free Society* (New York: W. W. Norton, 1945), pp. 17–38, 259–74. The positive reaction of American liberals to Beveridge's proposals is seen in Gerhard Colm to J. Weldon Jones, November 30, 1944, Box 1, Colm MSS, HSTL.

73. Bailey, *Congress*, p. 139.

74. Schmidt, *Can Government Guarantee*, p. 25. This pamphlet was mailed not only to the membership but also to lists of "community leaders" across the nation; the covering letter reminded these local luminaries that the outcome of the full employment debate would have important economic and political consequences. The preparation of such lists had been set down in 1944 as one of the basic tasks of the national affairs committee program. Howard Volgenau to "Community Leaders," May 28, 1945, in Department of Governmental Affairs, Campaign Book No. 3, September 4, 1944 to ——, 1945, COCUS; COCUS, *Congress Looks to Business* (Washington: COCUS, 1944), p. 5.

75. Charles P. Trussell, "Can Prosperity Be Dictated?" *Nation's Business*, April 1945, pp. 21–22, 80–81; "Transcript of Eric Johnston's Talk before Division Managers, September 13, 1945," in Presidential Speech File, 1942–1946, COCUS; Bailey, *Congress*, pp. 123–24.

76. Bailey, *Congress*, pp. 136–37, 155–56.

77. Regarding Whittington's crucial role, see ibid., pp. 164–65; Vinson to Truman, October 22, 1945; and Vinson's memo, "The Cabinet Committee Formula and the Full Employment Legislation," n.d., both in OF 264, HSTL. On Whittington's conservatism, see Patterson, *Congressional Conservatism*, p. 342; and James C. Patton and James Loeb, Jr., "Challenge to Progressives," *New Republic*, February 5, 1945, p. 191.

78. Whittington to Walter Sellers, November 21, 1945. See also Whittington to G. B. Benham, November 10, 1945; and "Whittington and the Full Employment Bill" press release, October 25, 1945, all in "Full Employment H.R. 2202" folder, Box 45, Whittington MSS, University of Mississippi.

79. Whittington to E. H. Blackstone (Secretary, Greenwood, Mississippi, Chamber of Commerce), February 5, 1942, in Box 34, ibid.; Blackstone to Whittington, March 17, 1944; and Whittington to Blackstone, March 20, 1944, both in Box 23, ibid.; Whittington, "Bureaucracy Rides the Rivers," *Nation's Business*, September 1945, pp. 31–33, 76–78.

80. Memo, Howard Volgenau to Ralph Bradford, November 8, 1945, in Department of Governmental Affairs, Letters and Statements Sent to Congress, 1945, COCUS; memo for the record from Volgenau, "Service to Congressmen in Respect to 'Full Employment Bill,'" October 26, 1945, ibid. Copies of two of the drafts are in the same place. These were apparently drafted by Mr. Kumm of the Department of Governmental Affairs. Emerson Schmidt, director of economic research for the Chamber, also prepared a substitute draft for Whittington, Letter, Schmidt to author, August 15, 1974. Schmidt's work very probably then served as the basis for Kumm's draft, although the evidence for this conclusion is not beyond question.

81. There were other suggestions, from other sources, submitted to Whittington. The Chamber's proposals, however, arrived first and, as it were, stayed longest. The congruence of the Chamber draft with the House substitute and with the final legislation is remarkable. The text of the Whittington substitute is found in U.S., Congress, House, *Employment-Production Act*, H. Rep. 1334 to Accompany S.380, 79th Cong., 1st sess., 1945, pp. 1–5.

82. "Basic Principles of the Full Employment Bill: Statement by Rep. George

E. Outland, September 14, 1945," in "Full Employment H.R. 2202" folder, Box 45, Whittington MSS; "'Federal Budget and Expenditures' by Dr. Fred Fairchild, reprinted from *Washington Review*, January 15, 1940," filed in COFF Papers, 1939–1940, COCUS.

83. COCUS, *Governmental Affairs. Legislative Daily*, vol. 2, no. 255, December 7, 1945.

84. Telegram, Howard Volgenau to District Managers, n.d. (notation in index "between November 26 and December 12, 1945"), in Department of Governmental Affairs, Campaign Book No. 3, September 4, 1944 to ——, 1945, COCUS; COCUS, *Proposed Program (for 1946)*(n.p., n.d.).

85. Volgenau to Whittington, January 14, 1946, in "Full Employment Conference Report —1946" folder, Box 33, Whittington MSS. The same letter to Hoffman is in Department of Governmental Affairs, Letters and Statements Sent to Congress, 1946, COCUS.

86. Truman, on December 20, 1945, sent identical letters to Senator Robert F. Wagner and Representative Carter Manasco, calling for passage of the Senate version. Press release, December 20, 1945, in "Full Employment Conference Report—1946" folder, Box 33, Whittington MSS; Bailey, *Congress*, pp. 221–22. For an overly harsh indictment of Truman's leadership in the full employment struggle, see Markowitz, *People's Century*, pp. 143–46 and especially n. 45, p. 158.

87. U.S., Congress, House, 79th Cong., 2d sess., February 6, 1946, *Congressional Record*, 92:984. Hansen is cited in Bailey, *Congress*, p. 48. The text of the Employment Act of 1946 can be found ibid., pp. 228–32.

88. U.S., Congress, House, 79th Cong., 2d sess., February 6, 1946, *Congressional Record*, 92:979. This reaction is seen also in Fred Vinson to HST, February 9, 1946, Box 121, PSF, General File/Full Employment, HSTL; and Colm to J. Weldon Jones, February 14, 1946, Box 1, Colm MSS.

89. Keyserling, "The Keynesian Revolution and Its Pioneers: Discussion," *American Economic Review* (May 1972), 62:136–37.

90. S.380, section 3(f).

91. COCUS, *A Program for Sustaining Employment: Report of the Committee on Economic Policy* (Washington: COCUS, 1945),pp. 20–25.

92. Victor A. Thompson, *Bureaucracy and Innovation* (University: University of Alabama Press, 1969), p. 10; David McClelland, *The Achieving Society* (Princeton: Van Nostrand, 1961), pp. 221–22.

93. Prefatory note, Schmidt, *Can Government Guarantee*.

5. THE STRUGGLE TO DEVELOP AN ALTERNATIVE

1. Luce, "The American Century," *Life*, February 17, 1941, pp. 61–65. American optimism concerning the postwar future is discussed in John Fenton, *In Your Opinion* (Boston: Little, Brown, 1960), pp. 28–43; and Joseph Goulden, *The Best Years, 1945–1950* (New York: Atheneum, 1976), pp. 3–13.

2. Eric Goldman, *The Crucial Decade* (New York: Knopf, 1956), p. 14.

3. Swanson and Schmidt, *Economic Stagnation*, p. 179.

4. Terborgh, *Economic Maturity*, p. 223.

5. Swanson and Schmidt, *Economic Stagnation*, p. 166.

6. COCUS, *A Program for Sustaining Employment: Report of the Committee on Economic Policy* (Washington: COCUS, 1945),pp. 20, 31.

7. Ibid., pp. 21–24.

8. Ibid., pp. 22–24; Terborgh, *Economic Maturity*, p. 224; Swanson and Schmidt, *Economic Stagnation*, pp. 196–97.

9. Swanson and Schmidt, *Economic Stagnation*, p. 159.

10. COCUS, *Sustaining Employment*, p. 23.

11. Swanson and Schmidt, *Economic Stagnation*, p. 193.

12. "Transcript of Eric Johnston's Talk before Division Managers, September 13, 1945," in Presidential Speech File, 1942–1946, COCUS.

13. Interview with Ralph Bradford, July 10, 1974. This was not Bradford's opinion, but he recalls that such feelings were in the air.

14. "Remarks by Eric Johnston before . . . the Board, September 14, 1945," Presidential Speech File, 1942–1946; COCUS "Middle-Roaders," *Business Week*, May 4, 1946, p. 16.

15. *Time*, May 13, 1946, p. 85; *Business Week*, May 4, 1946, p. 16; NYT, May 1, p. 29; May 2, p. 16; May 3, p. 12; May 5, 3:1, 6; *Newsweek*, May 18, 1946, p. 68.

16. The self-characterization is quoted in *Current Biography Yearbook, 1946* (New York: H. H. Wilson, 1947), p. 282. *Business Week* portrayed Jackson as "a Democrat in politics and a middle-of-the-roader in economics" who could thus "be counted on as a peacemaker between Johnston's young Turks and the chamber's conservatives." May 4, 1946, p. 8.

17. Speech of May 2, 1946, in Presidential Speech File, 1946–1947, COCUS.

18. Minutes of the 34th Annual Meeting, May 2, 1946, pp. 161, 164, COCUS.

19. John C. Beukema to Bradford, May 6, 1946, Bradford MSS.

20. Ibid.

21. Bradford to Beukema, May 9, 1946, Bradford MSS.

22. COCUS, *Federal Expenditure and Tax Policies: Reports of the Committee on Federal Finance* (Washington: COCUS, 1946), p. 3. See also COCUS, *Looking Toward a Balanced Budget* (Washington: COCUS, 1946); and "Federal Expenditure Policies: Report of the Committee on Federal Finance," in Reports to the Board of Directors (hereafter cited as BOD Reports), November 22–23, 1946, vol. 2, COCUS.

23. Barton Bernstein, "Charting a Course Between Inflation and Depression: Secretary of the Treasury Fred Vinson and the Truman Administration's Tax Bill," *Register of the Kentucky Historical Society* (January 1968), 66:53–64; Holmans, *Fiscal Policy*, pp. 45–55.

24. U.S., Congress, Senate, Committee on Finance, *Revenue Act of 1945*, Hearings on H.R. 4309, 79th Cong., 1st sess., 1945, pp. 180–95. Holmans asserts that the Chamber's contention was "obviously defective in that the increase in pro-

duction is matched by an increase in income somewhere in the economy, in addition to the increase in demand that is the direct result of the tax cut. The argument only has any validity if the tax rate is so high that entrepreneurs prefer to leave their plant idle. It could not be reasonably contended that this was happening in the United States in 1945." *Fiscal Policy*, p. 48. The point remains controversial as political leaders attempt to frame economic policy for the 1980's.

25. The account of the 1947–1948 tax debate which follows is based upon Holmans, *Fiscal Policy*, pp. 58–101; Stein, *Fiscal Revolution*, pp. 206–20; Susan Hartmann, *Truman and the 80th Congress* (Columbia: University of Missouri Press, 1971), pp. 11, 74–79; 95–96; 132–36; R. Alton Lee, "The Truman–80th Congress Struggle Over Tax Policy," *The Historian* (November 1970), 33:68–82; and James T. Patterson, *Mr. Republican: A Biography of Robert A. Taft* (Boston: Houghton Mifflin, 1972), pp. 373–75.

26. NYT, November 25, 1946, p. 27. The Chamber estimated that under its program, revenues would fall $11.1 billion to a total of $28.5 billion in fiscal year 1948. This, however, would more than cover the total budget of $25 billion or less which the Chamber thought feasible. See NYT, December 8, 1946, p. 26; March 20, 1947, p. 22.

27. U.S., Congress, Senate, Committee on Finance, *Individual Income Tax Reduction, Hearings* on H.R. 1, 80th Cong., 1st sess., 1947, pp. 320–21.

28. Truman veto message, June 16, 1947, in U.S., President, *Public Papers, Truman, 1947*, p. 279; Shreve's statement, June 16, 1947, in Presidential Speech File, 1947–1949, COCUS.

29. U. S., President, *Public Papers, Truman, 1947*, p. 147; Shreve's statement, July 18, 1947, Presidential Speech File, 1947–1949, COCUS.

30. NYT, January 28, 1948, p. 16; testimony of Ellsworth Alvord, in U.S., Congress, Senate, Committee on Finance, *Reduction of Individual Income Taxes, Hearings* on H.R. 4790, 80th Cong., 2d sess., 1948, pp. 446–50; "Reduction of Federal Expenditures, Taxes and Debt: Report of the COFF," in BOD Reports, January 23–24, 1948, COCUS.

31. Of course, conservatives were not advocating a tax reduction in order to produce a deficit; the issue was whether the budget surplus to be generated would be large or small.

32. U.S., Congress, Senate, Committee on Finance, *Individual Income Tax Reduction, Hearings* on H.R. 1, p. 320.

33. Statements of June 3 and June 16, 1947, in Presidential Speech File, 1947–1949, COCUS.

34. Testimony of Ellsworth Alvord, March 9, 1948, in U.S., Congress, Senate, Committee on Finance, *Reduction of Individual Income Taxes, Hearings* on H.R. 4790, p. 447.

35. Alvord testimony, October 1945, in U.S., Congress, Senate, Committee on Finance, *Revenue Act of 1945, Hearings* on H.R. 4309, p. 193.

36. The results of 1947 polling are in *Fortune*, January 1948, p. 69.

37. Testimony of Emerson Schmidt, in U.S., Congress, Joint Committee on the Economic Report, *Current Price Developments and the Problem of Economic*

Stabilization, Hearings, 80th Cong., 1st sess., 1947, p. 316. Schmidt was more receptive than most within the Chamber to the New Economics. Asked his opinion of the pending tax reduction, he replied, "The bill is based probably on the prediction of the [*sic*] recession in 1948. If a recession does take place, which I doubt, I think the tax reduction would be well-advised." Ibid., p. 304. The 1948 tax reduction did in fact cushion the recession that began in November 1948, and significantly aided the recovery in late 1949 and 1950. Holmans, *Fiscal Policy*, p. 121.

38. Annual Budget Message, January 10, 1950, in U.S., President, *Public Papers, Truman. 1949*, p. 45. In February, two of the three members of the CEA had told Truman that inflation remained the major economic problem. Edwin Nourse was the first Council member to recognize the recession. CEA to Truman, February 4, 1949, Box 5, Edwin Nourse MSS, HSTL.

39. U.S., President, *The Midyear Economic Report of the President to the Congress, July 11, 1949* (Washington: GPO, 1949), pp. 3, 8.

40. *The Economic Situation at Midyear 1949, A Report to the President by the Council of Economic Advisers* (bound with the *Midyear Economic Report* cited above), p. 12.

41. COCUS (Finance Department), *Taxing to Spend: An Analysis of the 1950 Federal Budget Which Proposes Increased Government Costs and Higher Taxes* (Washington: COCUS, 1949), p. 15; Earl Shreve, speeches of February 22 and April 13, 1949, in Presidential Speech File, 1947–1948, COCUS; NYT, May 4, 1949, p. 3.

42. NYT, June 14, 1948, p. 39. For a good treatment of the significance of the McClellan resolution, consult Holmans, *Fiscal Policy*, pp. 115-17. See also U.S., Congress, Senate, Committee on Expenditures in the Executive Departments, *Reducing Expenditures in Government for the Fiscal Year 1950 Consistent with the Public Interest*, S. Rept. 498 to accompany S. J. Res. 108, 81st Cong., 1st sess., 1949.

43. NYT, June 24, 1949, p. 15.

44. U. S., Congress, Joint Committee on the Economic Report, *Monetary, Credit, and Fiscal Policies, Hearings* before the Subcommittee on Monetary, Credit, and Fiscal Policies, 81st Cong., 1st sess., 1949, p. 547.

45. (New York: CED, 1944). Benton to John K. Galbraith, September 29, 1944, Benton MSS (NYC); Ruml, "National Fiscal Policy" (Merrill Foundation Lecture, Princeton University, May 2, 1950), Series 2, Box 6, Ruml MSS.

46. CED, *Postwar Tax Plan*, p. 7.

47. "Taxes After the War," *Fortune*, December 1944, pp. 121–44, 228–43; "Postwar Tax Plans—CED's Entry," *Business Week*, September 9, 1944, p. 16; *Time*, September 11, 1944, pp. 88–89; Oscar Gass, "A Rich Man's Tax Program," *New Republic*, October 16, 1944, p. 481. For a rejoinder to Gass's critical assessment, see his exchange of correspondence with Professor Harold Groves, a CED consultant, in *New Republic*, December 25, 1944, pp. 868–71.

48. "Business and Taxes," *The Nation*, September 16, 1944, p. 311.

49. CED, *Postwar Tax Plan*, pp. 23–24.

50. Ibid., p. 24.

51. "Taxes After the War," Fortune, December 1944, p. 236. See also Harold Groves' letter to the editor, New Republic, December 25, 1944, p. 868; and Groves, Production, Jobs and Taxes, CED Research Study, No. 1 (New York: McGraw-Hill, 1944), pp. 101–3.

52. CED, Taxes and the Budget: A Program for Prosperity in a Free Economy (New York: CED, 1947); Hoffman to Flanders, August 22, 1947, Box 102, Flanders MSS.

53. Stein, "Facing the Inflationary Boom," (cover letter, Yntema to members of the Research and Policy Committee and members of the Research Advisory Board, July 1, 1946) in 102517/36, U.S., General Records of the Department of Commerce, General Correspondence (Record Group 40), National Archives. This memo was passed to the President and Treasury Secretary Snyder on July 2. See also Sumner Slichter to Flanders, November 23, 1946, Box 102, Flanders MSS; Ruml, "Let's Talk Business," Collier's, March 29, 1947, pp. 57–59; Ruml, "The Next Depression," Cosmopolitan, April 1947, pp. 57, 73–74; and Ruml, "Urges Government Act to Bar Slump," NYT, May 4, 1947, 3:1.

54. Hoffman to Flanders, August 22, 1947, Box 102, Flanders MSS.

55. CED, Taxes and the Budget, pp. 20, 21.

56. Ibid., pp. 22, 32. Of course, the size of the surplus to be sought at the high-employment level of national income was a critical decision. The $3 billion figure was the result of considerable debate within the CED. See Stein, Fiscal Revolution, pp. 224–25.

57. CED, Taxes and the Budget, p. 22.

58. Flanders, "Tax Policy Statement, March 25, 1944," Box 128, Flanders MSS; Melvin de Chazeau, et al., Jobs and Markets: How to Prevent Inflation and Depression in the Transition, CED Research Study (New York: McGraw-Hill, 1946), pp. 65–67, 74–76, 123–25.

59. CED, Joint Meeting of the Research Committee and Research Advisory Board, November 17–18, 1945: Notes, Box 131, Flanders MSS; CED, Joint Meeting of Research Committee and Research Advisory Board, June 24, 1947: Notes, on Reel 1, CED Archives.

60. Ruml to Alvin Hansen, May 27, 1947, Series 2, Box 5, Ruml MSS.

61. CED, Taxes and the Budget, p. 25.

62. Folsom to Flanders, August 16, 1937, Folsom MSS.

63. Stein, "The CED on Budget Policy" (October 14, 1948), Series 2, Box 5, Ruml MSS.

64. (New York: CED, 1948). An example of the CED's shift in attention from recession to inflation is provided by Stein's memo of December 5, 1947, on Reel 2, CED Archives. The Committee realized that the weapon of monetary policy was more effective against inflation than against deflation. CED, Monetary and Fiscal Policy, p. 31; Stein, "Inflation and Monetary Policy" (September 23, 1952), on Reel 29, CED Archives.

65. CED, Monetary and Fiscal Policy, p. 45. Earlier, Hoffman, in rebutting the argument for flexibility in fiscal policy, had nevertheless recognized the need for

discretionary action in the "the field of credit." CED, Joint Meeting of the Research Committee and Research Advisory Board, November 17–18, 1945: Notes, Box 131, Flanders MSS.

66. See Stein, *Fiscal Revolution*, pp. 241–80; Allan Sproul, "The 'Accord'—A Landmark in the First Fifty Years of the Federal Reserve System," *Federal Reserve Bank of New York Monthly Review*, November 1964, pp. 227–36; James Knipe, *The Federal Reserve and the American Dollar: Problems and Policies, 1946–1964* (Chapel Hill: University of North Carolina Press, 1964), pp. 50–62; Daniel Ahearn, *Federal Reserve Policy Reappraised, 1951–1959* (New York: Columbia University Press, 1963), pp. 9–21.

67. CED, *Monetary and Fiscal Policy*, pp. 44, 48.

68. Howard S. Ellis, "The Rediscovery of Money" in *Money, Trade, and Economic Growth* (New York: Macmillan, 1951), pp. 253–69.

69. Ruml, "Remarks by Way of Introduction to the CED Tax and Fiscal Proposals of 1947," Series 1, Box 2, Ruml MSS.

70. "Report on Activities of the Research Division, Fourth Quarter, 1944," Box 53, Benton MSS (Chicago).

71. Flanders, "The Research Activity of the CED" (cover letter, Flanders to Benton, January 17, 1943), Box 50, Benton MSS (Chicago).

72. Stein, "Propositions on Tax and Fiscal Policy" (May 15, 1947), on Reel 1, CED Archives; Stein, "Stabilization Policy Statement" (August 19, 1948), on Reel 2, ibid.

73. Benton, Address to CED Trustees, May 11, 1949, Box 102, Flanders MSS. See also Howard Myers, "If Anti-Depression Policies Become Necessary . . . ?" (speech to the Conference of Business Economists, June 25, 1949), on Reel 33, CED Archives.

74. Ruml to Dudley Cates, September 17, 1945, Series 2, Box 3, Ruml MSS.

75. CED, *Taxes and the Budget*, p. 30. See also Stein, "Propositions on Tax and Fiscal Policy" (May 15, 1947), on Reel 1, CED Archives.

76. Flanders, "The Research Activity of the CED" (cover letter, Flanders to Benton, January 17, 1943), Box 50, Benton MSS (Chicago).

77. Jacoby, *Can Prosperity Be Sustained?* (New York: Henry Holt, 1956), p. 91. See also I. O. Scott, "Monetary and Debt Management Policies" (September 21, 1956), on Reel 29, CED Archives.

78. Stein, "What Can CED Say About Monetary Policy?" (February 11, 1952), on Reel 29, CED Archives.

79. Address to CED Trustees, May 11, 1949, Box 102, Flanders MSS.

80. Flanders, "The Research Activity of the CED," Box 50, Benton MSS (Chicago).

6. THE ASCENDANCY OF COMMERCIAL KEYNESIANISM

1. "Remarks of Donald David before CED Trustees, May 16, 1957," Box 102, Flanders MSS; Holmans, *Fiscal Policy*, pp. 296–99; Lewis, *Postwar Recessions*,

pp. 15–19; Robert A. Gordon, *Economic Instability and Growth: The American Record* (New York: Harper and Row, 1974), pp. 105–7, 133–36, 203–4; Heller, "Ced's Stabilizing Budget Policy After Ten Years," *American Economic Review* (September 1957), 47:634.

2. Norman Keiser, "The Development of the Concept of 'Automatic Stabilizers,'" *Journal of Finance* (December 1956), 11:436–37.

3. Folsom Memoir (Eisenhower Project), COHC; CED Executive Director H. R. Johnson, quoted in CED, Minutes, Board of Trustees, April 18, 1947, Folsom MSS. See also CED, Joint Research Meeting, September 25–26, 1943, Box 127, Flanders MSS.

4. "Report on the Press Coverage of Defense Against Inflation," on Reel 9, CED Archives. See also Nate White, "CED 'Idea Men' Scan Economic Horizons of U.S.," *Christian Science Monitor*, October 10, 1955, p. 10.

5. McCracken, "The Present Status of Monetary and Fiscal Policy," *Journal of Finance* (March 1950), 5:42.

6. The apt phrase was used by Robert Lenhart (CED Vice President, Administration) in an interview with the author, May 8, 1975.

7. Kolko, *Wealth and Power*, p. 33.

8. Flanders to Leeds, January 8, 1937, Box 32, Flanders MSS.

9. Kolko, *Wealth and Power*, p. 33; Polenberg, *War and Society*, pp. 27–28; Randolph Paul, *Taxation in the United States* (Boston: Little, Brown, 1954), pp. 294–326.

10. The account that follows is based upon Paul, *Taxation*, pp. 326–49; "The History of the Pay-As-You-Go Income Tax" (unpublished memorandum, dated January, 1957), Series 2, Box 2, Ruml MSS; "Chronology of Pay-As-You-Go Income Tax Plan 1942-1943" (Revised, September 1956), Series 2, Box 1, ibid.; John Morton Blum, *From the Morgenthau Diaries: Years of War, 1941–1945* (Boston: Houghton Mifflin, 1967), pp. 49–52, 58–64.

11. "Heritage—Beardsley Ruml #1" (transcript of television interview, May 13, 1958), Series 1, Box 3, Ruml MSS. See also the June 30, 1942 version of Ruml's Pay-As-You-Go Income Tax Plan in U.S., Congress, Senate, Committee on Finance, *Revenue Act of 1942, Hearings* on H.R. 7378, 77th Cong., 2d sess., 1942, 1:188, and Ruml's testimony, ibid., p. 1976.

12. Ruml to Morgenthau, March 30, 1942, Series 2, Box 2, Ruml MSS.

13. See for example, the testimony of Randolph Paul, General Counsel for the Treasury Department, in U.S., Congress, House, Committee on Ways and Means, *Individual Income Tax, Hearings* on a proposal to place income tax of individuals on a pay-as-you-go basis, 78th Cong., 1st sess., 1943, pp. 18–19. Representative Frank Carlson (R-Ka.) called the resulting legislative struggle "one of the hardest fights we had in Congress for years." Carlson to Ruml, May 26, 1943, Series 2, Box 2, Ruml MSS.

14. Gallup, *Gallup Poll*, 1:366.

15. Carlson to Ruml, May 26, 1943, Series 2, Box 2, Ruml MSS; Gearhart quoted in Paul, *Taxation*, p. 341.

16. Schriftgiesser, *Business Comes of Age*, p. 162.

17. Stein, interview with the author, Charlottesville, Virginia, June 20, 1977. Of course, Eisenhower did not retain his membership in the CED during his Presidency. Greater detail concerning the CED's old boy network is provided in R.A. Hummel, "The Impact of CED on U.S. National Policy" (covering letter, Hummel to Flanders, January 31, 1958), Box 102, Flanders MSS. This document expresses a conspiracy theory which should be handled gingerly; the raw biographical data contained therein are, however, useful. For a recent treatment, see Frank Fowlkes, "Washington Pressures: CED's Impact on Federal Policies Enhanced by Close Ties to Executive Branch," *National Journal*, June 17, 1972, pp. 1015–24. The interchange described above has characterized both Republican and Democratic administrations.

18. For citations regarding the Fed-Treasury dispute, consult note 66, chapter 5 above. See also the materials in OF 90, HSTL; and Box 2728, Federal Open Market Committee (1922–1954)—General, Records of the Federal Reserve System, Record Group 82, National Archives, Washington, D.C. (the Federal Reserve System Records are hereafter designated FRS).

19. CED, *The Committee for Economic Development: Its Past, Present and Future: An Address by Thomas B. McCabe . . . November 17, 1949* (New York: CED, 1949), p. 3.

20. McCabe, *The Role of CED Today* (New York: CED, 1951), p. 2. This is the published text of an address to the CED trustees, November 15, 1950. See also McCabe's speech, Birmingham, Alabama, December 12, 1950, Box 11, Subject File 001.411, FRS.

21. McCabe, "We Dared Not Leave Economic Solutions to Chance," in Walton, *Business and Social Progress*, p. 85. See also McCabe's comments in CED, *Report of Activities in 1963* (New York: CED, 1964), p. 1. Regarding the importance of McCabe's role in bringing about the accord, see the opinion of James O'Leary, chairman of the National Bureau of Economic Research, in *NYT*, January 11, 1978, p. 3(D).

22. Keyserling to HST, February 15, 1951, Subject File/Agencies/CEA, PSF, HSTL.

23. "Report of the Committee on Research and Statistics to the Presidents' Conference," October 6, 1943; "Minutes of the Meeting of Subcommittee of the Presidents' Conference Committee on Research and Statistics," October 21, 1943; "Cooperation of Federal Reserve Bank Research Departments with Other Research Agencies," February 26, 1944, all in Box 2256, Subject File 500.71, FRS; McCabe to J. Cameron Thomson, April 20, 1950, Box 2186; Hoffman to Eccles, August 12, 1946, Box 2185; Young to Stein, February 26, 1948, Box 2186; Henry Johnston (executive director, CED) to Young, March 15, 1948, Box 2186; Young to Fed Personnel Committee, April 3, 1950, Box 2186; F.A. Nelson to Young, April 5, 1950, Box 2186; Young to E. A. Goldenweiser, December 31, 1952, Box 2188; Young to Board of Governors, October 17, 1947; January 5, 1948; January 13, 1948; and February 9, 1948, Box 2186, all in Subject File 500.001, FRS.

24. Woodlief Thomas to Board of Governors, March 9, 1945, Box 2256, Subject File 500.71, FRS; R. M. Evans to Flanders, November 4, 1946, Box 2185, Subject

File 500.001, FRS; Flanders to Evans, November 6, 1946, ibid.; Ralph Young to Theodore Yntema, December 20, 1946, ibid.

25. U.S., Department of Commerce, *Markets after the Defense Expansion* (Washington: GPO, 1952), title page, iii–iv. On the CED's role, see Howard Myers to Folsom, March 11, 1952; Wesley Rennie to Folsom, September 12, 1952; and "CED, Summary Record of Meeting . . . September 18, 1952," all in Folsom MSS.

26. Gabriel Hauge to Robert Cutler, January 15, 1953, OF 114, DDEL.

27. Galbraith, *Economics and the Art of Controversy* (New York: Vintage Books, 1959), pp. 55–56.

28. Quoted in Herbert Parmet, *Eisenhower and the American Crusades* (New York: Macmillan, 1972), p. 36. Regarding the "surrender," see ibid., pp. 129–30; and Peter Lyon, *Eisenhower: Portrait of the Hero* (Boston: Little, Brown, 1974), pp. 478–79.

29. Quoted in Parmet, *Eisenhower*, p. 42. See also Henry Cabot Lodge, Jr., "Eisenhower and the GOP," *Harper's*, May 1952, pp. 34–39.

30. DDE to Russell Leffingwell, February 16, 1954, Box 3, Whitman File, Diary Series, DDEL. See also DDE to Milton Eisenhower, January 6, 1954, Box 12, Whitman File, Name Series, DDEL. This view of Eisenhower as more complicated—and moderate—than a traditional conservative is at odds with many contemporary assessments of his presidency. Gary Reichard, *The Reaffirmation of Republicanism: Eisenhower and the Eighty-third Congress* (Knoxville: University of Kentucky Press, 1975), pp. 227–37, continues to emphasize Eisenhower's ideological conservatism. Others, however, view Eisenhower differently. See, for example, Fred Greenstein, "Eisenhower as an Activist President: A Look at New Evidence," *Political Science Quarterly* (Winter 1979/1980), 94:575–99; and Robert Griffith, "Why They Liked Ike," *Reviews in American History* (December 1979), 7:577–83.

31. Sherman Adams, *Firsthand Report: The Story of the Eisenhower Administration* (New York: Harper and Brothers, 1961), p. 154.

32. DDE to Leffingwell, February 16, 1954, Box 3, Whitman File, Diary Series, DDEL. See also DDE to James Mitchell, December 21, 1957, Box 17, Whitman File, Diary Series, DDEL.

33. Box 18, Telephone Log, Whitman File, Diary Series, DDEL.

34. Hauge, speech, October 14, 1955, Box 19, Whitman File, Administrative Series, DDEL. See also Hauge to Humphrey, March 25, 1953, Box 7, Arthur Burns MSS, DDEL; Hauge to DDE, May 26, 1958, Box 20, Whitman File, Administrative Series, DDEL.

35. Adams, *Firsthand Report*, p. 156.

36. Burns, speech, June 16, 1955, Box 10, Whitman File, Administrative Series, DDEL. Regarding Burns's acceptance of Keynesianism, see Flash, *Economic Advice*, pp. 102–3; and Stein, *Fiscal Revolution*, pp. 293–94.

37. Both quotations are from Stein, *Fiscal Revolution*, p. 295. Humphrey's public statements are found in Nathaniel Howard, ed., *The Basic Papers of George M. Humphrey* (Cleveland: Western Reserve Historical Society, 1965).

38. NYT, March 7, 1953, p. 11. On the reestablishment of the Council, see

DDE to Styles Bridges, February 26, 1953; and Joseph Dodge to James Murray, March 26, 1953, both in OF 72(E), DDEL; Flash, *Economic Advice*, pp. 95–107.

39. DDE to Burns, June 6, 1953, Box 9, Burns MSS, DDEL.

40. Flash, *Economic Advice*, pp. 170–71. The minutes of several ABEGS meetings are in Box 5, Neil Jacoby MSS, DDEL. See also Burns, *Prosperity Without Inflation* (New York: Fordham University Press, 1957), pp. 86–89.

41. Wesley Rennie to Folsom, January 15, 1953; memo, Program Committee, CED to Eisenhower, January 14, 1953, both in Folsom MSS.

42. Cabinet Minutes, September 25, 1953, Box 2, Whitman File, Cabinet Series, DDEL. See also Cabinet Minutes, January 15, 1954, ibid.; and James Hagerty Diary, March 26, 1954, Hagerty MSS, DDEL.

43. Cabinet Minutes, September 25, 1953, Box 2, Whitman File, Cabinet Series, DDEL. See also "Counter-Depression Measures," September 23, 1953, Box 17, Burns MSS, DDEL.

44. Neil Jacoby, "An Evaluation of Federal Actions Since Mid-1953 to Promote a Prosperous Economy," October 23, 1954, Box 17, Burns MSS. The recession is treated in Stein, *Fiscal Revolution*, pp. 281–308; Holmans, *Fiscal Policy*, pp. 211–42; Lewis, *Postwar Recessions*, pp. 131–87.

45. DDE to Burns, February 2, 1954, Box 3, Whitman File, Cabinet Series, DDEL; Cabinet Minutes, February 5, 1954, ibid.

46. Diary entry, April 8, 1954, Box 3, Whitman File, Diary Series, DDEL.

47. Cabinet Minutes, May 14, 1954; Rowland Hughes to Maxwell Rabb, June 22, 1954; Adams to Lewis, July 8, 1954, all in Box 3, Whitman File, Cabinet Series, DDEL.

48. U.S., President, *Economic Report of the President, Transmitted to the Congress January, 1966* (Washington: GPO, 1966), p. 173. See also Neil Jacoby, "The President, the Constitution, and the Economist in Economic Stabilization," *History of Political Economy* (Fall 1971), 3:407–8; and Saul Engelbourg, "The Council of Economic Advisers and the Recession of 1953–1954," *Business History Review* (Summer 1980), 54:192–214.

49. Quoted in Stein, *Fiscal Revolution*, p. 283. See also Seymour Harris to Sherman Adams, March 29, 1954, OF 114, DDEL.

50. U.S., Congress, Joint Economic Committee, *January 1960 Economic Report of the President, Hearings*, 86th Cong., 2d sess., 1960, p. 455. See also Anderson, speech, December 29, 1959, Box 3, Whitman File, Administrative Series, DDEL; and Anderson to DDE, December 12, 1960, Box 2, ibid.

51. U.S., Congress, Joint Committee on the Economic Report, *January 1949 Economic Report of the President, Hearings*, 81st Cong., 1st sess., 1949, pp. 601–2.

52. "Reports of the Department of Manufacture Committee" in BOD Reports, March 25-26, 1949, vol. 2; Minutes, Board of Directors, March 25, 1949, both in COCUS.

53. "Interim Report on Depression Policy: Submitted by the Committee on Economic Policy," in BOD Reports, November 18–19, 1949, COCUS.

54. "An Annually Balanced Budget: Preparatory Memo (No.9) for Committee

on Federal Finance," in COFF Papers, January 13, 1950, COCUS. The Committee on Federal Finance was a membership committee serviced by and attached to the Finance Department of the Chamber. The Committee on Economic Policy, also a membership committee, was attached to the Economic Research Department.

55. Minutes, Meeting of the Committee on Federal Finance, in COFF Papers, January 13, 1950, COCUS; Minutes, Board of Directors, March 24, 1950, COCUS.

56. "Committee on Economic Policy Suggestions in Regard to Chamber Policies," in Policy Committee Notes, 1953, vol. 2, COCUS.

57. COCUS, Policy Declarations of the Chamber of Commerce of the United States (Washington: COCUS, 1953), p. 33.

58. Memo, "Proposed Policies on Economic Stability and the Federal Budget," (Covering letter, Emerson Schmidt to Clem Johnston, February 12, 1954) in Clem Johnston MSS (privately held, Roanoke, Virginia). See also Minutes, Board of Directors, January 21–22, 1954; and "Economic Stability: Recommended Policy Declarations of the Economic Policy Committee," Policy Committee Notes, 1954, vol. 1, both in COCUS.

59. COCUS, Policy Declarations (Washington: COCUS, 1952), pp. 76–77.

60. COCUS, Policy Declarations (Washington: COCUS, 1954), pp. 32–33.

61. Ibid., pp. 2–3.

62. May 7, 1954, p. 10.

63. Schmidt to Clem Johnston, February 12, 1954, Clem Johnston MSS.

64. Emerson Schmidt, "Industrial Expansion Program of CEP," Business Action, May 29, 1944, p. 3.

65. Schmidt to the author, August 15, 1974.

66. Quoted in "Words on Enterprise," Newsweek, May 16, 1949, p. 67.

67. "Memo: Committee on Economic Policy" in BOD Reports, March 24–25, 1950, vol. 2, COCUS.

68. "An Annually Balanced Budget: Preparatory Memo (No. 9) for Committee on Federal Finance," in COFF Papers, January 13, 1950, COCUS.

69. Minutes, Board of Directors, September 27, 1948, and November 19, 1948, COCUS; "A National Monetary Commission: Report of the Finance Department Committee," in BOD Reports, November 19–20, 1948, COCUS.

70. U.S., President, Public Papers, Truman, 1949, pp. 1–7. The measures are discussed in James E. Murray, "A Plan to Maintain Prosperity," New Republic, July 11, 1949, pp. 12–14; "The Dispensers of Fear," Fortune, August 1949, pp. 47–48; Hamby, Beyond the New Deal, pp. 331–32. For the Chamber's reaction, see COCUS, The Drive for a Controlled Economy Via Pale Pink Pills (Washington: COCUS, 1949); Minutes, Board of Directors, March 26, 1949; and "All-Out Control of Enterprise System (Proposed Economic Stability Act of 1949): Report of the Department of Manufacture Committee" in BOD Reports, March 25-26, 1949, vol. 2, COCUS.

71. Interviews with Emerson Schmidt, July 20, 1974; and George Terborgh, November 15, 1974.

72. COCUS, A Program for Expanding Jobs and Production: Report of the Committee on Economic Policy (Washington: COCUS, 1953), unnumbered intro-

ductory page. See also "Committee on Economic Policy Suggestions in Regard to Chamber Policies" in Policy Committee Notes, 1953, vol. 2, COCUS.

73. "The Economic Outlook: Report to the Board of Directors, January 21, 1954," in Clem Johnston MSS.

74. "Proposed Policies on Economic Stability and the Federal Budget," (covering letter, Schmidt to Johnston, February 12, 1954), ibid.

75. "The Year Ahead," *Economic Intelligence*, January 1954, p. 1. This was a monthly publication of the Chamber's Economic Research Department. See also COCUS, *Program for Expanding Jobs*, p. 1; "The Boom Fed Boom," *Economic Intelligence*, April 1954, p. 1.

76. "Remarks by Clark Warburton at a Meeting of the COEP, February 27, 1953," in the author's possession, courtesy of Dr. Schmidt; letter, Schmidt to the author, July 31, 1974; interview with Schmidt, July 29, 1974. For a full development of Warburton's thought, see his *Depression, Inflation, and Monetary Policy: Selected Papers, 1945–1953* (Baltimore: Johns Hopkins University Press, 1966). A critical assessment of his theory is available in Rendigs Fels, "Warburton vs. Hansen and Keynes," *American Economic Review* (September 1949), 39:923–29.

77. Schmidt, "Memoire: Dr. Clark Warburton and the Money Supply," (February 21, 1967), in the possession of the author, courtesy of Dr. Schmidt.

78. "Why Balance the Budget?" *Economic Intelligence*, July 1954, p. 2.

79. "The Economic Outlook: Report to the Board of Directors, January 21, 1954," in Clem Johnston MSS.

80. COCUS, *Annual Report, 1954*, p. 50.

81. Alan Otten and Charles Seib, "There Goes the Man Who Cut the Budget," *Nation's Business*, May 1954, p. 43; "National Affairs Are Personal Affairs" (draft of speech to be delivered in September 1954), Clem Johnston MSS. On the general business reaction to the return of the Republicans to the White House, see Krooss, *Executive Opinion*, pp. 246–47.

82. "Proceedings, 41st Annual Meeting, Policy Luncheon Session, April 29, 1953," in Policy Committee Notes, 1953, vol. 2, COCUS. By this time, budget balancing was given a higher priority by the public at large than by the supposedly rigid businessmen of the Chamber. A Gallup poll published in August, 1953, found 52 percent opposed to a tax reduction that would leave the budget unbalanced. Gallup, *Public Opinion*, 2:1164–65.

83. Interview with Emerson Schmidt, July 29, 1974; letter, Schmidt to author, July 31, 1974.

84. Clem Johnston in COCUS, *Annual Report. 1955* (Washington: COCUS, 1955), p. 55; "Statement to the Democratic National Committee, May 12, 1960," Clem Johnston MSS; Minutes, Board of Directors, January 30–31, 1959, COCUS. The Chamber's dismissal of the annually balanced budget is evident in Walter Fackler (Assistant Director of Economic Research, COCUS), "Government Spending and Economic Stability," in U.S., Congress, Joint Economic Committee, *Federal Expenditure Policy for Economic Growth and Stability: Papers*, Joint Committee Print, 85th Cong., 1st sess., 1957, p. 330. The change in the Chamber's position can be seen by comparing the above with the Chamber's statement to the Douglas

subcommittee in 1949. See U.S., Congress, Joint Committee on the Economic Report, *Monetary, Credit, and Fiscal Policy, Hearings*, 81st Cong., 1st sess., 1949, pp. 544–58.

85. Chamber statement in U.S., Congress, Joint Economic Committee, *Employment, Growth, and Price Levels, Hearings* pursuant to S. Con. Res. 13, 86th Cong., 1st sess., 1959, pt. 9-B, p. 3154. See also "Economic Prospects," *Economic Intelligence*, April 1954, p. 1; Fackler, "Government Spending," in U.S., Congress, Joint Economic Committee, *Federal Expenditure Policy for Economic Growth and Stability: Papers*, pp. 338–42; COCUS, *Economic Lessons of Postwar Recessions* (Washington: COCUS, 1959), pp. 20–31.

86. (2 vols.; New York: McGraw-Hill, 1946), pp. 949–63.

87. U.S., Congress, Joint Committee on the Economic Report, *Monetary, Credit, and Fiscal Policy, Hearings*, 81st Cong., 1st sess., 1949, pp. 366–85.

88. "Comment on CED: 'Jobs and Markets,'" memo by Bradford Bixby Smith (Advisory Group to the NAM Committee on Economic Stability), May 3, 1946, drawer 73 (yellow), storage, NAM MSS.

89. Robey, "Federal Spending and Economic Stability," in U.S., Congress, Joint Economic Committee, *Federal Expenditure Policy for Economic Growth and Stability: Papers*, p. 402.

90. NAM, *Money and Credit Management* (New York: NAM, 1955), p. 26.

7. BUSINESS AND THE NEW ECONOMICS OF THE KENNEDY ERA

1. Stein, "The CED on Budget Policy," (speech, October 1948), Series 2, Box 5, Ruml MSS.

2. Stein, "Budget Policy to Maintain Stability," in CED, *Problems in Anti-Recession Policy*, CED Supplementary Paper (New York: CED, 1954), p. 97.

3. CED, *Defense Against Recession: Policy for Greater Economic Stability* (New York: CED, 1954), pp. 10-48.

4. Robert Lenhart, "Case Study of 'Defense Against Recession'" (March 31, 1954), Reel 6, CED Archives.

5. Stein recalls, "When it released the statement in March, the committee considered whether its policy called for extraordinary action then and decided that the situation did not fall within even the milder terms of its new position." *Fiscal Revolution*, p. 499 (n. 45).

6. See, for example, the remarks of Donald David, May 16, 1957, in Folsom MSS.

7. Statistics from U.S., President, *Economic Report of the President . . . January 20, 1959* (Washington: GPO, 1959), pp. 139, 160.

8. Press release, March 22, 1958. See also Stein to Members, Research and Policy Tax Subcommittee, February 25, 1958; and Edward F. Denison, "Anti-Recession Policy for the Federal Government in 1958" (February 25, 1958), all on

Reel 9, CED Archives. The program committee was a small group empowered to issue interpretations of established CED policy in "crisis" situations.

9. U.S., Congress, Joint Economic Committee, *Fiscal Policy Implications of the Current Economic Outlook, Hearings* before the subcommittee on fiscal policy, 81st Cong., 2d sess., 1958, pp. 160–86.

10. Allan Sproul to Stein, May 13, 1958; memo, Stein to the Program Committee, May 15, 1958; "Program Committee Meeting, May 19, 1958 (Lenhart Notebook)," all on Reel 9, CED Archives.

11. Raymond Saulnier Memoir, COHC. Saulnier supported tax reduction. See Saulnier to DDE, February 10, 1958, Box 10, Whitman File, Cabinet Series, DDEL; and Saulnier to DDE, May 23, 1958, Box 2, Whitman File, Administrative Series, DDEL.

12. DDE to H. Christian Sonne, April 23, 1958, OF 114, DDEL; DDE to Nelson Rockefeller, Box 19, Whitman File, Diary Series, DDEL. Evidence of the schism within the administration is found in Hauge to Whitman, May 15, 1958, Box 20, Whitman File, Diary Series, DDEL. Old advisers helped not at all: George Humphrey, retired from public life and thus freed from any necessity to temper his innate conservatism, warned that "if you give an inch, they'll take a mile, and the only way to save a runaway is to stand pat on everything." Humphrey to DDE, May 13, 1958, Box 23, Whitman File, Administrative Series, DDEL. Arthur Burns, on the other hand, supported a tax reduction as "a solution based on free enterprise, in contrast to the public works programs which can only serve to expand the role of government in our economy." Burns to DDE, March 10, 1958, Box 10, Whitman File, Administrative Series, DDEL. See also Burns to DDE, May 5 and 12, 1958, ibid.

13. Hauge to Whitman, March 13, 1958, OF 114, DDEL; DDE to Knowland and Martin, March 8, 1958, Box 19, Whitman File, DDEL. As in 1954, however, the administration did accelerate public works spending within budget limits.

14. DDE to Donald Kennedy, April 14, 1958, OF 114, DDEL.

15. Hauge to Whitman, May 15, 1958, Box 20, Whitman File, Diary Series, DDEL; Cabinet Minutes, May 2, 1958, Box 11, Whitman File, Cabinet Series, DDEL.

16. DDE to Donald Kennedy, April 14, 1958, OF 114, DDEL.

17. DDE to Burns, May 15, 1958, Box 10, Whitman File, Administrative Series, DDEL; DDE to Owen Cheatham, OF 114, DDEL.

18. "A Modern Tax Policy for a Recession," *Vital Speeches*, May 15, 1958, p. 474.

19. The following discussion of the political economy of the New Frontier is based upon Arthur Schlesinger, Jr., *A Thousand Days: John F. Kennedy in the White House* (Boston: Houghton Mifflin, 1965), pp. 620–31, 644–51, 1002–14; Theodore Sorensen, *Kennedy* (New York: Harper and Row, 1965), pp. 393–433; Seymour Harris, *Economics of the Kennedy Years and a Look Ahead* (New York: Harper and Row, 1964); Walter Heller, *New Dimensions of Political Economy* (Cambridge: Harvard University Press, 1966), pp. 1–82; Tobin, *Intellectual Revolution*; Bernard Nossiter, *The Mythmakers: An Essay on Power and Wealth* (Boston: Houghton Mifflin, 1964), pp. 1–42; Hobart Rowen, *The Free Enterprisers:*

Kennedy, Johnson and the Business Establishment (New York: G. P. Putnam's Sons, 1964); Jim Heath, *John F. Kennedy and the Business Community* (Chicago: University of Chicago Press, 1969), pp. 22–47, 114–22; and Stein, *Fiscal Revolution*, pp. 373–453.

20. Harris, *Economics of the Kennedy Years*, p. 23. JFK's primary advisers included Keynesians John Kenneth Galbraith, Paul Samuelson, James Tobin, Kermit Gordon, Walter Heller and Seymour Harris. Treasury Secretary Douglas Dillon, an important influence on economic policy questions, was a moderate; he shunned the Keynesian label but exhibited a flexibility much like that of the CED on fiscal issues.

21. Quoted in Schlesinger, *Thousand Days*, p. 649.

22. Stein, *Fiscal Revolution*, p. 391; U.S., President, *Public Papers, Kennedy, 1961*, pp. 41–53; Council of Economic Advisers, "The First Six Months of the Kennedy Administration: Economic Policy" (revised July 27, 1961), Walter Heller MSS, JFKL.

23. Quoted in Schlesinger, *Thousand Days*, p. 629. See also Paul Samuelson's remarks (p. 174) in the Council of Economic Advisers Oral History Memoir, JFKL (hereafter CEA Memoir).

24. On July 21, Kennedy actually approved a tax increase of just under $2 billion. The decision was later rescinded. Dillon to Sorensen, July 21, 1961, Box 40, Theodore Sorensen MSS, JFKL.

25. Yale Commencement Address, June 11, 1962, in U.S., President, *Public Papers, Kennedy, 1962*, pp. 470–75.

26. Quoted in Schlesinger, *Thousand Days*, p. 628.

27. See for example, Council of Economic Advisers, "Memo, The Problem of Full Recovery" (May 24, 1961), Box 21, Heller MSS.

28. Samuelson, CEA Memoir, p. 171. See also "Prospects and Policies for the 1961 American Economy: A Report to President-elect Kennedy by Paul A. Samuelson" (January, 1961), Box 21, Heller MSS.

29. Heller to Colwell, Brown and Kaplan, March 23, 1961. See also Heller to Tobin and Gordon, February 20, 1961, both in Box 21, Heller MSS.

30. Heller to JFK, March 21, 1962, Box 31, Sorensen MSS. See also Heller, CEA Memoir, p. 173.

31. Heller to JFK, June 2, 1962, Box 31, Sorensen MSS; CEA, "Possible Government Action," May 29, 1962, Box 40, ibid.; CEA, "Proposals for Tax Reduction," June 5, 1962, ibid. In the wake of the stock market collapse, the CEA warned that "the odds on a recession beginning in 1962" had fallen from 20 to 1 to 10 or even 5 to 1. Heller to JFK, June 5, 1962, Box 29, ibid.

32. CEA, "Proposals for Tax Reduction," June 5, 1962, Box 40, Sorensen MSS.

33. U.S., President, *Public Papers, Kennedy, 1962*, p. 457.

34. Heller to JFK, August 9, 1962, Box 22, Heller MSS.

35. Memo, CEA to JFK, June 16, 1962, Box 22, Heller MSS.

36. On fears of congressional disapproval, see Sorensen, *Kennedy*, pp. 425–26. The reduction planned by the administration in mid-July—designed as an adjunct

to reform—was only $3 billion, far smaller than that envisaged by the tax cutters. Heller to JFK, July 13, 1962, Box 22, Heller MSS.

37. This paragraph is based on Karl Schriftgiesser, *The Commission on Money and Credit: An Adventure in Policy-Making* (Englewood Cliffs, N.J.: Prentice-Hall, 1974), pp. 3-43.

38. CMC, *Money and Credit, Their Influence on Jobs, Prices and Growth: The Report of the Commission on Money and Credit* (Englewood Cliffs, N.J.: Prentice-Hall, 1961), p. 137.

39. Schriftgiesser, *Commission on Money and Credit*, pp. 37, 43.

40. U. S., President, *Economic Report of the President, 1962*, pp. 18, 21–22.

41. Press release, June 29, 1962; "Summary of the Business Outlook Conference, June 29, 1962"; "Meet the Press" transcript, July 15, 1962, all in Presidential Speech File, 1962–1963, COCUS; Minutes, Board of Directors, June 29-30, 1962, COCUS.

42. Letter, Byrd to Plumley, July 6, 1962, *Congressional Record*, 108:1283–84.

43. Plumley to Byrd, July 11, 1962, Presidential Speech File, 1962–1963, COCUS. See also Plumley to Byrd, July 5, 1962, and J. Kirk Eads to Byrd, July 2, 1962, ibid.; and Byrd to Arch Booth (executive vice-president, COCUS), July 11, 1962, in *Congressional Record*, 108:1332–36.

44. Heller to JFK (cable), June 29, 1962, Box 22, Heller MSS.

45. Schlesinger to JFK, July 17, 1962, Box 22, Heller MSS.

46. See, for example: Heller to JFK, July 12, 1962, Box 22; October 9, 1962, Box 5; November 10, 1962, Box 22; November 15, 1962, Box 22, all in Heller MSS.

47. Cabinet Committee on Economic Growth to JFK, December 1, 1962, Box 40, Sorensen MSS.

48. Galbraith's importunities are recounted in Schlesinger, *Thousand Days*, pp. 648–49. See, for example, Galbraith to JFK, March 25, 1961; undated memo, Galbraith to JFK, "Tax Reduction, Tax Reform and the Problem in this Path," both in Box 2, John Kenneth Galbraith MSS, JFKL; and Galbraith to Schlesinger, February 8, 1963, Box 11, Arthur M. Schlesinger, Jr., MSS, JFKL.

49. Hansen to David McCord Wright, July 30, 1945, Box 2, HUG (FP)-3.10, Hansen MSS.

50. The characterization of Keyserling is in Neil Jacoby to Hauge, June 30, 1955, Box 7, Burns MSS. See, for example, Keyserling's *Consumption—Key to Full Prosperity* (Washington: Conference on Economic Progress, 1957); Keyserling Oral History Memoir, HSTL; Hansen, "The Task of Promoting Economic Growth and Stability," February 20, 1956, Box 1, HUG(FP)-3.42, Hansen MSS; "Spontaneous Prosperity Versus Contrived Prosperity," n.d. [1963], Box 2, HUG(FP)-3.10, ibid.; Hansen, *The American Economy* (New York: McGraw-Hill, 1957).

51. "The American Economy 1925, 1955, and 1965," n.d. [1955], Box 1, HUG(FP)-3.42, Hansen MSS. In 1969, Galbraith wrote to Hansen, "I never doubted that you had anticipated points that I had made in *The Affluent Society*." Galbraith to Hansen, May 27, 1969, Box 1, HUG(FP)-3.10, ibid.

52. Hansen to Ackley, April 23, 1963, Box 2, HUG(FP)-3.10, Hansen MSS;

Hansen, "Stagnation and Under-employment Equilibrium," *Rostra Economica Amstelodamensia* (November 1966), p. 9, n.1.

53. Heller to JFK, December 16, 1962, Box 22, Heller MSS.

54. Heller, *New Dimensions*, p. 34; Sorensen, *Kennedy*, pp. 429–30.

55. U.S., President, *Public Papers, Kennedy, 1962*, p. 88.

56. Sorensen, *Kennedy*, p. 430; Heller, *New Dimensions*, p. 35.

57. NYT, December 19, 1962, p.1; NAM, *The Federal Budget for 1964: Report of the Government Economy Committee, February–April, 1963* (New York: NAM, 1963), p. 7.

58. CED, *Reducing Tax Rates for Production and Growth* (New York: CED, 1962), p. 7.

59. Heller to Stein, December 22, 1962, Box 22, Heller MSS.

60. Paul Sarbanes to Heller, December 21, 1962, ibid.

61. Heller to JFK, December 16, 1962, ibid.

62. Heller, *New Dimensions*, p. 35; Sorensen, *Kennedy*, p. 430; U.S., President, *Public Papers, Kennedy, 1963*, pp. 73–92.

63. Prothro, *Dollar Decade*, pp. 120–36; Francis Sutton, et al., *The American Business Creed* (Cambridge: Harvard University Press, 1956), pp. 196–99.

64. "Realism in Fiscal and Monetary Policy," in CED, *Taxes and Trade: Twenty Years of CED Policy* (New York: CED, 1963), p. 19. See also COCUS, *The United States Balance of Payments Position* (Washington: COCUS, 1961), p. 15.

65. Heller, *New Dimensions*, p. 35.

66. Press release, June 29, 1962, in Presidential Speech File, 1962–1963, COCUS. See also "Hidden Tax Rise Limits Your Prosperity," *Nation's Business*, April 1962, p. 70.

67. U.S., Congress, Joint Economic Committee, *State of the Economy and Policies for Full Employment, Hearings*, 87th Cong., 2d sess., 1962, p. 326. See also the testimony of W. P. Gullander in U.S., Congress, Senate, Committee on Finance, *Revenue Act of 1963, Hearings* on H.R. 8363, 88th Cong., 1st sess., 1963, pt. 3, pp. 1030–32. The Chamber was also concerned over "our current creeping business stagnation." See press release, June 29, 1962, in Presidential Speech File, 1962–1963, COCUS; and testimony of Joel Barlow in U.S., Congress, House, Committee on Ways and Means, *President's 1963 Tax Message, Hearings*, 88th Cong., 1st sess., 1963, pt. 4, p. 2308.

68. CED, *Reducing Tax Rates*, pp. 7, 35. Concern for growth was not new for the CED. In 1947 it had called for "reasonable stability of total demand at an adequate level—which means a steadily rising level of demand as our productive capacity grows." CED, *Taxes and the Budget, A Program For Prosperity in a Free Economy* (New York: CED, 1947), p. 10.

69. Heller, *New Dimensions*, p. 64.

70. U.S., President, *Public Papers, Kennedy, 1962*, p. 472; U.S., President, *Economic Report of the President, 1962* (Washington: GPO, 1962), pp. 77–78. The administrative budget is particularly inappropriate as a guide to fiscal policy because it does not include transactions involving federal trust funds, such as unemployment compensation payments and social security revenues and benefits.

Such transactions, of tremendous impact upon the economy, are covered in the consolidated cash budget format. The national income accounts budget also includes trust fund activities and has the further advantage of recording transactions between business and government on an accrual basis, i.e., when liabilities are incurred rather than when cash changes hands.

71. CED, *Taxes and the Budget*, p. 17; CED, *Fiscal and Monetary Policy for High Employment* (New York: CED, 1962), p. 29; Testimony of Emerson Schmidt in U.S., Congress, Joint Economic Committee, *January 1962 Economic Report of the President, Hearings*, 87th Cong., 2d sess., 1962, pp. 668–69; "Report of the Committee for Improving the Federal Budget, Approved by the Board October 19, 1962," in Presidential Speech File, 1962–1963, COCUS.

72. Heller, *New Dimensions*, pp. 66–67; U.S., President *Economic Report of the President, 1962*, pp. 78–81; and Heller, "Why We Must Cut Taxes," *Nation's Business*, November 1962, p. 100.

73. Tobin, *Intellectual Revolution*, p. 19.

74. Ruml, "Free Enterprise and Post-War Planning," November 12, 1943, Series 2, Box 3, Ruml, MSS; Ruml and H. Christian Sonne, *Fiscal and Monetary Policy*, National Planning Association Planning Pamphlet no. 35 (Washington: National Planning Association, 1944), pp. 8–9; CED, Joint Research Meeting, September 25–26, 1943, Discussion Notes, Box 127, Flanders MSS; CED, *Taxes and the Budget*, p. 22. At about this same time, Milton Friedman independently developed a version of the high employment budget. "A Monetary and Fiscal Framework for Economic Stability," *American Economic Review* (June 1948), 38:248. See also Keith Carlson, "Estimates of the High-Employment Budget: 1947-1967" *Federal Reserve of St. Louis Review*, June 1967, pp. 6–13; and Robert Soloman, "A Note on the Full Employment Budget Surplus," *Review of Economics and Statistics* (February 1964), 46:105–8.

75. CED, *Taxes and the Budget*, p. 24. See also "Hidden Tax Rise," *Nation's Business*, pp. 70–72.

76. Fred Maytag II, *Taxes and America's Future* (New York: NAM, 1954), pp. 5, 7. See also NAM, *A Tax Program for Economic Growth* (New York: NAM, 1955).

77. NAM, *Tax Rate Reform Means Faster Economic Growth* (New York: NAM, 1960); "Creating More Jobs . . . Now," *NAM News*, March 24, 1961, p. 3.

78. The Chamber also feared that unless taxes were cut the administration would turn to increased government spending. It found particularly disturbing Kennedy's request for stand-by authority to spend up to $2 billion for public works in case of rising unemployment. Kennedy later appended to this proposal a request for an immediate $600 million public works program for depressed areas. A watered-down version of the act was signed into law on September 14, 1962. For the Chamber's response, see its biweekly, *Here's the Issue*, May 14, 1962; and Ladd Plumley's speech, September 24, 1962, in Presidential Speech File, 1962–1963, COCUS.

79. Joseph Pechman, "Individual Income Tax Provisions of the Revenue Act of 1964," *Journal of Finance* (May 1965), 20:266. A detailed history of the congressional battle over the Kennedy-Johnson tax cut is beyond the purview of this study.

It was surely as complex as the struggle over full employment in 1945–1946 and deserves the close attention of scholars.

80. Gardner Ackley notes, Troika Meeting with Johnson, November 25, 1963, Box 23, Heller MSS. See also Lyndon Johnson, *The Vantage Point: Perspectives of the Presidency, 1963-1969* (New York: Holt, Rinehart and Winston, 1971), pp. 35–37.

81. Heller to LBJ, November 29, 1963, Box 31, Sorensen MSS; Stein, *Fiscal Revolution*, p. 511 (n. 38); Heath, *Kennedy and the Business Community*, p. 171 (n. 46). A membership list (as of September 1, 1963) is in Box 175, John W. Snyder MSS, HSTL. On the formation and membership of the Business Committee, see U.S., Congress, Senate, Committee on Finance, *Revenue Act of 1963, Hearings on H.R. 8363*, 88th Cong., 1st sess., 1963, pt. 3, pp. 1263–78; and Frazar Wilde, "Some Comments on the History and Position of the Business Committee for Tax Reduction in 1963" (September 10, 1963), in Box 23, Heller MSS. Regarding JFK's endorsement, see U.S., President, *Public Papers, Kennedy, 1963*, pp. 351, 667.

82. U.S., Congress, Senate, Committee on Finance, *Revenue Act of 1963, Hearings*, pt. 3, pp. 1248–50, 1231–32.

83. Ibid., pt. 2, pp. 475–77.

84. Speech, December 12, 1962, Presidential Speech File, 1962–1963, COCUS. See also U.S., Congress, Senate, Committee on Finance, *Revenue Act of 1963, Hearings*, pt. 2, pp. 529, 534–35.

85. U.S., Congress, House, Committee on Ways and Means, *President's 1963 Tax Message, Hearings*, 88th Cong., 1st sess., 1963, pt. 4, pp. 2310–11, 2375.

86. U.S., Congress, Senate, Committee on Finance, *Revenue Act of 1963, Hearings*, pt. 2, pp. 513–14, 535–56.

87. U.S., Congress, House, Committee on Ways and Means, *President's 1963 Tax Message, Hearings*, pt. 4, pp. 2097–98. In commenting on an article by Seymour Harris ("Why Business Buys the New Economics," *Challenge*, May–June 1966, pp. 11–12, 39), NAM president W. P. Gullander cautioned that while "a greater degree of understanding exists between business and government than at some times in the past," it remained true that "few people in business . . . would want to accept this approach [Keynesian economic theory] as holding all the answers for all time." *Challenge*, July–August 1966, p. 2.

8. RETROSPECT AND PROSPECT

1. Lippmann, "The Permanent New Deal," *Yale Review* (June 1935), 24:665.

2. *Business Week*, February 12, 1949, p. 20.

3. James Bryce, *The American Commonwealth* (2 vols.; Chicago: Charles H. Sergel, 1891), 2:474; Richard Hofstadter, *The American Political Tradition* (New York: Knopf, 1948); Louis Hartz, *The Liberal Tradition in America* (New York: Harcourt, Brace and World, 1955); Daniel Boorstin, *The Americans* (3 vols.; New York: Random House, 1958–1973).

4. The literature on American business in the twentieth century is hardly unanimous in its recognition of this flexibility. Implicit in much of Progressive history is a rigidity on the part of business which serves as a backdrop for the theme of recurrent conflict. James Prothro, *Dollar Decade*, emphasized inflexibility in his study of business ideas in the 1920s. Such views are not limited to critics. Albert Steigerwalt's unabashed apologia, *National Association of Manufacturers*, concluded that, for NAM, "the past is ever present." The most detailed description of business ideology to date, Sutton, et al., *Business Creed*, found that as of 1948–1949 the classical exposition of the creed remained dominant, although a managerial version thereof had developed. The authors' argument that the creed itself serves mainly to resolve certain basic conflicts inherent in the business role in America implies that, barring a dramatic change in the nature of that role, the major components of the creed will remain unchanged.

Several recent works, however, emphasize the adaptability of the business community. Accommodation to a changing and threatening political environment is the main theme in Robert Wiebe's *Businessmen and Reform*. Gabriel Kolko's *The Triumph of Conservatism* (New York: Free Press, 1963) and *Railroads and Regulation, 1877–1916* (Princeton: Princeton University Press, 1965) go a step further in portraying business as *initiating* political reform in order to meet the exigencies of a changing economic environment.

5. Clark Teitsworth, "Growing Role of the Company Economist," *Harvard Business Review* (January-February 1959), 37:97; "Symposium on the Industrial Economist," *Harvard Business Review* (Spring 1942), 20:375–92.

6. Loren Baritz, *The Servants of Power: A History of the Use of Social Science in American Industry* (Middletown, Conn.: Wesleyan University Press, 1960), pp. 142–43.

7. John Kenneth Galbraith, *The New Industrial State* (Boston: Houghton Mifflin, 1967), pp. 294, 292.

8. Keynes, *General Theory*, p. 383.

9. Compare, for example, the attention afforded the Chamber and the NAM with that given the CED in David Truman, *Governmental Process*; and V. O. Key, Jr., *Politics, Parties, and Pressure Groups* (5th ed.; New York: Thomas Crowell, 1964).

10. Herring, *Group Representation Before Congress* (Baltimore: Johns Hopkins Press, 1929), pp. 30–77, 126. See also Truman, *Governmental Process*, pp. 213–14.

11. For examples of this tendency, see Herman Krooss, *Executive Opinion*, p. 275; and Robert Heilbroner, "The View from the Top: Reflections on a Changing Business Ideology," in Earl Cheit, ed., *The Business Establishment* (New York: Wiley, 1964), p. 32; Ronald Radosh, "The Myth of the New Deal," in Radosh and Rothbard, eds., *Leviathan* pp. 156–58, 187.

12. Hawley, "The Discovery and Study of a 'Corporate Liberalism,'" *Business History Review* (Autumn 1978), 52:312 (n. 3).

13. See the references in note 19, chapter 4.

14. Hawley, *Problem of Monopoly*; Kim McQuaid, "The Business Advisory Council," pp. 171–97; McConnell, *Private Power*.

15. See, for example, Kim McQuaid, "Henry S. Dennison and the 'Science' of Industrial Reform, 1900-1950," *American Journal of Economics and Sociology* (January 1977), 36:79-98.

16. Evan Metcalf, "Secretary Hoover and the Emergence of Macroeconomic Management," *Business History Review* (Spring 1975), 49:60–80; Carolyn Grin, "The Unemployment Conference of 1921: An Experiment in National Cooperative Planning," *Mid-America* (April 1973), 55:83–107. For a critical view, see Robert Zieger, "Herbert Hoover, the Wage-earner, and the 'New Economic System,' 1919–1929," *Business History Review* (Summer 1977), 51:161–89.

17. Benton, speech to CED trustees, 1949, Box 1518, OF 638-A, HSTL.

18. Alfred D. Chandler and Louis Galambos define primary organizations as large-scale, complex bureaucracies which essentially organized people in order to provide goods or services. Secondary organizations coordinated the activities of primary organizations. Their important essay, "The Development of Large-Scale Economic Organizations in Modern America," is reprinted in Edwin Perkins, ed., *Men and Organizations: The American Economy in the Twentieth Century* (New York: G. P. Putnam's Sons, 1977), pp. 188–201.

19. McConnell, *Private Power*, pp. 264–75.

20. Gabriel Hauge, speech, October 14, 1955, Box 19, Whitman File, Administrative Series, DDEL; Arthur Larson, *A Republican Looks at His Party* (New York: Harper and Brothers, 1956).

21. Keyserling, Oral History Memoir (p. 15), HSTL.

22. Schlesinger, *Thousand Days*, p. 679; U.S., President, *Public Papers, Kennedy, 1962*, p. 422.

23. Galbraith to Hansen, May 27, 1969, Box 1, HUG(FP)-3.10, Hansen MSS.

Selected Bibliography

The following selected bibliography is designed to acquaint the reader with the study's major sources of inspiration and evidence. For reasons of space and clarity, citations of government documents, periodical literature, and organizational publications have been omitted. Extensive use was made of all three types of material, and the interested reader can find particular citations in the Notes.

Manuscript Collections

William Benton Papers, privately held, New York, N. Y.
William Benton Papers, University of Chicago.
Thomas C. Blaisdell, Jr., Papers, Harry S. Truman Presidential Library.
Roy Blough Papers, Harry S. Truman Presidential Library.
Ralph Bradford Papers, privately held, Ocala,Florida.
Arthur F. Burns Papers, Dwight D. Eisenhower Presidential Library.
Harry F. Byrd Papers, University of Virginia.
Chamber of Commerce of the United States Archives, Washington, D.C.
Stuart Chase Papers, Library of Congress.
John Clark Papers, Harry S. Truman Presidential Library.
Will Clayton Papers, Harry S. Truman Presidential Library.
Clark Clifford Files, Harry S. Truman Presidential Library.
Clark Clifford Papers, Harry S. Truman Presidential Library.
Gerhard Colm Papers, Harry S. Truman Presidential Library.
Committee for Economic Development Archives, Washington, D.C.
Dwight D. Eisenhower Papers, Eisenhower Presidential Library.
Ralph Flanders Papers, Syracuse University.

Marion Folsom Papers, University of Rochester.
John Kenneth Galbraith Papers, John F. Kennedy Presidential Library.
James Hagerty Papers, Dwight D. Eisenhower Presidential Library.
Alvin Hansen Papers, Harvard University.
Gabriel Hauge Papers, Dwight D. Eisenhower Presidential Library.
Walter Heller Papers, John F. Kennedy Presidential Library.
Leon Henderson Papers, Franklin D. Roosevelt Presidential Library.
Lou Holland Papers, Harry S. Truman Presidential Library.
Harry Hopkins Papers, Franklin D. Roosevelt Presidential Library.
Neil Jacoby Papers, Dwight D. Eisenhower Presidential Library.
Clem Johnston Papers, privately held, Roanoke, Virginia.
Jesse H. Jones Papers, Library of Congress.
J. Weldon Jones Papers, Harry S. Truman Presidential Library.
Meyer Kestnbaum Records, Dwight D. Eisenhower Presidential Library.
James Loeb Files, Harry S. Truman Presidential Library.
Henry Morgenthau, Jr., Papers, Franklin D. Roosevelt Presidental Library.
Charles Murphy Files, Harry S. Truman Presidential Library.
National Association of Manufacturers Archives, Eleutherian Mills Historical Library, Wilmington, Delaware.
Edwin G. Nourse Papers, Harry S. Truman Presidential Library.
Office of the Chairman, Council of Economic Advisers, Records, Dwight D. Eisenhower Presidential Library.
Office of the Council of Economic Advisers, Records, Dwight D. Eisenhower Presidential Library.
Franklin D. Roosevelt Papers, Roosevelt Presidential Library.
Beardsley Ruml Papers, University of Chicago.
Walter S. Salant Papers, Harry S. Truman Presidential Library.
Arthur M. Schlesinger, Jr., Papers, John F. Kennedy Presidential Library.
Paul Shoup Papers, Stanford University.
John W. Snyder Papers, Harry S. Truman Presidential Library.
Theodore Sorensen Papers, John F. Kennedy Presidential Library.
Harry S. Truman Papers, Truman Presidential Library.
Rexford Tugwell Diary, Franklin D. Roosevelt Presidential Library.
U.S., General Records of the Department of Commerce, General Correspondence (Record Group 40), National Archives.
U.S., General Records of the Department of the Treasury, Office of the Secretary, General Correspondence (Record Group 56), National Archives.
U.S., Records of the Federal Reserve System (Record Group 82), National Archives.
Will Whittington Papers, University of Mississippi.
Aubrey Williams Papers, Franklin D. Roosevelt Presidential Library.

Oral History Materials

Paul Appleby Memoir, Oral History Collection, Columbia University.
Will Clayton Memoirs, Oral History Collection, Columbia University.
Council of Economic Advisers Memoir, John F. Kennedy Presidential
    Library.
Marion Folsom Memoirs, Oral History Collection, Columbia University.
Leon Keyserling Memoir, Harry S. Truman Presidential Library.
Walter Salant Memoir, Harry S. Truman Presidential Library.
Raymond Saulnier Memoir, Oral History Collection, Columbia University.

Interviews

Thomas Boushall, Richmond, Virginia, December 20, 1973.
Ralph Bradford, Ocala, Florida, July 10–12, 1974.
Clem Johnston, Roanoke, Virginia, November 26–28, 1973.
Robert Lenhart, Washington, D.C., May 8, 1975.
Emerson Schmidt, Washington, D.C.,July 29, 1974.
Herbert Stein, Charlottesville, Virginia, June 20, 1977.
George Terborgh, Washington, D.C., November 15, 1974

Books

Adams, Sherman. *Firsthand Report: The Story of the Eisenhower Administration.* New York: Harper and Brothers, 1961.
Ahearn, Daniel. *Federal Reserve Policy Reappraised, 1951–1959.* New York: Columbia University Press, 1963.
Allen, Frederick Lewis. *Since Yesterday, 1929–1939.* New York: Harper and Brothers, 1940.
Alsop, Joseph, and Robert Kintner. *Men Around the President.* New York: Doubleday, Doran, 1939.
Altmeyer, Arthur. *The Formative Years of Social Security.* Madison: University of Wisconsin Press, 1966.
American Economic Association. *Readings in Fiscal Policy.* Homewood, Ill.: Irwin, 1955.
Bailey, Stephen. *Congress Makes a Law.* New York: Vintage Books, 1950.
Bakeless, John, ed. *Report of the Round Tables and General Conferences at the Twelfth Session.* Institute of Politics, Williams College. New Haven: Yale University Press, 1932.
Baritz, Loren. *The Servants of Power: A History of the Use of Social*

Science in American Industry. Middletown, Conn.: Wesleyan University Press, 1960.

Benveniste, Guy. *The Politics of Expertise.* Berkeley, Calif.: Glendessary Press, 1972.

Bernstein, Barton. "American in War and Peace: The Test of Liberalism." In *Towards a New Past.* New York: Vintage Books, 1968.

Bernstein, Irving. *The Lean Years: A History of the American Worker, 1920–1933.* Boston: Houghton Mifflin, 1960.

——*Turbulent Years: A History of the American Worker, 1933–1941.* Boston: Houghton Mifflin, 1969.

Beveridge, William. *Full Employment in a Free Society.* New York: W. W. Norton, 1945.

Blum, John Morton. *From The Morgenthau Diaries: Years of Crisis, 1928–1938.* Boston: Houghton Mifflin, 1959.

——*From the Morgenthau Diaries: Years of Urgency, 1938–1941.* Boston: Houghton Mifflin, 1964.

——*From the Morgenthau Diaries: Years of War, 1941–1945.* Boston: Houghton Mifflin, 1967.

——, ed. *The Price of Vision: The Diary of Henry A. Wallace, 1942–1946.* Boston: Houghton Mifflin, 1973.

——*V Was for Victory: Politics and American Culture During World War II.* New York: Harcourt Brace Jovanovich, 1976.

Boorstin, Daniel. *The Americans.* 3 vols. New York: Random House, 1958–1973.

Bradford, Ralph. *Along the Way.* Washington, D.C.: Judd and Detweiler, 1949.

Brady, Robert. *Business as a System of Power.* New York: Columbia University Press, 1943.

Breit, William, and Roger Ransom. *The Academic Scribblers: American Economists in Collision.* New York: Holt, Rinehart and Winston, 1971.

Bryce, James. *The American Commonwealth.* 2 vols. Chicago: Charles H. Sergel, 1891.

Burner, David. *Herbert Hoover: A Public Life.* New York: Knopf, 1979.

Burns, Arthur. *Prosperity Without Inflation.* New York: Fordham University Press, 1957.

Burns, James MacGregor. *Roosevelt: The Lion and the Fox.* New York: Harcourt Brace and World, 1956.

——*Roosevelt: The Soldier of Freedom.* New York: Harcourt Brace Jovanovich, 1970.

Canterbery, E. Ray. *The President's Council of Economic Advisers.* New York: Exposition Press, 1961.

Chazeau, Melvin de, et al. *Jobs and Markets: How to Prevent Inflation and Depression in the Transition.* CED Research Study. New York: McGraw-Hill, 1946.

Childs, Harwood Lawrence. *Labor and Capital in National Politics.* Columbus: Ohio State University Press, 1930.

Childs, Marquis. *They Hate Roosevelt.* New York: Harper and Brothers, 1936.

Cochran, Thomas. *Business in American Life: A History.* New York: McGraw-Hill, 1972.

——*The Pabst Brewing Company: The History of an American Business.* New York: New York University Press, 1948.

Complete Presidential Press Conferences of Franklin D. Roosevelt. 12 vols. New York: Da Capo Press, 1972.

Conkin, Paul. *The New Deal.* New York: Crowell, 1967.

De Armond, Fred. *Merle Thorpe, Champion of the Forgotten Man.* Springfield, Mo.: Mycroft Press, 1959.

Dennison, Henry S., et al. *Towards Full Employment.* New York: Whittlesey House, 1938.

Donovan, Robert J. *Eisenhower: The Inside Story.* New York: Harper and Brothers, 1956.

Douglas, Lewis. *The Liberal Tradition: A Free People and a Free Economy.* New York: Van Nostrand, 1935.

——*There Is One Way Out.* Boston: The Atlantic Monthly Co., 1935.

Drury, Allen. *A Senate Journal, 1943–1945.* New York: McGraw-Hill, 1963

Eccles, Marriner. *Beckoning Frontiers.* New York: Knopf, 1951.

Ellis, Howard. "The Rediscovery of Money." In *Money, Trade, and Economic Growth.* New York: Macmillan, 1951.

Fabricant, Solomon. *The Trend of Government Activity in the United States since 1900.* New York: National Bureau of Economic Research, 1952.

Fenton, John. *In Your Opinion.* Boston: Little, Brown, 1960.

Filene, Edward A. *Speaking of Change.* Freeport, N.Y.: By Former Associates of Edward A. Filene, 1939.

Fitch, Lyle, and Horace Taylor, eds. *Planning for Jobs: Proposals Submitted in the Pabst Postwar Employment Awards.* Philadelphia: Blakiston, 1946.

Flash, Edward S., Jr. *Economic Advice and Presidential Leadership: The Council of Economic Advisers.* New York: Columbia University Press, 1965.

Flynn, John. *As We Go Marching.* Garden City, N.Y.: Doubleday, Doran, 1944.

Free, Lloyd A., and Hadley Cantril. *The Political Beliefs of Americans: A Study of Public Opinion.* New Brunswick, N.J.: Rutgers University Press, 1967.

Freedman, Max, ed. *Roosevelt and Frankfurter: Their Correspondence, 1928–1945.* Boston: Little, Brown, 1967.

Freeman, Ralph, ed. *Postwar Economic Trends in the United States.* New York: Harper and Brothers, 1960.

Freidel, Frank. *Franklin D. Roosevelt: The Triumph.* Boston: Little, Brown, 1956.

——*Franklin D. Roosevelt: Launching the New Deal.* Boston: Little, Brown, 1973.

Fried, Joseph. *Housing Crisis U.S.A.* New York: Praeger, 1971.

Galambos, Louis. *Competition and Cooperation.* Baltimore: Johns Hopkins University Press, 1966.

Galbraith, John Kenneth. *The Affluent Society.* Boston: Houghton Mifflin, 1958.

——*Economics and the Art of Controversy.* New York: Vintage Books, 1959.

——*Economics and the Public Purpose.* Boston: Houghton Mifflin, 1973.

——"How Keynes Came to America." In *Economics, Peace and Laughter.* Boston: Houghton Mifflin, 1971.

——*The New Industrial State.* Boston: Houghton Mifflin, 1967.

Gallup, George, ed. *The Gallup Poll: Public Opinion, 1935–1971.* 3 vols. New York: Random House, 1972.

Gilbert, Richard, et al. *An Economic Program for American Democracy.* New York: Vanguard, 1938.

Goldman, Eric. *The Crucial Decade.* New York: Knopf, 1956.

Goodrich, Carter. *Government Promotion of American Canals and Railroads, 1800–1890.* New York: Columbia University Press, 1960.

Gordon, Robert. *Economic Instability and Growth: The American Record.* New York: Harper and Row, 1974.

Goulden, Joseph. *The Best Years, 1945–1950.* New York: Atheneum, 1976.

Graham, Otis, Jr. *Toward a Planned Society.* New York: Oxford University Press, 1976.

Greer, Thomas H. *What Roosevelt Thought: The Social and Political Ideas of Franklin D. Roosevelt.* East Lansing: Michigan State University Press, 1958.

Hamby, Alonzo. *Beyond the New Deal: Harry S. Truman and American Liberalism.* New York: Columbia University Press, 1973.

Hansen, Alvin. *The American Economy.* New York: McGraw-Hill, 1957.

—— *Economic Issues of the 1960's.* New York: McGraw-Hill, 1960.

—— *Fiscal Policy and Business Cycles.* New York: W. W. Norton, 1941.

—— *Full Recovery or Stagnation.* New York: W. W. Norton, 1938.

—— "Social Planning for Tomorrow." In *The United States after War.* Ithaca, N.Y.: Cornell University Press, 1945.

—— "Stability and Expansion." In *Financing American Prosperity: A Symposium of Economists,* ed. Paul Homan and Fritz Machlup. New York: The Twentieth Century Fund, 1945.

Harrington, Michael. *The Other America: Poverty in the United States.* Baltimore: Penguin Books, 1962.

Harris, Seymour. *Economics of the Kennedy Years and a Look Ahead.* New York: Harper and Row, 1964.

—— "Fiscal Policy." In *American Economic History.* New York: Mc-Graw-Hill, 1961.

—— *The New Economics: Keynes' Influence on Theory and Public Policy.* New York: Knopf, 1947.

—— *Saving American Capitalism.* New York: Knopf, 1948.

Hartmann, Susan. *Truman and the 80th Congress.* Columbia: University of Missouri Press, 1971.

Hartz, Louis. *Economic Policy and Democratic Thought: Pennsylvania, 1776–1860.* Cambridge: Harvard University Press, 1948.

—— *The Liberal Tradition in America.* New York: Harcourt, Brace and World, 1955.

Hawley, Ellis. *The Great War and the Search for a Modern Order.* New York: St. Martin's Press; 1979.

—— "Herbert Hoover and American Corporatism, 1929–1933." In *The Hoover Presidency: A Reappraisal,* ed. Martin Fausold and George Mazuzan. Albany: State University of New York Press, 1974.

—— "The New Deal and Business." In *The New Deal: The National Level,* ed. John Braeman, Robert Bremner, and David Brody. Columbus: Ohio State University Press, 1975.

—— *The New Deal and the Problem of Monopoly.* Princeton: Princeton University Press, 1966.

Hazlitt, Henry. *The Failure of the "New Economics."* Princeton: Van Nostrand, 1959.

Heath, Jim. *John F. Kennedy and the Business Community.* Chicago: University of Chicago Press, 1969.

Heilbroner, Robert. "The View from the Top: Reflections on a Changing Business Ideology." In *The Business Establishment,* ed. Earl Cheit. New York: Wiley, 1964.

Heller, Walter. *New Dimensions of Political Economy.* Cambridge: Harvard University Press, 1966.

Herring, E. Pendleton. *Group Representation before Congress.* Baltimore: Johns Hopkins Press, 1929.

Hickman, Bert. *Investment Demand and U.S. Economic Growth.* Washington, D.C.: The Brookings Institution, 1965.

Himmelberg, Robert. *The Origins of the National Recovery Administration.* New York: Fordham University Press, 1976.

Hofstadter, Richard. *The American Political Tradition.* New York: Knopf, 1948.

—— *Anti-Intellectualism in American Life.* New York: Knopf, 1963.

Holmans, A. E. *United States Fiscal Policy, 1945–1959.* London: Oxford University Press, 1961.

Homan, Paul, and Fritz Machlup, eds. *Financing American Prosperity: A Symposium of Economists.* New York: The Twentieth Century Fund, 1945.

Hoover, Herbert. *Addresses Upon the American Road, 1933–1938.* New York: Scribner's, 1938.

—— *The Memoirs of Herbert Hoover: The Great Depression, 1929–1941.* New York: Macmillan, 1952.

Howard, Nathaniel, ed. *The Basic Papers of George M. Humphrey.* Cleveland: Western Reserve Historical Society, 1965.

Huthmacher, J. Joseph. *Senator Robert F. Wagner and the Rise of Urban Liberalism.* New York: Atheneum, 1968.

—— , and Warren Susman. *Herbert Hoover and the Crisis of American Capitalism.* Cambridge, Mass.: Schenkman, 1973.

Hyman, Sidney. *The Lives of William Benton.* Chicago: University of Chicago Press, 1969.

—— *Marriner S. Eccles: Private Entrepreneur and Public Servant.* Stanford: Graduate School of Business, Stanford University, 1976.

Ickes, Harold. *The Secret Diary of Harold L. Ickes: The First Thousand Days, 1933–1936.* New York: Simon and Schuster, 1953.

—— *The Secret Diary of Harold L. Ickes: The Inside Struggle, 1936–1939.* New York: Simon and Schuster, 1954.

Income, Employment and Public Policy: Essays in Honor of Alvin H. Hansen. New York: W. W. Norton, 1948.

Jacoby, Neil. *Can Prosperity Be Sustained?* New York: Henry Holt, 1956.

Johnson, Lyndon. *The Vantage Point: Perspectives of the Presidency, 1963–1969.* New York: Holt, Rinehart and Winston, 1971.

Johnston, Eric. *America Unlimited.* Garden City, N.Y.: Doubleday, 1944.

Karl, Barry. *Charles E. Merriam and the Study of Politics.* Chicago: University of Chicago Press, 1974.

—— *Executive Reorganization and Reform in the New Deal.* Cambridge: Harvard University Press, 1963.

Keller, Morton. *In Defense of Yesterday: James M. Beck and the Politics of Conservatism, 1861-1936.* New York: Coward-McCann, 1958.

Key, V. O., Jr. *Politics, Parties and Pressure Groups.* 5th ed. New York: Crowell, 1964.

Keynes, John Maynard. *The Collected Writings of John Maynard Keynes.* London: Macmillan, 1971–.

—— *The General Theory of Employment, Interest and Money.* London: Macmillan, 1936.

Keyserling, Leon. *Consumption—Key to Full Prosperity.* Washington: Conference on Economic Progress, 1957.

Kimmel, Lewis. *Federal Budget and Fiscal Policy, 1789–1958.* Washington, D.C.: The Brookings Institution, 1959.

Kirkendall, Richard. *Social Scientists and Farm Politics in the Age of Roosevelt.* Columbia: University of Missouri Press, 1966.

Knipe, James. *The Federal Reserve and the American Dollar: Problems and Policies, 1946–1964.* Chapel Hill: University of North Carolina, 1965.

Kolko, Gabriel. *Railroads and Regulation, 1877–1916.* Princeton: Princeton University Press, 1965.

—— *The Triumph of Conservatism.* New York: Free Press, 1963.

—— *Wealth and Power in America: An Analysis of Social Class and Income Distribution.* New York: Praeger, 1962.

Kristol, Irving. "Ten Years in a Tunnel: Reflection on the Thirties." In *The Thirties: A Reconsideration in the Light of the American Political Tradition,* ed. Morton Frisch and Martin Diamond. DeKalb: Northern Illinois University Press, 1968.

Krooss, Herman. *Executive Opinion: What Business Leaders Said and Thought on Economic Issues, 1920's–1960's.* Garden City, N.Y.: Doubleday, 1970.

Lampman, Robert J. *The Share of Top Wealth-Holders in National Wealth.* Princeton: Princeton University Press, 1962.

Larson, Arthur. *A Republican Looks at His Party.* New York: Harper and Brothers, 1956.

Lekachman, Robert. *The Age of Keynes.* New York: Vintage Books, 1966.

Leuchtenburg, William. *Franklin D. Roosevelt and the New Deal.* New York: Harper and Row, 1963.

——— "The New Deal and the Analogue of War." In *Change and Continuity in Twentieth-Century America*, ed. John Braeman, Robert Bremner, and Everett Walters. Columbus: Ohio State University Press, 1964.

Lewellen, Wilbur. *Executive Compensation in Large Industrial Corporations.* New York: Columbia University Press, 1968.

Lewis, Wilfred, Jr. *Federal Fiscal Policy in the Postwar Recessions.* Washington, D.C.: The Brookings Institution, 1962.

Lindley, Ernest. *Half Way With Roosevelt.* New York: Viking Press, 1936.

Lingeman, Richard. *Don't You Know There's a War On?* New York: Putnam's, 1970.

Lowi, Theodore. *The End of Liberalism.* New York: Norton, 1969.

Lyon, Leverett S., et al. *The National Recovery Administration: An Analysis and Appraisal.* Washington, D.C.: The Brookings Institution, 1935.

Lyon, Peter. *Eisenhower: Portrait of the Hero.* Boston: Little, Brown, 1974.

Lyons, Eugene. *Herbert Hoover: A Biography.* Garden City, N.Y.: Doubleday, 1964.

McClelland, David. *The Achieving Society.* Princeton: Van Nostrand, 1961.

McConnell, Grant. *Private Power and American Democracy.* New York: Knopf, 1966.

McKean, Dayton David. *Party and Pressure Politics.* Boston: Houghton Mifflin, 1949.

McKinley, Charles, and Robert Frase. *Launching Social Security: A Capture-and-Record Account, 1935–1937.* Madison: University of Wisconsin Press, 1970.

McQuaid, Kim. "The Business Advisory Council of the Department of Commerce." In *Research in Economic History, 1976,* ed. Paul Uselding. Greenwich, Conn.: JAI Press, 1976.

Maier, Charles. *Recasting Bourgeois Europe.* Princeton: Princeton University Press, 1975.

Markowitz, Norman. *The Rise and Fall of the People's Century: Henry A. Wallace and American Liberalism, 1941–1948.* New York: Free Press, 1973.

Miller, Arthur. *The Modern Corporate State: Private Governments and the American Constitution.* Westport, Conn.: Greenwood Press, 1976.

Miroff, Bruce. *Pragmatic Illusions: The Presidential Politics of John F. Kennedy.* New York: David McKay, 1976.

Mitchell, Broadus. *Depression Decade: From New Era Through New Deal, 1929–1941.* New York: Rinehart, 1947.

Moley, Raymond. *After Seven Years.* New York: Harper and Brothers, 1939.

—— *The First New Deal.* New York: Harcourt, Brace and World, 1966.

National Planning Association. *The Employment Act Past and Future: A Tenth Anniversary Symposium,* ed. Gerhard Colm. Washington, D.C.: National Planning Association, 1956.

Nelson, Donald. *Arsenal of Democracy: The Story of American War Production.* New York: Harcourt, Brace, 1946.

Noble, David. *America by Design: Science, Technology, and the Rise of Corporate Capitalism.* New York: Knopf, 1977.

Nossiter, Bernard. *The Mythmakers: An Essay on Power and Wealth.* Boston: Houghton Mifflin, 1964.

Okun, Arthur. *The Political Economy of Prosperity.* Washington, D.C.: The Brookings Institution, 1970.

Pabst Brewing Company. *The Winning Plans in the Pabst Postwar Employment Awards.* Milwaukee: Pabst Brewing Company, 1944.

Parmet, Herbert. *Eisenhower and the American Crusades.* New York: Macmillan, 1972.

Patterson, James. *Congressional Conservatism and the New Deal.* Lexington: University of Kentucky Press, 1967.

—— *Mr. Republican: A Biography of Robert A. Taft.* Boston: Houghton Mifflin, 1972.

Paul, Randolph. *Taxation in the United States.* Boston: Little, Brown, 1954.

Peek, George. *Why Quit Our Own.* New York: Van Nostrand, 1936.

Perkins, Dexter. *The New Age of Franklin Roosevelt, 1932–1945.* Chicago: University of Chicago Press, 1957.

Perkins, Edwin. *Men and Organizations: The American Economy in the Twentieth Century.* New York: Putnam's, 1977.

Perkins, Frances. *The Roosevelt I Knew.* New York: Harper and Row, 1964.

Perrett, Geoffrey. *Days of Sadness, Years of Triumph: The American People, 1939–1945.* New York: Coward, McCann and Geohegan, 1973.

Polenberg, Richard. *War and Society: The United States, 1941–1945.* Philadelphia: Lippincott, 1972.

Prothro, James. *The Dollar Decade.* Baton Rouge: Louisiana State University Press, 1954.

Radosh, Ronald, and Murray Rothbard. *A New History of Leviathan: Essays on the Rise of the American Corporate State.* New York: Dutton, 1972.

Rauch, Basil. *The History of the New Deal, 1933–1938.* New York: Creative Age Press, 1944.

Rayback, Joseph. *A History of American Labor.* Rev. ed. New York: Free Press, 1966.

Reichard, Gary. *The Reaffirmation of Republicanism: Eisenhower and the Eighty-Third Congress.* Knoxville: University of Kentucky Press, 1975.

Richberg, Donald. *The Rainbow.* Garden City, N.Y.: Doubleday, 1936.

Robinson, Joan. *Economic Philosophy.* Chicago: Aldine, 1962.

Romasco, Albert. *The Poverty of Abundance.* New York: Oxford University Press, 1965.

Roosevelt, Elliott, ed. *F.D.R.: His Personal Letters.* 4 vols. New York: Duell, Sloan and Pearce, 1947–1950.

Roosevelt, Franklin D. *The Public Papers and Addresses of Franklin D. Roosevelt.* Compiled by Samuel Rosenman. 13 vols. New York: Random House, 1938–1950.

Roper, Daniel. *Fifty Years of Public Life.* Durham, N.C.: Duke University Press, 1941.

Rosen, Elliott. *Hoover, Roosevelt, and the Brains Trust.* New York: Columbia University Press, 1977.

Ross, Davis R. B. *Preparing for Ulysses.* New York: Columbia University Press, 1969.

Rossiter, Clinton. *The American Presidency.* Rev. ed. New York: New American Library, 1960.

Rowen, Hobart. *The Free Enterprisers: Kennedy, Johnson and the Business Establishment.* New York: Putnam's, 1964.

Ruml, Beardsley, and H. Christian Sonne. *Fiscal and Monetary Policy.* National Planning Association Planning Pamphlet no. 35. Washington, D.C.: National Planning Association, 1944.

Schapsmeir, Edward L., and Frederick H. Schapsmeir. *Prophet in Politics: Henry A. Wallace and the War Years.* Ames: Iowa State University Press, 1970.

Schlesinger, Arthur M., Jr. *The Age of Roosevelt: The Coming of the New Deal.* Boston: Houghton Mifflin, 1958.

—— *The Age of Roosevelt: The Crisis of the Old Order.* Boston: Houghton Mifflin, 1957.

—— *The Age of Roosevelt: The Politics of Upheaval.* Boston: Houghton Mifflin, 1960.

—— *A Thousand Days: John F. Kennedy in the White House.* Boston: Houghton Mifflin, 1965.

Schriftgiesser, Karl. *Business Comes of Age: The Story of the Committee*

for Economic Development and Its Impact upon the Economic Policies of the United States, 1942–1960. New York: Harper and Brothers, 1960.

—— Business and Public Policy: The Role of the Committee for Economic
Development, 1942–1967. Englewood Cliffs, N.J.: Prentice-Hall,
1967.

—— The Commission on Money and Credit: An Adventure in Policy-
Making. Englewood Cliffs, N.J.: Prentice-Hall, 1974.

Schwarz, Jordan A. The Interregnum of Despair: Hoover, Congress, and
the Depression. Urbana: University of Illinois Press, 1970.

Shannon, Fred. The Farmer's Last Frontier: Agriculture, 1860-1897. New
York: Farrar, 1945.

Sorensen, Theodore. Kennedy. New York: Harper and Row, 1964.

Steigerwalt, Albert. The National Association of Manufacturers, 1895–
1914: A Study in Business Leadership. Ann Arbor: University of
Michigan Press, 1964.

Stein, Herbert. The Fiscal Revolution in America. Chicago: University
of Chicago Press, 1969.

Sutton, Francis, et al. The American Business Creed. Cambridge: Harvard
University Press, 1956.

Swanson, Ernst, and Emerson P. Schmidt. Economic Stagnation or Progress: A Critique of Recent Doctrines on the Mature Economy, Oversavings, and Deficit Spending. New York: McGraw-Hill, 1946.

Taylor, Albion Guilford. Labor Policies of the National Association of
Manufacturers. Urbana: University of Illinois Press, 1927.

Taylor, George Rogers. The Transportation Revolution, 1815-1860. New
York: Rinehart, 1951.

Terborgh, George. The Bogey of Economic Maturity. Chicago: Machinery
and Allied Products institute, 1945.

Thompson, Victor. Bureaucracy and Innovation. University: University
of Alabama Press, 1969.

Tobin, James. The Intellectual Revolution in U.S. Economic Policy-Making. London: Longmans, 1966.

Truman, David. The Governmental Process: Political Interests and Public
Opinion. 2d ed. New York: Knopf, 1971.

Tugwell, Rexford. The Brains Trust. New York: Viking Press, 1968.

—— The Democratic Roosevelt. Baltimore: Penguin Books, 1957.

Turner, Carl. An Analysis of Soviet Views on John Maynard Keynes.
Durham, N.C.: Duke University Press, 1969.

U.S., President, Public Papers of the Presidents of the United States.
Washington: National Archives and Records Service, 1953–

Vatter, Harold. *The U.S. Economy in the 1950's.* New York: W. W. Norton, 1963.

Veritas Foundation. *Keynes at Harvard.* New York: Veritas Foundation, 1960.

Walker, S. H., and Paul Sklar. *Business Finds Its Voice: Management's Effort to Sell the Business Idea to the Public.* New York: Harper and Brothers, 1938.

Wallace, Henry A. *Sixty Million Jobs.* New York: Simon and Schuster, 1945.

Walton, Clarence, ed. *Business and Social Progress: Views of Two Generations of Executives.* New York; Praeger, 1970.

Warburton, Clark. *Depression, Inflation, and Monetary Policy: Selected Papers, 1945–1953.* Baltimore: Johns Hopkins University Press, 1966.

Warren, Harris Gaylord. *Herbert Hoover and the Great Depression.* New York: W. W. Norton, 1959.

Weinstein, James. *The Corporate Ideal in the Liberal State.* Boston: Beacon Press, 1968.

Wiebe, Robert. *Businessmen and Reform: A Study of the Progressive Movement.* Chicago: Quadrangle, 1962.

Winch, Donald. *Economics and Policy.* New York: Walker and Company, 1969.

Wolfskill, George. "The New Deal Critics: Did They Miss the Point?" In *Essays on the New Deal,* ed. Harold Hollingsworth and William Holmes. Austin: University of Texas Press, 1969.

—— *The Revolt of the Conservatives: A History of the American Liberty League, 1934–1940.* Boston: Houghton Mifflin, 1962.

—— , and John Hudson. *All but the People.* New York: Macmillan, 1969.

Dissertations

Brady, Patrick G. "Toward Security: Postwar Economic and Social Planning in the Executive Office, 1939–1946." Rutgers University, 1975.

Brown, Linda Keller. "Challenge and Response: The American Business Community and the New Deal, 1932–1934." University of Pennsylvania, 1972.

Cleveland, Alfred S. "Some Political Aspects of Organized Industry." Harvard University, 1947.

Fisher, Galen. "The Chamber of Commerce of the United States." M.A. thesis, University of California, 1950.

—— "The Chamber of Commerce of the United States and the Laissez-Faire Rationale, 1912–1919." University of California, 1960.

Gable, Richard. "A Political Analysis of an Employers Association: The National Association of Manufacturers." University of Chicago, 1951.

Kelly, Alfred. "A History of the Illinois Manufacturers' Association." University of Chicago, 1938.

Stalker, John, Jr. "The National Association of Manufacturers: A Study of Ideology." University of Wisconsin, 1951.

Tilman, Lee. "The American Business Community and the Death of the New Deal." University of Arizona, 1966.

Warken, Philip. "A History of the National Resources Planning Board, 1933-1943." Ohio State University, 1969.

Index

Contemporary American History Series

WILLIAM E. LEUCHTENBURG, GENERAL EDITOR

Robert M. Hathaway, *Ambiguous Partnership: Britain and America, 1944–1947*

1981

Leonard M. Dinnerstein, *America and the Survivors of the Holocaust*

1982

Laurence S. Wittner, *The Americans in Greece, 1943–1949: A Study in Counterrevolution*

1982